ECO PATRIARCHY

The Origins & Nature of Hunting

ria montana

ISBN: 978-1-7003-7414-1

This thesis is not in final form.
It is a somewhat collective living document, open for your input.
VeganPrimitivist.wordpress.com

Cover painting "PRIMITIVE MAN HUNTING ANIMALS"
At the Museum of Vietnamese History
Zdeněk Burian: Neandertálci pod vrchem Kotoučem, olej, 1958.
Zdeněk Burian: Neandertals under Kotouč Hill, oil, 1958.
Contributed by HappyMidnight
https://commons.wikimedia.org/w/index.php?curid=23975540

DEDICATION

to the animals who suffered and succumbed under 'man the hunter'

and to Frank C. Cook:

Flow happens through connection…
When you go into a forest,
you're not just simply walking through,
there's an invisible link up that's happening.
Everything in the forest knows that you're there.
If you slow down enough you can hear that through the birds talking…
We need to get back to that recognition that we're linked up…
When you start to open up,
there's that term empath, to be empathic,
to reach out and feel empathy,
and to go in to the other organisms that are around you.
there's this interplay that goes on, that relationship,
that interplay going back and forth between is how we're going to grow.
It's really our next level of evolution,
of us being conscious of it.
Flow has been going on all the time,
but now that we're becoming conscious of it,
we're able to interrelate with it.

FLOW by Frank Cook
youtube

CONTENTS

APPRECIATIONS

Appreciation for input or support from several anonymous people

&

C.
M.B.
TJ Long
Lee Hall
Hayduke
Jim Mason
Yi-Fu Tuan
Ken Damro
David Hunt
David Watts
Possum Riot
Linda Hogan
Dave Mayton
Flower Bomb
Julian Langer
Pattrice Jones
David Skrbina
Emily Victoria
Ryan the Green
Nicolas Dupont
Ricardo Martins
Anushka Aanush
Robert Mossberger
Conrad Justice Kiczenski
Kollibri terre Sonnenblume
Kerry M Redwood Atjecoutay
and counterpoints from Steve Kirk

Illustrations by Miles Lucas

Please note:

The overarching theme of this thesis is distinct from the views of cited authors.
Citations are rocks plucked & remixed binding intuitive to reasoned substratum.

Replica of *Panthera spelaea*, extinct cave lions,
painted in the Chauvet Cave, France ~30,000 years ago.

What inspired the Paleolithic ice age artist to symbolize cave lions? What did she sense in them, how did she feel and think about them? With shoulder height ~ 4', head-body length (without tail) ~ 7', and weighing up to 800 pounds, what was the nature of interactions between humans and cave lions?

Cave lions originating ~ 370,000 years ago went extinct ~12,000 years ago. Scientists suggest climate warming possibly played a role by reforming savanna into forest and reducing abundance of their prey, which recovered substantially later. Did competitor expansion play a role in cave lion extinction, the human ape outhunting their food with weaponized organization? How exactly did cave lions, once dominating the land spanning Eurasia to Alaska-Yukon, along with herbivorous wooly mammoths and numerous others, come to no longer exist?

eco-patriarchy:

a human parasitic power over others
disconnecting and disintegrating wildness

or, an emotional commitment to remain in supremacist ignorance

or, to re-apply the words of Fredy Perlman

the beast that is destroying the only known home of living beings

In *Stories of the Gorilla Country*, Paul Du Chaillu, 1895

Ria Montana

Group of Animals with Warning Coloration
by Frank Evers Beddard, 1892
scan, Swan Sonnenschein, London

1 INTRODUCTION

I was raised by the forest. ~Kat Philbin

We need to uncover our ability to be humans-in-nature and humans-as-nature in a new, creative, and liberatory way.[1] ~Chaia Heller

By now you're fortunate if you can relate to my earliest years, lived in a field along woods in community with other animals - ants, spiders, beetles, gnats, mosquitos, bees, wasps, flies, fireflies, caterpillars, butterflies, moths, dragonflies, grasshoppers, frogs, toads, worms, lizards, snakes, fish, birds, mice, gophers, squirrels and raccoons. The life energy of the place incited an awe and respect for all. As a toddler I refused fish because I knew they were animals - the act of eating, much less harming an animal would have been intrinsically disturbing. The first time I heard 'vegan', my being attached to it as completely as any born truth, with a relief of rejoining the community of life. At the same time, it separated me from most other humans. Only if I had known then, what I have come to know now...

> *Veganism is essential to wildness. Not only is exploiting and killing animals a humanape-constructed activity and form of authority, but it socially evolved into the leading political regime worldwide. Very often humans want to pinpoint about such questions as origins, saying that "it has always been so even prior to civilization", and extreme rationalization has destroyed the last bits of remorse that could be left - nonetheless, if there is any initial "project" for humans, here we are, and we fail.[2]*

A vegan primitivist involved with indigenous activism for more than a decade observes,

> *People close to nature all over the world thrive on a plant-based and even strict vegetarian diet. They are the most disease-free and long living people in the world. This says something about the ideal human diet and how a lot of people have misconceptions about how we are supposed to find our place in nature as a species.[3]*

Schooling[4] removed me from my wild home, drove me into a modern artificial worker-consumer life, but worst of all separated me from and mediated my wild relationships. At midlife my brother was murdered by my sister's son, and in grief I rediscovered nature's solace. In reconnecting with wild I heard the plight of animals in their encroached, fragmenting habitats, and the malice in humans' excuses for their strange supremacy.

It is ignorant and foolish to believe that the human experience is more emotionally elevated, sentient, or important than it is for other animals. We aren't better or more worthy than non-humans. We were taught to believe that we are the height of creation, because it gives us an excuse to benefit from their oppression and their bodies. ~ Karen Ellis-Ritter

Priest River winding through Whitetail Butte with
'lots' of forestry, since the mid-19th century.
An astronaut observed this checkerboard pattern along Priest River in northern Idaho. The quarter-mile squares in this landscape checkerboard are the result of civilization's forest management. Similar patterns originated in the 1800s, when alternate parcels of land were granted by the U.S. government to railroads such as the Northern Pacific. Many parcels in the Pacific Northwest were later sold off and harvested for timber. White patches reflect areas with younger trees with snow cover. Dark squares are parcels of denser, intact forest. The checkerboard is used as a method of maintaining purported sustainability of forested tracts while still enabling a harvest of trees. For nearly a century, Priest River, winding through the scene from top to bottom, was used to transport logs...
Astronaut photograph ISS050-E-28519, January 4, 2017,
Caption excerpt by Andi Hollie, and M. Justin Wilkinson, Texas State University

I shifted my energies from assisting civilization's humans to recovering forests and wetlands. Wild liberation became my life-force, which expressed itself in actions of a restoration ecologist, but with an anti-civilization, primitivist bent.

In trying to understand how my species came to normalize being an atrocious world tyrant, I researched, following intuitions in sifting out human supremacist bias, to arrive as close to the core as I could. I found and released my authoritarian indoctrination where possible.

> *...every individual mind is a rushing, wild waterway of ideas that spill out when the dam of social subordination breaks down. Society collectively discourages any wildness, domesticating the individual and ultimately creating a caged animal within the mind. Beneath all the social conditioning there is a unique individual that discovers itself in chaotic contradiction with society.* [5]

With my hard fought freedom of thought de-subduing, what emerged was the hearing of an unfettered story, locating deep origins.

Drawing from Toynbee[6], Fredy Perlman positions the birth of the violent Leviathan spirit in Ur, Mesopotamia's ancient Sumerian city-state, in its determination to make farm of forest.[7] But it was the birth of eco-patriarchy that set the stage for events in Ur. Track Ur's violent spirit stepping stones back, and arrive in moments the spirit first forced steps outside wildness itself. Perhaps out of sheer will to survive, very early folio-frugivore humans used a desperate ingenuity to devour dead others as if they themselves were carnivores.

Much later, perhaps out of need or simple curiosity, or thrill seeking joy or the powerful feeling of supremacy, early humans used this newfangled predatory spirit to ignore wild's invisible walls. They stepped beyond belonging in habitat, outside nature's reach, not accidentally, but in time with intent. This intention was more than wild will to propagate their own kind; it was to explore other lands in a spirit of conquest. While this spirit at times blended with survival, or a freedom to roam, at its core grew a colonizing supremacy, extracting and engineering nature, unwilding themselves into Earth's top invaders, human apes perceiving themselves above animality. Eco-patriarchy was the original transition into humans killing wildness with an inventive, empowered violent spirit. Eco-patriarchy wrought Leviathan. By the time Ur took on statehood, this project had been long underway, springing from seeds more ancient than *Homo sapiens* themselves.

Ur's Leviathan was another stepping stone, a transition point into artificial lifeway in modern form (at least to those who can still see outside their subjugated artifices) – an intensified taming, domestication through stratified institutions and business of war documented on tablets. Before, Ur had generally been a semblance of human commune with nature and wild altruism between themselves. But something was buried in their ecstatic myth making, ceremonies, visions, dreams and gods that mingle in the human realm. This mysticism was outside belongingness with wild lifeway of animals embedded in wildness.

The ecstatic spirit supplanted wildness of origins, shriveling and surrendering it with an excited constraint, the becoming of machine parts that later propel the Leviathan. Perlman seems aware of the depth of his-story, speaking of it as a *"masculine affair"* that revolves *"around phallus shapes: the spear, the arrow... the dagger and of course later the bullet and the missile... all made to penetrate and kill."*[7] The pre-story of Leviathan told how troops of wild human apes became hunter, predator and parasite, paving a path of eco-patriarchy to later become Leviathan's hunter of profits, embers sweltering through ages before setting the world ablaze in a frenzied fire.

Long before Ur deviations manifested from conscious fears. As stated in *Ape and Essence* by Aldous Huxley, *"fear is the very basis and foundation of modern life."*[9] Eco-patriarchy's story origins began long ago, with emotion-actions in humans' relationships with other animals shifting, at times in dire response to shifts toward harsher climate. *"In our panic to avoid the*

16

darkness of death, we sacrifice the light of our lives. "[10] Humanity might have ended before it began with wet and dry, warm and cold fluctuations shrinking the pre-human habitat. But

> *...in a confluence of events, evolution took a different turn, producing a new species of ape with a different strategy for dealing with its changing world... While the deep forest apes simply hunkered down and reacted to the events, unaware of their causes and patterns, the marginal apes became proactive in coping with the mosaic of change presented to them. These new apes began to see the world differently, to recognize its patterns, to predict its cycles, and to act more effectively to minimize the negative consequences of change and to maximize the positive. In short, nature invented the 'human strategy', a survival repertoire that offered better solutions to the problems of life on the forest margins. This strategy embodies the concept of 'control'...*[11]

Snowbound, by Charles R. Knight, 1911
Staten Island Museum
An arthritic "Old Man of La Chapelle" skeleton likely influenced this painting. Knight renders a trio of hunched, hapless Neanderthals enduring a snowstorm. "Poor little devils," Knight reportedly remarked, "they had such a hard time."

Over stretches of time human apes over-adapted themselves into what sometimes became colonizing parasitic predators. The general ethos began leaning toward power over others, born in earliest instances of preying upon animals. That sense of power took on the tone as conveyed today - privilege, undeserved ease, opted obliviousness to suffering of others, or even enjoyment, a relishing in higher hierarchal position, super-natural control over life and death. Then as humans self-domesticated, they constructed inorganic hierarchies of value assigned to everything of use to their domestication. With the aids of fire, weapons, and other taming technologies, they took charge. Over more time, their designed domesticating animals and plants assisted them. Wild struggles and serenities of life within habitat converted into struggles and serenities maintaining and expanding a dominating power, unwilding self and others.

Early humans on the eco-patriarchy path.
from an original drawing by Alan Sorrell

Even social justice movements, politics, all the soft and even the hard sciences, are tainted in unwild hegemony. In *Wild Children-Domesticated Dreams: Civilization and the Birth of Education*, comparative anthropologist Layla AbelRahim speaks to civilizing indoctrination in considering Bentham's *The question is not, Can they 'reason'? Nor, Can they 'talk'? But, Can they 'suffer'?*:

> *To conceive a question like this, one must first be able to imagine the other's experience and hear her, which cannot happen through abstraction and representation. The more we are taught to know the world through perverted words and formulae, the dumber we grow, for intelligence only devolves in artificial "educational" settings, where the civilized are taught to listen to the voices representing their needs and woes. In this way, the civilized are taught how to not hear the other, but overwrite her voice with civilized generalizations.*[12]

When a friend asked me to write an essay on hunting, it dawned on me that the civilized mind's abrogating the experiences of wild others is eco-patriarchy - a closing of empathy for, a rejection of, and rule over wildness. Human apes adapted for empathy also acclimate away from empathy, some biologically such as psychopaths, but most by choice. I sensed origins of the human hunt as primary origins of human nonparticipation in the ecological community of Kropotkin's empathetic mutual aid.[13]

Modernity is challenged to grasp mutual aid in its raw form, embedded in wildness. The term 'wildness' here is adopted from "Will-of-the-land: Wilderness Among Primal Indo-Europeans" as summarized by John Moore:

> *(A) state inhabited by willful, uncontrollable, natural energies. In such states, humans surrendered their individuality, renounced personal volition to the will-of-the-land, and merged individuated desire within the expansive needs of the wild. In doing so, they became channels or mediums through which the wilderness could*

> *become articulate and operative in the human sphere... the*
> *merging of individuation within holism... there were no*
> *established journeys to be undertaken, no predetermined*
> *paths to traverse. All social codes were annulled: vision,*
> *emotion and behavior were no longer subject to regulation*
> *and control.*[14]

Notions such as egalitarianism, equality, hierarchy, specialization, division of labor, leisure time, etc., seem oblivious to ways of wildness at the core of animality. Indeed, for the modern human species, who have devastated others, to consider applying such notions as equality to the context of wildness could be deemed by civilization's rational mind as eco-patriarchal speciesism.

Wildness is more than shape-shifting relationships of dynamics like energy transfers, symbiotic assemblages, electro-magnetic-chemical-hormonal communications within and between bodies, flowing transformations of complex networks, all charged with emotion. *"The natural world is a culture of vigilance based on carefully tended relationships and connections, maintained through recognition, mutual respect, and "jungle etiquette."*[15] Through bio-social animal-plant-fungi-protista-bacteria relations, beings hone one another's bodies and lifeways. In this way, all life co-participates in a sort of spontaneous, unintentional 'ecosystem management'. But there is a missing element beneath it all.

> *Ostensibly, the evolution of life on earth is merely a*
> *succession of adaptations that can either benefit a species*
> *or lead them down a dead-end path of overspecialization...*
> *Call it biological blasphemy, but despite nature's apparent*
> *indifference in the harsh struggle for survival, life is*
> *evolving along a continuum of compassion"*[16]

With compassion, what matters is togetherness, striving toward abundant homeostasis, thriving wild communities of life in which all who belong sense a feeling of belonging. The indigenous Kalahari man /I!ae remained and died in his homeland Omaheke, *"his spirit captive to the sense of belonging..."*[17]

Owl remaining after humans razed the home where she belonged.

...what we call knowledge is merely another form of Ignorance-highly organized, of course, and eminently scientific...[18]

The dominance of 'reason' has proven itself a destructive force since its origins, justifying carnages based on authority, then in hindsight, maliciously forgetting or too easily forgiving the harm. Carolyn Merchant's 1980 classic *The Death of Nature: Women, Ecology and the Scientific Revolution*[19] details how reason's apocalyptical scientific revolution fueled objectifying and mutilating carnages. Even in writing about other animals, channeling my perception of their being into abstraction de-beings them from their essence. I am wary of reasoning, use it with intentions to arouse animality, staying vigilant of my modern human bias. The primitive remains despite civilization – that *Homo* constructed inorganic artificiality severing intrinsic life. This study focuses on the process of how, and origin at which humans relinquished their primal lifeway. Emotion as opposed to reason is central to that understanding. By losing conviction in reasoned kindness of humankind, humans can recuperate their primal empathy for others.

Even when reason evidences human atrocities against nonhuman animals, ending cruelty lags, seemingly disconnected from empathy or even an appropriate reasoned response.[20] When a stimulus is impenetrable to the mind but detected with the body, modern humans still tend to let the mind dominate. As in Ogla Tokarczuk's novel *Drive Your Plow Over the Bones of the Dead*, *"We have a view of the world, but Animals have a sense of the world."*[21] These senses have powerful abilities. A mind that views wild as having 'functions' and providing 'services' is dominating, not sensing. *"From nature's point of view no creatures are useful or not useful. That's just a foolish distinction applied by people."*[22] Domination bias invades and overtakes narratives to feed the mind, silencing real experiences.

Reality is what we take to be true.
What we take to be true is what we believe.
What we believe is based upon our perceptions.
What we perceive depends upon what we look for.
What we look for depends upon what we think.
What we think depends upon what we perceive.
What we perceive determines what we believe.
What we believe determines what we take to be true.
What we take to be true is our reality.
~Theoretical Physicist David Bohm who warned of the dangers of rampant reason and technology.

I am imprisoned in a global human culture guarding its cataclysmic pseudo-supremacy. Anthropologist Robert Sussman concluded, *"I am forced to believe that 'Man the Hunter' is a myth, and that the myth will continue in Western European view on human nature long into the future."*[23] This thesis peels hands off the human-beast's hidden eyes, exposing the flawed killer myth. My thinking may come off as hubris to some or many, but this is what I sense as a rawer reality, sans mythology. In this time of humans' mass annihilation of all, an emerging awareness that even the global science is beginning to meld into its 'objective' truth, more closely aligns with return to wildness of deep origins.

In writing this thesis I draw from lucid decisions of de‹ before the domestic, developments perhaps deeper than the advent of cooking and clothing.[24] The 'man the hunter' bias dominating institution controlled archaeology makes searches challenging the propagandized narrative a tussle. *"The popularity and persistence of scientific narratives often have more to do with how well they support dominant mythologies than with their scientific veracity."*[25] Further, noted by James C. Scott in his deep history study *"...if you were hunter-gatherers or nomads, however numerous, spreading your biodegradable trash thinly across the landscape, you were likely to vanish entirely from the archaeological record,"*[26] Not only do hunter-gatherers leave little evidence, foraging gatherers leave even less, likely resulting in greatly overexaggerated claims of inherent human hunting. *"For the most part the Pleistocene, and even the earliest post-glacial, is a blank when it comes to evidence of humans eating plants. No wonder the old men's stories, of chaps who hunt great mammals and eat their meat, still dominate our unthinking visions of hunter-gathering in that period."*[27] With eco-patriarchal structures *"denying validity or even recognition to alternative interpretations, access to alternative values and beliefs capable of freeing a society from its own self-destruction is closed."*[28]

In documenting the research leading to this notion of eco-patriarchy, varied sources snugged together, from academic anthropology articles to qualitative case studies to intensely insightful illustrations (which are open for your interpretation), assembled as pieces to form a puzzle. A diversity of perspectives patched together tells the tale of the origins and nature of human supremacy, resulting in wild animals and habitats struggling under human control. Within this main theme, subthemes interweave that may appeal to or challenge feminists, anarchists, earth and animal liberationists and others. For example, ecofeminists may resist anthropocentric focus replacing the androcentric. The primary audience was initially intended to challenge Western anti-civers, particularly anarcho-primitivists, who view hunting as central to a future primitive. I find that the ethos and act of hunting is origins of and central to civilization, and if continued, prevents return to wildness.

Others are evolving into this ethos and connecting with one another with similar stories.

> ...*strong opposition to animal farming within anarcho-primitivism is not new and odd at all. It is just a part of the reflection on the issue of the commodification of life.*
>
> *I remember having conversations about this with Zerzan and reading/watching articles/documentaries online. They have always been supportive of ALF as well as ELF.*
>
> *I believe I didn't turn vegan at the time largely out of cowardice (perceived conflict with family) and not understanding the dimension and relevance of the issue. I was focused on this kind of Kaczynski idea of "hitting where it hurts" and didn't take personal responsibility for something that is important. Still, at the time, I understood, like most anarcho-primitivists must understand, that animals/Life doesn't belong in factories.*
>
> *I think veganism is more than an important issue. I would argue that it is right at the core of this movement. Isn't anarcho-primitivism about challenging anthropocentrism*

24

and a desire to be a part of a healthy ecosystem? As a political ideology it points out that our social problems/injustices are rooted in this breakdown with life and nature. Civilization is the antithesis of veganism.[29]

Reports roll in from distant places, such as *Deviance Project – Siate Consapevoli. Deviate!* in Italy, and *Coletivo Erva Daninha* and *Coletivo Menta* in Brazil, collectives of anarcho-primitivists following their intuition with including veganism. Too often I have met someone who explored rewilding, who enrolled in a wilderness awareness program, or who started listening to my anarcho-primitivist friend John Zerzan's Anarchy Radio guests, or read or listened to his friend Kevin Tucker, and gave up after feeling their approach to animal liberation or their veganism was rejected and even mocked. This thesis is the response to people with those experiences. Anarcho-primitivism does not necessitate hunting, and perhaps the two are separate matters altogether.

Agonizing discomfort with cultural conditions can incite wild beings to soothe themselves in a co-mingling band of resistance and re-gathering, but the civilized mind is easily incited to search for nonexistent utopia., In *Personal Narrative of a Journey to the Equinoctial Regions of the New Continent during the years 1799–1804* scientist Alexander von Humbold observed: *"When nations are mentally exhausted and see the seeds of depravity in their refinements, the idea that in some distant region infant societies enjoy pure and perpetual happiness pleases them."*[30] The question is, will anarcho-primitivism be able to step away from idealizing 'hunter-gatherism' and recognize ancestral origins of the human ape's weaponized hunting as a tyrannical early form of objectification and disintegration of nature, just as they repel the agricultural revolution?

Over focus on domestication removes the actual agency that other species have on determining human behavior, and part of undermining a concept of "human exclusivity" is removing the centrality of human agency to demonstrate that "human" is actually not really human at all, but is produced by complex ecological relations in which other animals are constantly defining human behaviors and being. ~ Justin Gortva Scheibel

Under mighty-man social conformity, veganism has waned in anarcho-primitivist circles, with social pressure to keep it suppressed.

> *Seen it all before, there is this cyclic reject that comes as no surprise :*
>
> *1) because the anthropocentric approach of their own freedom is a recurring thing with humans, having been confronted to that since late 80s as far as i'm concerned, the right to eat meat and dairy products thus to exploit and kill animals is of course an essential aspect of liberty, obviously ;*
>
> *2) veganism nowadays seems to be perceived as some neo-liberal element, coming out of the underground of radicals to become trendy and mainstream, integrating mass consumption in ways that are pushing forward synthetic products as well as 'PC' and mundane attitudes ;*
>
> *3) there has been some recent Kevin Tucker feature in a podcast [http://www.petermichaelbauer.com/episode-2-rewilding-anarchy-with-kevin-tucker/check at 00:16:45] in which such issues as eg. saying "hunter-gatherers" rather than "gatherer-hunters" has been heavily debated - hunting's so cool, hunting's so wild, hunting shows a dude's got balls, hunting's a primal man thing, ya know.*
>
> *Among all of these points, i tend to find that, animals themselves are very absent.*[31]

Others report similar anthropocentric experiences with anarcho-primitivism.[32] I would love to read Kevin Tucker, but to me the man-the-hunter hype is an insurmountable barrier. I only made it through Shepard to critique him. Horrified with even anarchists continuing their tyranny on nonhuman animals, both domesticated and wild, especially when based in malicious machismo, anarcho-vegans of all shades are simmering just beneath boiling point.

Edwin Henry Landseer
Wikimedia Commons

Use of the term 'eco-patriarchy' in this essay is distinct from the assumed connotations. Here humans' eco-patriarchy is not opposite matriarchy or women, rather opposite unfettered ecology. Eco-patriarchy is human domination at the root of disintegrating wildness. This topic's exemplar is human hunting vis-à-vis gathering. While the containers have evolved, the act of gathering – picking wild food – remains similar from primitive to modern humans. While the weaponry has evolved, the act of human hunting – *"deliberate, direct, violent killing of unrestrained wild animals"*[33] – also remains similar from primitive to modern humans.

The hunt is by definition an armed confrontation between humanness and wildness, between culture and nature. Because it involves confrontational, premeditated, and violent killing, it represents something like a war waged by humanity against the wilderness."[34]

Some of eco-patriarchy's targets, sometimes with allies, resist or fight back, but the battle is undoubtedly one-sided, and unless humans shift paths soon, all is soon lost.

Five years' hunting adventures in South Africa-
being an account of sport with the lion, elephant.
Roualeyn George Gordon-Cumming, London, Simpkin, Marshall & Co., 1892
Broward College Archives and Special Collections

The eco-patriarchal path leads to mass extinctions and ecosystems annihilation. Modern humans tend to want hopeful endings with specific suggestions of how to make things better, to prevent the path's inevitable outcome. Suggestions tend to be oversimplified, too easy, too unrealistic, remaining on the ecocidal path in blissful denial, retaining lifeway in cognitive-emotional dissonance. While I share my ideas, they are my own, and align with my perspective. I offer an invitation to authentically, responsively actively participate in the situation at hand. I challenge the human species to expand its empathy to include wild animals, and respond accordingly. I assert that resisting and deconstructing civilization, and protecting and recovering thriving ecosystems, is wild's requisite. The calling I sense is not anti-human, but pro-human, especially in that it prevents upcoming mass human anguish of civilization's certain apocalypse. The calling is humans defending and rewilding wildlife and habitats as rewilding humans.

The theory of eco-patriarchy, evidenced in the nature of human relations with other animals strewn in assorted cultural forms all the way back to some earliest *Homo sapiens*, reflects a narrative based on interpretations of this author. Undeniably, my perspective cannot reflect pure reality. In the words of Adorno, *"The more reified the world becomes, the thicker the veil cast upon nature, the more the thinking weaving that veil in its turn claims ideologically to be nature, primordial experience."*[35] Further, thinking and communicating in the realm of language is confining and imprecise. Words and dichotomies like natural-unnatural have thorny connotations underlying perceivers' individualized interpretations of their perceptions.

Here's more on dichotomy word play. In this writing, eco-patriarchy is to ecofeminism as humanity is to animal. That is, animal is the form to which all humanity innately longs for return. Ecofeminism is the form to which all eco-patriarchy innately longs for return. So too civilization innately longs for return to the form of wildness. None of these are actually dichotomous, but skewed notions of given essences. The de-formed are entrenched in themselves and are a bit lost in their way back.

I am aware that 'radical' paleoanthropology, archeology, sociology, psychology, evolutionary biology, etc. interpretations of human nature can have the effect of demeaning some who hold opposing values or identities. My 'radical' thesis intends no harm. My method is an ecofeminist, ecological look through various other lenses to focus on that which has come to ail free living communities suffering and dying at ever quickening rates. Ecofeminism aspires for a more aware, wild connected, mutualistic, compassionate human remediating the harm of their species through multi-sensory, deep feeling actions. Analysis into human origins is essential for identifying both what may be helpful to salvage, and mishaps to avoid repeating. Inspiration and conflict prowl in evolutionary understandings of origins and nature. They create clear vision, motivate healing of and preventing harm to nothing less than life on Earth.

From origins to now, the human ape's attempt to morph into Earth's apex predator is entirely unnatural, fully centered on dominating and killing, reliant on inciting anguish and annihilation. Adaptation from a modest, prey primate species to Earth's apex predator is not the way of wild, but anti-wild. Pro-hunting, meat eating humans, and those shocked at the notion of humans as anything but apex predators, may be tempted to misread this essay as moralistic condemnation of all hunters through all times, but it comes from a corporeal compassion expressed into languaged analysis. There is no Peter Singer or *Animals, Men and Morals* in the bibliography. Further, I resist and reject the moralizing politics of identities humanity bestows. I am the feeling flesh of hominid animal compassionately and belligerently interacting with others in a severely wounded habitat. That emotions or compassion are undervalued or rejected by civilization is eco-patriarchy. Compassion is a, if not the, key feature of human life. It's an intense spark for action, despite and sometimes contrary to morals, more valid than intelligence or inventiveness. Compassion and all emotions are our species' essence.

Is conjuring up a pre-civ ideal to recreate an act of morality? My aim is not future utopia based on past utopia, but to draw from the past toward a wild future. To adopt an ancient diet with scanty to unknowable awareness, such as illusory 'paleo' foodways of select early hunter-gatherers, is moralistic idealism as much so as the intensified agrarian culture being defied. Even if a rewilder opts for moralism through replication of inaccessible past ways, why not opt for one of co-existence or kinship with other animals in lifeway and dietway, counter to current practices? Adaptation to conditions of the land was an early human hallmark, as was the commonality of plant-based diets. If one senses today's landscape and responds intuitively, kinship over killing is the wildway.

Rewilders will never be able to reproduce past in such a harmed ecology. The greatest shortfall in many rewilders is lack of intuitive and tangible awareness of the indigenous community. Too often they implant modern notions onto struggling remnant habitats, oblivious of their impact, sometimes intentionally. Paradoxically, their morality is not aligned with their cultural ideal in that, to be sustainable, early cultures would have repelled moralistic human supremacy. Indeed, supremacist ethos is what caused the degraded world from which rewilders seek refuge. To go feral requires prolonged observation to re-open senses,[36, 37, 38, 39] noticing nuances, actions and exchanges, inter-relations. Prolonged. Something the eco-patriarchal rewilder seems to have little time for, too busy imposing their will.

How can a rewilder whose ideal is based on early cultures with spiritual hunting honed through generations, communicate with the spirit of the hunted animal? Sometimes instead they supplant eco-patriarchal notions, *I am wild by hunting and eating animals.* How is the intimate connection between animal persons formed, when they don't experience other animals as persons? Their rewilding is artificial. They are a babe thinking themselves into a virile doer of civilization's 'rewilding'. Observing a lifetime would not bring them a step closer to their goal with their mindset. They cannot accept that ancient knowledge of ecological embeddedness has vanished, and reconstructing wild knowledge takes generations. In today's hurting wildscape, wildness requires immense healing first, lifetimes of giving back. When your friend is hurting, you don't use her, you offer aid. Wild is hurting, and if you sense the pain and don't give aid, instead exploit wild even more, your relationship is based in the disconnected aloofness of disregarded pain. Despite their justifications, they flail in attempts at ecological embeddedness by hunting animals, without perceiving their harm to the habitat. In this way a vegan rewilder at least causes less harm.

Humans' harms are too often unknown. Westerner Jean Liedloff lived in southeast Venezuela among rainforest aboriginals. Her experience coalesced into her treatise on human nature toward closer human relations, *The Continuum Concept: In Search of Happiness Lost.* She conveys an incident of a Yequana boy Wididi, seemingly lost to deeper understanding, perhaps a missed interpretation of how compassion is conquered and eco-patriarchy coerced via the need to belong.

> *Anchu was preparing to go hunting and Wididi watched him with mounting apprehension. His face reflected dreadful conflict and his lips began to quiver as he followed the man's every move with his eyes. When Anchu's bow and arrows were ready, the boy's chest was shaken with spasms and then sobs. Anchu had said nothing, nor had he given any sort of look of judgment upon him, but Wididi knew that boys went out hunting with their leaders and he did not want to go. There was no one to argue with but himself, for Anchu was simply going hunting and what Wididi did was up to Wididi. His antisocial side said no, his innate sociality, now in the process of being liberated by Anchu, said yes. Anchu took the bow and arrows and started up the path. Wididi's whole body shook as he screamed. By now his motive and countermotive were evenly matched and he simply stood and howled, racked by indecision. I understood nothing of the principles at work. I only saw a boy in torment because he had not gone with Anchu. I went to him and putting my hands on his shoulders hurried him along the path... I pushed Wididi ahead and bade him hurry. I thought I was helping Wididi and preventing Anchu from being disappointed, but of course I was interfering, and with the clumsiness typical of my culture, I was substituting my will for the child's, trying to make him do the right thing when Anchu had been working*

32

on the far sounder principle of freeing him to want to do the right thing. My contribution may have set Wididi's progress back several weeks. Anchu's system may have been on the verge of throwing the balance by removing all pressure from Wididi so his natural urge to be part of things could overcome whatever had caused him to rebel.[40]

This sex division scenario in childhood may correlate to a possible finding with early Neolithic pottery culture Linearbandkeramik, that after weaning about age 3, young boys were fed a less plant-based diet than girls.[41] How many individual humans' resistance to harming animals was forever lost to enculturation will never be known, as patterns of eco-patriarchy persistently etch into muscle memory, dictated learning by culture's group habit.

The suppression of compassion supplanted with eco-patriarchy, rooted into children through thousands of generations, however gently, is a traumatic process. Ecofeminist activist Pattrice Jones wrote *Aftershock: Confronting Trauma in a Violent World* to help activists cope with trauma, but it applies to all trauma.

By "breaking" children and then encouraging them to fear and forget their own wild feelings, we discourage their natural empathy for other animals, thereby socializing them into the exploitation of animals... At the heart of the problem is alienation, separation, and dissociation. Estrangement is both cause and consequence of the problem. We are cut off from earth, other animals, each other, and ourselves. These disconnections allow us to do terrible things to earth, other animals, each other, and ourselves. The terrible things we do increase the distance between us and within ourselves. And the cycle of traumatic violence continues.[42]

Ignoring human-on-nonhuman violence reveals supremacy and prerogative of a dominator, colonizer species. Steven Pinker is an example of focus on human violence stonily neglecting and thereby normalizing human violence on other animals.

This orangutan held out their hand to a help man who was clearing snakes from a river as part of efforts to protect the endangered apes. February 7, 2020
Animals guide humans back to their basics of interspecies compassion.
Photo: Anil T. Prabhakar

Perhaps as today, Paleolithic individual, patches and waves of humans resisted suppression of their innate interspecies compassion. For *"...we are born with a repugnancy to the killing, and consequently the eating of animals; for it is impossible that a natural appetite should ever prompt us to act on... what we have an aversion to... "*[43] Earlier humans too may have been put into a hard place of wanting a lifeway of compassion with other animals while still needing social belonging. Some, at least in moments, decide or intuitively sense that compassion supersedes a feeling of belongingness with their own culture. Some mindfully decide or innately act on their compassion, defending nonhuman animals from other humans. Known examples today are only the most recent. Here is one of the innumerable waves of compassion action for other animals:

Pamphlet – 2006
The Western Wildlife Unit of the Animal Liberation Front,
An amazing inspiring story of how a small, well organized group of compassionate individuals brought the US fur industry to the brink of destruction and liberated countless animals.

-- A fairly lengthy history of the birth of Animal Liberation in North America through the successes (and failures) of the 80s/early 90s, ending with the repression of the mid-90s, and (first) jailing or Rod Coronado. It is unsparing in its analysis of the ongoing triumphs and failures of the Animal Liberation movement.
Includes Coronado's 'open letter' from prison, in 1995.

Biche morte (Dead hind) by Gustave Courbet, 1857

When compassion is suppressed, 'others' become objects, opening the way for harming them, as objects don't feel pain. This thesis analyzes Deep Ecologist Paul Shepard's connecting nature to women, and mystifying, idealizing, and romanticizing nature into the *"cult of the romantic."*[44] This ostensibly inadvertent eco-patriarchy deflects from anarchic liberation, thereby propagating the *"exploitation of both woman and nature, while also impeding an authentic love for and knowledge of women and the natural world."*[45] Subconscious manifestations of eco-patriarchy conceal desire for supremacy, which is at the origins of objectifying and degrading ecology, the opposite of the kind of action required for recovery. During transition out of eco-patriarchy, authentically knowing and caring incites allied aid in autonomous action.

> *...we will strive to know and care for the resistance of all living things that dwell in poisoned eco-communities, offering ourselves as allies in resistance to social and*

> *ecological degradation... forcing those in power to completely relinquish economic and psychological privileges... the romantic drama of ecology is over...the ecology movement must also become an anarchist movement...*[46]

This is not moralizing, but a way of the wild, ecology's shifting energies resurging toward liberation.

In the words of environmental studies professor, author of *Rogue Primate* and Deep Ecology darling John Livingston, *"cultural perspectives on Nature and our treatment of the non-human are monstrous and unnatural. That is not a moral judgment. It is a naturalist's interpretation of the phenomena that surround him."*[47] This essay is an earthy exploration of the role of hunting in humans' detachment from and domination over wildness. The thesis is that the human ape's hunting is eco-patriarchy. Wild lives are central, and inciting return of all animals to wild belonging, humans included, is the aim. As with Perlman's Leviathan, eco-patriarchy dies when humans withdraw and let the beast rot, as this anti-wild spirit has no life of its own.

Compassion instincts are the instigator of re-belonging.

Female elephant pursued with javelins, protecting her young.

"She often stood after she had crossed a rivulet, and faced the men, though she received fresh spears. It was by this process of spearing and loss of blood that she was killed, for at last, making a short charge, she staggered round and sank down dead in a kneeling posture. I did not see the whole hunt, having been tempted away by both sun and moon appearing unclouded. I turned away from the spectacle of the destruction of noble animals, which might be made so useful in Africa, with a feeling of sickness, and it was not relieved by the recollection that the ivory was mine, though that was the case. I regretted to see them killed, and more especially the young one, the meat not being at all necessary at that time; but it is right to add, that I did not feel sick when my own blood was up the day before. We ought perhaps to judge these deeds more leniently in which we ourselves have no temptation to engage. Had I not been previously guilty of doing the very same thing, I might have prided myself on superior humanity, when I experienced the nausea in viewing my men kill these two." [1]

2 ORIGINS OF RATIONALIZING

"Now, years after I've quit hunting and fishing, I look back and realize how deep into the tribal mentality I was. I was (almost) hopelessly addicted to the high of the hunt and my inflated ego, shunning introspective feelings of compassion... I cannot explain the freedom I have felt since. [2] *~Kenneth Damro*

"The human hunter in the field is not merely a predator, because of hundreds of centuries of experience in treating the woman-prey with love, which he turns back into the hunt proper. The ecstatic consummation of this love is the killing itself. Formal consummation is eating... The prey must be eaten for ethical not nutritional value, in a kind of celebration."[3] ~Paul Shepard

The quote above by another Deep Ecology darling, Paul Shepard depicts civilization's blending of man's power over woman and animal rooted in a primordial mythicized hunt. The list of self-deceptive vindications is lengthy: The urge to lovingly kill animals is only natural as it is linked to instinct to sexually surmount women. Hunting and sex are biological drives fulfilling ecological functions. Man's hunt intrinsically connects him to wild through expression of his predatory, primal essence. Man's hunt is natural if all the animal parts are used, if he expresses gratitude, respects his prey, if he only takes animals that offer themselves to him. Man's hunt must be, because it is his deep primitive calling. Suffering and killing of the hunted must be, because it is the circle of life, the food chain. As much as some seemingly revel in the hunt, some are still attached with their empathy enough to grapple with the unease of what 'must be done.' Man's ability to withstand his hesitations and kill an animal is honorable; it is what makes him a man. The most repulsive of the rationalizations are those attempting to *"disguise their self-interest as 'concern' for animals and for other people."*[4]

Raymond Dart, the first archaeologist to find early human bones in 1924, interpreted pre-civilized humanway as *"carnivorous creatures, that seized living quarries by violence, battered them to death... slaking their ravenous thirst with the hot blood of victims and greedily devouring living writhing flesh."* With Western civilization's intensifying authoritarian, patriarchal context of the day, the narrative resonated in the minds of the masses. Despite Raymond Dart's 'man the killer ape' hypothesis being annulled decades ago[5, 6, 7] including by Shepard himself[8], the narrative's seeds still sprout from neo-global uni-culture down into individual minds. Modern humans embrace the narrative because they forgot how to be part of the nature their species conquers. Long ago their ancestors stepped off the path that would not have progressively seized habitats of all, and they need a story explaining, mollifying their participating in the resulting anti-nature, tyrannical, cultivated lifeway.

Humans' inventive power self-justifies their Top Ape dominant, evolutionarily prophesized status. Their fabled predatory instincts morphed into civilization's mechanization of *Homo* supremacy via specializations enforced by customs. Civilization reinforces and re-creates man's hegemonic hunt, propelling eco-patriarchal wars of all manners toward apocalypses of all scales on all fronts. [9, 10, 11] While hunting became primarily man's activity, sexual division of labor is not the root of the problem, but assigned by the problem.

Eco-patriarchy creates ingrained quagmires rife in self-hypocrisy. In today's modernity, how aware are vegans that animal liberation requires much more than buying local organic farmed plants and adopting rescue dogs? How aware are rewilders that going feral requires resisting deepest roots of a human supremacist narrative, becoming traitors to their own species?

> *There is a war to be waged against society, alongside the non-human animals who refuse domesticated subservience, and who are evicted from their homes due to mass deforestation, human development and technology. Veganism burdened by the millstone of liberalism, fails to critically acknowledge capitalist, industrial civilization itself as the massified, embodiment of anthropocentric domination. Anarchism that fails to challenge speciesism on an individual level reproduces the internalized authoritarian values of human domination. Since speciesism is pervasive in society, it is insulated and well preserved by a comforting normalization - a normalization that aids cultural indoctrination and apathy. Confrontation is necessary in unsettling the socially established comforts*

and moral order of non-human animal domination. My vegan anarchy embodies solidarity not just with dietary intake, but also armed with attack; attack defined by the material actions of an incendiary desire to destroy the social manifestations of human supremacy.[12]

With human supremacy running rampant, unseen in plain sight, domesticated humans fear supremacy's antithesis: anarchy, simply the organic in action.

Women and children gathering nuts.
The Late Cave-Men, by Katharine Elizabeth Dopp, 1904

Do power dynamics between femininity-gathering and masculinity-hunting reveal sex hierarchy? Why does the index section in Shepard's *The Others: How Animals Made Us Human*, in Colin Turnbull's writings and so many others, include a listing for 'women' but not 'men'?[13] Or when Shepard claims, *"the hunt made us human"*, to which 'us' is he referring?[14] Discussion of 'men' is expected and generalized, marginalizing 'women' into a special indexed topic. Stories and perspectives of the dominated are overpowered, left untold. Bias is found in the lack of recognition of the indigenous role, knowledge and training of gathering and sowing wild seeds into the habitat, i.e. wild tending, compared to the glorified role, knowledge and training of hunting.

> *Met a native survival instructor near Klamath Falls. Very knowledgeable about primitive traps but knew nothing about Yampah or biscuit root, or how to tend first food gardens. It's funny how this man vs wild mentality is so prevalent in primitive skills courses but I hardly hear anything about planting back, working with the wild to create abundance.*
>
> Commenter replied: *Domination and conquest verses harmony and co-creation.*[15]

A common retort: But if 'man the hunter' is a fable, why is there no evidence of primitive people who don't hunt? Name one.

Scientific narratives are processed and molded through cultural values. For example, when modern meat eating paleoanthropologists find any evidence of hunting, they routinely deem all individuals comprising an entire group over vast areas and times as 'hunters'. Mainstream-embraced evolutionary narratives tend to be value-laden. Being that alternative narratives tend to be silenced, scorned and sternly denied before considered, even when alternative 'proof' is discovered, is it recognized for what it is, or explained away with acceptable culturally mediated ideology?

Margaret A. McIntyre "The Cave Boy of the Age of Stone"
Illustration by Irma Deremeaux

Anthropological narratives are created, not described realities. Repetitively reinforcing the myth of the virile, heterosexual, animal slaying, meat gorging caveman not only naturalizes eco-patriarchy by projecting it into human origins, but ignores and denies the possible existence of other ways of being. Challenges to inaccurate, propagated narratives do manifest, but face uphill battles in gaining mainstream acceptance. For example, paleobiologist Amanda Henry finds evidence supporting a plant-based early human diet. *"We need plant-derived nutrients to survive – vitamin C and fibre, for example…Hominins were probably predominantly vegetarians."*[16, 17] Archaeologist Lyn Wadley concludes, *"I'm afraid the paleo diet is really a misnomer."* Narratives on early human diets are bias in that botanical remains are less likely to leave behind evidence, and in that researchers seldom look for plant remains. *"Many archaeologists are not interested in botanical remains,"* says

43

Wadley.[18, 19] In challenging modern eco-patriarchal culture, ecofeminsm naturalizes a broader ancestral life narrative by undermining the values behind eco-patriarchal science and rejecting the rigidity of its evolutionary normative. Until the realm of potentials is open for consideration, the 'caveman' experience remains an oblique mystery.

Archaeologist Penny Spikins and her team utilized new technology, such as neuro-imaging, to draw scientific evidence of feelings of early humans. Tracking archaeological remains in search of elusive, intangible emotions, York University's Department of Archaeology marks the beginnings of human empathy at six million years ago when the common ancestor of humans and chimpanzees began to 'help' others. Between 500,000 and 40,000 years ago humans tended to sick and wounded people over a period of many years. Researchers found a child with a congenital brain abnormality was not abandoned but taken care of for years until death. A Neanderthal with a withered arm, deformed feet and blindness in one eye was taken care of for decades. The team concluded that compassion in *Homo erectus* 1.8 million years ago began to be regulated as an emotion integrated with rational thought. Starting 120,000 years ago, innate compassion was extended to strangers, animals, objects and abstract concepts. Compassion is an essential human emotion, inspiring and connecting humans.[20]

In *How Compassion Made Us Human: The Evolutionary Origins of Tenderness, Trust & Morality* Spikins theorizes that compassion set early humans apart from archaic ancestors.[21] Her theory is drawn from and honed into this essay's notion of eco-patriarchy. An evolved human ape brain and lifeway include not only intensified, overflowing compassion but abilities both to hunt and to rationalize. Rationalizing serves as an evolved strategy to overcome distress elicited by internal incongruence with the increasingly compassionate human ape hunting animals.

Some hunters insist that they love the animals they pursue and kill... Does the hunter's alleged "love" for a cougar or bear he or she intends to kill justify the killing? No. Such claims... mask a deep confusion. More likely, the sentiment is admiration that is mistaken for love. In any case, it is patently obvious, upon reflection, that the alleged love of the quarry pursued by the trophy hunter is really self-love that is both inflated and masked through self-identification of the hunter with the defeated quarry. If the defeated quarry is loved, the love is secondary to and dependent upon the ego-gratification obtained by conquering and destroying it. And the greater the challenge (or the perceived challenge), the greater the conqueror is presumed to be... True love of a wild animal would be best shown by leaving it alone, not by killing it; and certainly not by shooting it.[22]

Rationalizing, an adaptation to cope by suppressing emotional discomfort incited by killing, creates a cognitive dissonance easily apparent to those aware of the adaptation, whose empathy does not succumb under its pressure. As astutely stated by Olga Tokarczuk, *"The psyche is our defense system-it makes sure we'll never understand what's going on around us."[23]*

Human ape hunting and exploiting other animals is an adaptation corroding innate compassion at best, and a human-constructed authoritarianism upon all at worst. Like civilization, harming other animals becomes habituated, rote, institutionalized, jading humans to needless inflicting of pain and death. As an unnatural force, human hunting triggers yearning for more hunting than subsistence would require, for mere pleasure. Living free avoids this unnatural trap, retains intact compassion. Blocked compassion fuels unwildness, domination, and civilization, leading to lifeways detrimental to self and others. Compassion is malleable, capable of being fully restored, rewilded. Rationalizing entwines humans and other animals into an escalating apocalypse-bound trajectory, unless compassion is unblocked.

"Nutcracker Man" Challenges Ideas on Evolution of Human Diet,
Human ancestor's teeth yields new clues, April 30, 2008
*Tooth wear challenges assumptions of why specializations occur in nature.
Researchers examined the teeth of Paranthropus boisei, also called the
"Nutcracker Man," an ancient hominin that lived between 2.3 and 1.2 million
years ago. The "Nutcracker Man" had the biggest, flattest cheek teeth and the
thickest enamel of any known human ancestor and was thought to have a
regular diet of nuts and seeds or roots and tubers. But analysis of scratches on
the teeth and other tooth wear reveal the pattern of eating for the "Nutcracker
Man" was more consistent with modern-day fruit-eating animals.
https://www.nsf.gov/news/news_summ.jsp?cntn_id=111457*

About 4 million years ago *Homo*'s early ancestral Australopithecines evolved an ability to walk upright, releasing them from the forest canopy.

Australopithecus afarensis jaw fossil.
Exhibit in the Arppeanum, Helsinki, Finland.
DSC05509.JPG AL 206-1, 17 August 2012

With diminutive canines that persist to this day, they were foliofrugivores, a prey species on the run, ever cautious of fierce predators like now extinct saber-toothed cats. One theory, contrary to mainstream narrative, is that human canines are not for tearing and ripping meat, but male mating fights, evolving smaller and smaller as humans stopped using canines for sex skirmishes.[24] After coming down from the trees with bipedalism, early hominins retained curved hand bones and huge finger muscles, remaining semi-arboreal. They might have used rocks and sticks to protect themselves on the open ground.

Australopithecine Troop

Australopithecus' emotional and social repertoire may have been similar to their closest kin chimpanzees or bonobos. *Homo* first evolved from *Australopithecus* retaining their viable dietway from trees and shrubs of persisting woodland plants. Contrary to modern mythology, they did not directly shift to hunting in the expanding grassy savannah.[25] As the grassland gradually replaced forest, they moved out into the opening, moving amongst different animals.

Footprints of a group of Australopithecus afarensis walking together 3.6 million These ancient footprints preserved in volcanic ash were found at Laetoli in northern Tanzania.Other Pliocene animals—giraffes, elephants and an extinct horse called a hipparion, hares and birds —also left their tracks in the ash.

In time, to survive as prey of the large carnivorous animals of the African savanna - lions, hyenas, leopards, cheetahs, wild dogs and three species of saber-toothed cats - with unpredictable plant food sources on the expanding savannah overtaking forest, *Australopithecus and Homo* passively scavenged from the leftovers of their predators, then actively competed for them, causing the extinction of some large mammals to the point of substantial impact on biodiversity starting millions of years ago.[26] Interviewed on their study titled "Brain Expansion in Early Hominins Predicts Carnivore Extinctions in East Africa", researchers stated, *"substantial anthropogenic influence on biodiversity started millions of years earlier than currently assumed... the impact of our lineage on nature has been far greater and longer-lasting than we ever could ever imagine."*[27] While carbohydrates were likely essential for *Australopithecine* evolution,[28] scavenging from animal kills, pounding bones with stones to reach fatty marrow and brain, may have triggered the human brain to enlarge and reform,[29] giving cognitive abilities to dominate carcasses of other species' kills, like that of saber-toothed tigers, reducing their susistence.[30]

Early hominins scavenging bone marrow.
Image: Ninara, Wikimedia Commons

While scavenging went on and off for a million years or so, the folio-frugivore foraging primate transformed into the origins of an inventive, invasive, big brained hunting human. Under attack and with an Ice Age climate shift destabilizing food opportunities, the hominin gradually converted from prey to predator. Extreme survival conditions instigated extreme survival reactions.

> *But as the crisis became prolonged, sensibilities became lethally deformed and vested interests in deprivation developed amongst emerging control groups. We have all lived in a permanent state of emergency ever since...forming the basis of the biocidal mentality... The war on animals became a war on humans and thence a war on nature, a war ultimately against all life waged in the name of total domination and disconnexion.*[31]

Socially and biologically adjusting to nourishment initially obtained by passive scavenging from predators' kills fueled early humans internalizing becoming killers themselves.

Using stone tools to slice raw meat and grind raw vegetables, and fire to tenderize food further, shifted chewing energy into brain development. Chimpanzees, humans' close DNA kin, eat some meat but they spend about half their awake time chewing and have much stronger jaw muscles. Mechanically, inventing objects and controlling fire is how humans evolved into behavioral predators, but the social and emotional impacts comprised more than clever tools and weapons, but a change in attitude.

By about 1.7 million years ago it's as if marrow and brain fat triggered not only brain growth and body strength, but something more.

> *Indeed, it was the form and symmetry of handaxes which convinced early geologists that... they represented humanity... Humans started to make handaxes at a time when climates became more variable, oscillating radically between wet and dry or warm and cold. Therefore food must have become more difficult to find...The makers of handaxes... seem... touchingly like us in their willingness to go beyond the practical.*[32]

Paleolithic Handaxe
between 500,000 BC and 245,000 BC, Essex
Sussex Archaeological Society, Laura Burnett,
Lower Palaeolithic, Acheulean, bifaced ovate flint hand axe, symmetrical in plan and profile. The axe is completely covered in shallow flake removal scars with evidence for more precise retouch. Such hand axes were in widespread use from c.600, 000 to 245,000 years ago in Britain during warmer climate, produced by the hominid species Homo heidelbergensis.

Homo erectus ergaster developed advanced lithic technology in the form of bifacial oval and pear shaped stone hand axes. *Ergaster* had features separating them from *Australopithecenes*, such as reduced sexual dimorphism, smaller face, and a larger brain capacity, closer resembling modern humans. Diminished size difference between sexes seems to correspond to diminished male-male aggression. *Ergaster* was likely the first hominin species to use fire, complexly socially organize, and distinguish sounds to talk. Spikins suggests a desire to prove trustworthiness was the inspiration behind finely crafting symmetrical handaxes, as opposed to the accepted interpretation of demonstrating skill for sexual selection.

> *The attention to detail is about showing an ability to care about the final form, and by extension, people too... overcoming the significant frustrations of imposing form on stone displays considerable emotional self-control and patience, traits needed for strong and enduring relationships... that it was an instinct towards trust which shaped the face of stone tool manufacture is particularly significant to our understanding of Lower Paleolithic societies. It sets a challenge for research into how our emotions, rather than our complex thinking skills, made us human... As small vulnerable primates in risky environments where they faced dangerous predators our ancestors needed to be able to depend on each other to survive -- displaying our emotional capacities was part of forming trusting relationships with the kind of 'give and take' that they needed.*

Studying social dynamics of modern chimpanzees and human foragers, Spikins finds that long-term altruistic alliances of many small goodwill gestures hone a sense of trust. The handaxe may be the first object manifestation of trust and reputation for trustworthiness. *"The form of a handaxe... may demonstrate trustworthiness not only in its production, but also each time it is seen or re-used, when it might remind others of the emotional reliability of its maker."*[33]

With an updated brain, humans adapted quickly to unpredictable changes in ecological conditions on the expanding savannah, morphing into lifeways interplaying with updated emotions, thinking, social strategies and creations. Early humans in various places transitioned from prey on the run to predator with weapons, from rocks to chipped handaxes, from sticks to sharpened spears, from digging baked roots from natural fires' ensuing 'hot spots' to controlling fire for protection and cooking.

> *(T)he control of fire ultimately led us so far down the path of control and supremacy. Manipulation of fire allowed us to eat outside of our species specific diet, migrate to cold climates, and ultimately fueled industrialization. Our domination of nature is all fueled by fire… Fire leads to degradation. When we add something to fire, it rapidly decays. If I had a piece of wood and did not add it to fire, it would remain in-tact for a while, slowly decaying and composting. But when I add it to flames, it begins to decay rapidly, turning to ash right before my eyes. Same goes for food; if I add foods to fire, it begins to decay and destroy its life-forces. It's best to eat fresh, ripe, raw wild fruits with its life-energies in-tact, only cooked by the fire of the sun… (O)ur domination of nature is rooted in our manipulation of fire… (D)omination led/leads to domestication.*[34]

Fire led to both killing and cooking animals, an ethos of domination, which in time led to colonizing outside their embedded habitat, to domesticating others.

Controlling fire was transformative. With fire, early humans evolved from foraging with passive scavengers to weaponized, organized dominant hunters. Relationships with other animals and between themselves were profoundly altered. The new ethos set the stage for what came next. *"Then the downward spiral to industrialization. None of it would run without heat/fire/fuel energy."*[35]

Mammoth Hunt

To form the level of cooperation required for perilous fight with fierce predators, commitment, trust and self-control were vital social strategies. Spikins turns to evolutionary and developmental psychologist Andrew Whiten and David Erdal's theory on the psychological evolution of sharing.[36] They propose five pillars of early humans' shift into hunting: cooperation, egalitarianism, mindreading (i.e. 'theory of mind'), language and cultural transmission,

> *By facing predators together to find food or defend each other, by sharing food among the whole group and by maintaining egalitarianism, humans moved from being a group of small vulnerable apes to what (Whiten and Erdal) describes as a highly competitive predatory organism'... neither intelligence nor technology would be enough to turn small primates into professional hunters. It was new ways to work together which moved humans into an entirely new niche. Only changing how we feel would change who we were.[37]*

54

Tight group cohesion was premised on profound care and attachment deeper and more complex than their ancestral groups. A drive to be accepted, appreciated, to maintain a good reputation needed to be strong for the group to function as one. The group regulated itself with intricate norms and routines. With this intense compassion paired with symbolic communication, *"...language would prompt a common opinion to come to bear on anyone's behavior or attitudes."*[38]

Human's distinctive spoken language interacts with compassion. Anthropologist Camilla Power's thesis on egalitarianism speaks to its basis, compassion. *"Language as the mutual exploration of each other's minds, conversation as a necessarily consensual process, expresses the quintessential opposite of the relations of dominance.*[39] Human's distinctive gazing 'cooperative eyes', are invitations into the mindworld of others, the kind of empathy rooted in and compelling compassion. The human baby instinctively gazes into the eyes of her caregiver and exchanges babble with a smile, pre-cursor to conversation. Human's dance of eyes and language is rooted in the emotion of compassion.

Homo erectus using fire, preparing tools, hunting
altering human relation with other animals.
Peking Man, 360,000 years ago, Choukoutien Cave, China
The Natural History Museum, London

As humans grew accustomed to hunting animals, acculturation and symbolism functioned as compassion's 'cut off' switch to other animals, channeling anxiety through various abstract outlets. *"Our emotional minds... are a hotchpotch of differing drives and motivations which often seem to make life harder."*[40] The most recent cave art discovery is an anxiety outlet in the form of a mythological drawings of human-like hunters and fleeing mammals dated to nearly 44,000 years old in Indonesia.[41] Complex thinking and language paired with combined with hunting anxiety instigating rationalization, the ability to tame powerful emotions, to detach from stressful feelings. Outlets of suppression through rationalization may be evidenced in impractical finely crafted handaxes during dire times, and in kept trophies of animal parts, like teeth.

Makira hunters string flying fox bat teeth together into necklaces.

Primatologist Frans de Waal deduced that humans have *"emotional biases toward cooperation that can only be overcome with effortful cognitive control."*[42] As emotions of sympathy, gratitude, guilt, shame, anger and pride wove in, rationalization took form in socially constructed mythologies, mysticisms, rituals and rites of passage. To hunt, some human ape individuals and groups need to overcome their innate resistance to methodical killing by inciting themselves into a hyped up altered mental state, masking their true feelings and instincts.

Humans' incongruous rationalizing-compassion interplay with harming animals remains strong, even while anxiety over hunting has settled into comfort of customary routines, societies' normalization mainstays. Yet worldwide humans retain an interspecies drive to care and protect, and an ability to expand their 'circle of compassion' with their organic empathy for other animals, as portrayed in this 2019 tweet:

> #SIBERIAISBURNING
> Siberia is burning!
> The forests are burning, the animals are burning alive…
> …We must be concerned! All of us…
> …it broke my heart by thinking at the poor animals burned alive. Thousands animals dead!
> …when all of our forests will die in a fire, we will be the next one to go. We and the animals.
> Here a testimony by one of the volunteers in Siberia:
>> "A bear walked out of the burning forest: thin, part of its fur burned, exhausted.
>> He approached the men who were trying to put down the fire, not menacing at all, as if it was asking for help.
>> The bear drank the water and the biscuits (they only had that) that the men gave him, and then it walked away toward that part of the forest still not reached by the flames.
>> Many men started crying watching the bear walk away.
>> What may have happened to the other animals of the forest?"
> …This is a catastrophe! The russian government finally started handling the fire after the info blasted everywhere. But it's not enough. The forest is still burning because the fire is too much big![43]

The interspecies empathy extended even to insects is demonstrated in this report of another fire, "'Screaming Animals in Pain': Beekeepers Traumatised as They Check on Hives after Fires"

> *SW Apiarists Association president Stephen Targett said the situation in north-eastern NSW was 'truly devastating' to beekeepers and extremely traumatic.*
>
> *'It's doing their heads in, the screaming animals, the animals that are in pain, that are crying out in the forest, it's absolutely horrific,' Mr Targett said.*
>
> *One beekeeper employs some young people and it has really traumatised them.*
>
> *'So the beekeeper has arranged counselling for these young beekeepers who went into the forest and he won't allow them back into the forest for a period of time.'* [44]

When modern human drive to care remains tangibly strong for so long, why have the origins and nature of human compassion been unstudied? To evidence 'man the hunter' eco-patriarchy bias, ask people to close their eyes, imagine Neanderthal and describe the image. Almost every mind will envision the modern culturally indoctrinated belief: powerful weaponized male hunter dominant over other animals. Something like this

Le Moustier Neanderthals, 1920
by Charles R. Knight

Perhaps consciously people know or can deduce that it is likely half of early humans were women, about half children, many of them gathered food, not all of them hunted, some tended to one another when they ailed, and many of them likely cared deeper than many modern humans. Eco-patriarchy bias is laced through societies' pre-history notions based on scientific narratives. In *Erect Men/Undulating Women*, Melanie Wiber exposes subliminal beliefs indoctrinated through popularized illustrations of human evolution. She encourages readers of writings on the Paleolithic to carefully critique messages and values behind 'first world' culture constructs embedded in scientific perspectives.[45]

Challenges to the western 'Man the Hunter' model are underway in archaeological explorations gaining insights into experiences of the sex and genders previously excluded from record. Alternative narrative interpretations emerge through lenses including anthropology, history and hard sciences. Today's culturally oppressed peoples tell the stories of early women and genders in books such as

The Invisible Sex: Uncovering the True Roles of Women in Prehistory

Invisible Women of Prehistory: Three Million Years of Peace, Six Thousand Years of War

The Invisible Sex

Gender Archaeology

Gender in Archaeology: Analyzing Power and Prestige

Ancient Bodies, Ancient Lives: Sex, Gender, and Archaeology

Exploring Sex and Gender in Bioarchaeology

Engendering Archaeology: Women and Prehistory

In Pursuit of Gender: Worldwide Archaeological Approaches

What This Awl Means: Feminist Archaeology at a Wahpeton Dakota Village

Ancient Maya Women (Gender and Archaeology); *Women in Prehistory*

Women in Ancient America and

Women in Prehistory: North America and Mesoamerica (Regendering the Past).

Neanderthal Museum in Krapina, Croatia

Stories of another dominated people, children, are recently beginning to be explored as in the book *Unearthing Childhood: Young Lives in Prehistory*, from Australopithecines to Stone Age foragers, to first farming villages. Even scientific methodologies focusing on children are outlined in

Paleopathology of Children: Identification of Pathological Conditions in the Human Skeletal Remains of Non-Adults and

Children and Childhood in Bioarchaeology: Bioarchaeological Interpretations of the Human Past: Local, Regional, and Global Perspectives.

Untold stories of the dominated next in line for telling are those of nonhuman animals. While eco-patriarchy seems to be navigating planetary ecocide, its authority is being chipped away.

Philosopher and animal liberationist Brian Luke explains how humans subordinating emotion to reason maintains an authoritarianism.[46] Perhaps that is how *"Man has become an expert at rationalizing his destructiveness."* [47] When Spikins raised the role of compassion in early humans, many of her professional colleagues found the notion to be *"deeply subversive."*[48] Feminist archaeologist focusing on gendered power in prehistory, Joan Gero, challenges male-centered explanations of tool-making on several levels, including emphasis in research time and money towards studies of the most "masculine" of stone tools, such as projectile points, while tools likely made and used by women remain relatively ignored.[49]

Perhaps the most obvious, self-deluding example of this rationalizing is when Derrick Jensen, in all seriousness, wrote that when he opens his refrigerator to get pieces of dead salmon flesh, the salmon speaks to him:

> *Remember the bargain... I know you don't like killing. If you help take out the dams that will help us survive. Then you can kill and eat all the salmon you'd like. We will even jump out of the water and right to where you are waiting. You won't feel bad about killing us, because you have helped our community. We will gladly do this for you, if you will help us survive.*[50]

His mind co-opted Indian culture to come up with feeble validation.

Ironically and sadly, the compassion-rationalizing tension in harming animals may be the tension fueling the making of humans' material world overtaking wild habitat. Just as tension made the axe weapon that brought on the tension, tension may also be making humans' civilization in twisted spiral of tension harming all. *"We have all inherited minds which are capable both of the heights of compassion and the depths of cruelty."*[51] The fundamental unanswered question is, do humans, with their updated brains, have the ability to adapt off the eco-patriarchal path of the perpetual apocalypse they've incited; and if they do, will they choose to?

Maidu woman preparing acorn mush.
Sturtevant, William C. *Handbook of the North American Indians.*
Smithsonian Institution, 1978, p. 394.
Photograph Notes: Probably feast at Bidwell Bar, March 1903.
Photo by Dr. John W Hudson, from the Field Museum of Natural History.
Information taken from Sturtevant, William C, et al California Vol. 8.
The Field Museum of Natural History

3 HUNTING AS TRANSITORY

In *The Artificial Ape: How Technology Changed the Course of Human Evolution*, archaeologist Timothy Taylor posits that human honed hunting weapons and other technologies created a synthetic life, shifting humans from simply wild to managing the wild, which *"undermined the logic of evolution... Through technology, the laws of nature are supplanted by the will of humans. "*[1] For Taylor, once humans overcame nature there was no return. Others, such as anarcho-primitivists, hold that return to wildness is possible.

Hunter-turned-vegan Kenneth Damro details the perpetual apocalypse of human hunted animals, affecting both the hunted and the hunter. He includes examples of how some primitive hunting methods cause more suffering than modern methods.

> *Bow hunting is particularly cruel as it often leaves deer with arrows protruding from nasty wounds. I once watched a wounded deer that had an arrow protruding from its shoulder. Each time the arrow would brush a tree or limb, the deer would flinch as it endured the pain... I came upon a deer track from an apparently wounded deer. Splotches of dark green intestinal bile were displayed on bright white snow among its tracks – it was unmistakable. If you hunt, sooner or later you will wound your quarry, which (though it may be subconscious) will wound your heart.*[2]

How hunters cope with their wounded hearts varies.

Generally found in hunting cultures,
shamanism may be the oldest mystical tradition.
Tungus shaman, detail of an engraving from
Nicholaas Witsen's Noord en Oost Tartarye ("North and East Tartary"), 1785.
the trustees of the British Museum; photograph, J.R. Freeman & Co. Ltd.

Novelist Joy Williams' satirical yet reality-based essay "The Killing Game: Why the American Hunter is Bloodthirsty, Piggish, and Grossly Incompetent" details how frequent 'poorly placed' shots leave wounded animals scampering away for miles in fear and pain before they collapse.[3] She details the suffering intentionally inflicted by bow hunting:

> *These guys are elitists. They doll themselves up in camouflage, paint their faces black, and climb up into tree stands from which they attempt the penetration of deer, elk, and turkeys with modern, multiblade, broadhead arrows shot from sophisticated, easy-to-draw compound bows. This "primitive" way of hunting appeals to many, and even the nonhunter may feel that it's a "fairer" method, requiring more strength and skill, but bow hunting is the crudest, most wanton form of wildlife disposal of all... An animal that flees, wounded by an arrow, will most assuredly die of the wound, but even with a "good" hit, the time elapsed between the strike and death is exceedingly long.*

Modern hunters look to current indigenous hunting methods as models. While contemporary 'traditional societies' are not Paleolithic or Neolithic relics for conveying experiences of early human lifeways, certain generalities can be considered. For example, hunting mysticisms signal anxiety and ambivalence. Numerous rituals, taboos and mythologies are common among hunters, facilitating man's overcoming innate aversion to premeditated killing, blocking interspecies empathy.

> *(O)ur nurturing and empathetic urges do not discriminate on the basis of species. Only the wordy, rational, hair-splitting parts of our mind and culture do that. We 'learn' to discriminate; the prevailing culture and our elders teach it to us... since we have been actively using and killing animals... we have put together a hodge-podge of cultural devices that repress many of these feelings. The device-making began with the hunt rituals in primal society...[4]*

Technological prowess as inspiration for art and ritual.
Artists in the cave of Font-de-Guame. By Charles R. Knight
Neg. no. 2A21479. AMNH Photo Studio, Wikimedia Commons
The American Museum of Natural History

Hunt anxiety may have channeled into early symbolic art or language. Or sometimes empathy is buried so deep in the gut that the routine killing comes rote, jaded in routine, or is even enjoyed, leaving aghast others still attached to their compassion. Myths, rituals, taboos, etc. are mechanisms for warding off intrinsic compassion, which if experienced, would incite terror at oneself, risking discovering the enormity of deeply held self- and group-delusions.

The sense that Earth's living communities need finality to human domination is rising. Especially while hunting in these times is contributing to extirpations and extinctions,[5, 6, 7] human reconnection with the withered wild is feasible in today's degraded bioregions only with responsive healing action based in ethos of compassion and liberation. For example, some Māori are adapting to current conditions by going vegan based on their sense of what the land needs, as well as the people. For Laura O'Connell Rapira (Te Ātiawa, Ngāpuhi, Te Rarawa, Ngāti Whakaue) being Māori is integral to her veganism

"In the Māori worldview, the rivers, lakes, and forests are our ancestors. They are part of us and we are part of them. But right now, our rivers and forests are sick, and intensive animal agriculture, and especially dairy in New Zealand, have played a huge role in that. By not eating meat and dairy, I don't contribute as much to the sickness of my ancestors." She points out that the confiscation of Māori land has been used to support the proliferation of dairy farms throughout the country. *"I consider not buying into the dairy industry to be an act of decolonisation,"* she says.*"*[8]

Increasingly, native people are challenging their cultural normatives. Perhaps the most effective challenges respect native traditions by incorporating cultural mythologies into the challenge.

Margaret Robinson strives to adapt her veganism into her native heritage. Part of her struggle is that *"when you challenge hunting traditions, you challenge the way Mi'kmaq men understand their masculinity."*[9]

Bison Hunt

Foraged tuber from groundnut, *Apios Americana* –
*Groundnut is a long vine that likes to grow along the edge of flowing water.
Mi'kmaq harvested the tubers. Before the founding of the village where I grew
up (1860) the area was the summer campground of the Mi'kmaq. They called
groundnut 'sequbbun', 'sequbbunakade means 'groundnut-place'. Other names
for groundnut are Hopniss, Mi'kmaq potato, Indian potato and traveler's
delight. The plant will have at least two and upwards of 20 tubers, ranging in
size from a grape to a grapefruit, containing 11-14% protein. They are crunchy
and nutritious and the taste is supposed to resemble chestnut, which is slightly
sweet, becoming sweeter after the first frosts. They also have a somewhat nuttier
flavor when baked. Groundnut beans (from the flowers) can be eaten raw or
boiled like peas. The tubers can be boiled, fried or baked. Since they have a low
sugar content they have tendency to not over-brown when fried. Tubers can also
be dried for storage and ground into flour. Groundnut can be harvested all year
round, but are best between fall and spring.
http://www.docaitta.com/2011/08/foraging-26-groundnut-or-apios.html*

Robinson interprets Mi'kmaq legends and their relationship with animals as one of dependence, not dominion. According to Mi'kmaq legends, only survival can justify killing animals, as they have personhood equal to humans, not existing for human consumption. Robinson contemplates that if animal consent is traditionally required to justify their consumption, then it opens the possibility that consent might be revoked. Or Mi'kmaq could not ask animals for their sacrifice.[10] Many Mi'kmaq food traditions empower women to be gatherers of fruit, vegetable and nuts. Robinson reasons that since those traditions are recognized as fully native, then Indigenous counter-narratives can challenge meat customs. As Robinson puts it: *"There is more to my culture and to our relationship with the land, particularly as women, than hunting and killing animals."* [11]

Choctaw Village near the Chefuncte
Women preparing dye to color cane strips for making baskets.
by Francois Bernard, 1869, *The Peabody Museum – Harvard University.*

Choctaw and Cherokee Dr. Rita Laws writes on the historical connections between Native Americans and vegetarianism. Laws observes that it is the introduction of European meat-eating customs that has forever changed contemporary Indigenous relations to animals. Laws sees that the stereotype of the Indian as a *"killer of buffalo, dressed in quill-decorated buckskin, elaborately feathered headdress, and leather moccasins, stranger to vegetables"* is historically inaccurate and the direct result of European influence. At time of first European contact Choctaws had plant-based shelter and clothing, agriculture and orchards of native foods such as persimmon, pawpaw, hickory, walnuts, blueberries, blackberries, plums and mulberries.

A Cherokee legend describes origins as 'mutual helpfulness'.

> *The needs of all were met without killing one another. When man became aggressive and ate some of the animals, the animals invented diseases to keep human population in check. The plants remained friendly, however, and offered themselves not only as food to man, but also as medicine, to combat the new diseases.*

> *More tribes were like Choctaws than were different. Aztec, Mayan, and Zapotec children in olden times ate 100% vegetarian diets until at least the age of ten years old.*

> *In the past, and in more than a few tribes, meat-eating was a rare activity, certainly not a daily event. Since the introduction of European meat-eating customs, the introduction of the horse and the gun, and the proliferation of alcoholic beverages and white traders, a lot has changed. Relatively few Indians can claim to be vegetarians today.*

> *But it was not always so. For most Native Americans of old, meat was not only not the food of choice, its consumption was not revered.*[12]

The dietary practice of forager indigenous children not eating meat, and meat being a rarity, has also been observed in South America.[13]

Ojibwe/Cherokee artist and activist Linda G. Fisher also notes frustrations of stereotyping Indigenous culture.

> *We almost always associate the Indian – even today's Indian – with wearing and using nonhuman animals' hides, furs and feathers... I have often wondered why some people witness pain and suffering, yet turn and walk away, never giving that suffering another thought, while others empathize, are affected, and are changed by such suffering forever...I believe, if my Indian ancestors could comment on our present "right to hunt" in a world with so many people and so few nonhuman animals, that they, who listened to the land and killed only as was necessary, would not be wasteful. I think my ancestors would tell us that it is time to stop the suffering and the killing.*[14]

Fisher emphasizes that although she avoids hides and furs and follows a vegan diet, her Indianness is still critical to whom she is, not through a culture of hunting, but the teachings of her ancient Ojibwa ancestors. She describes how her ancestors' only killed animals out of absolute necessity. Nature had agency, nature had interests, nature made the decisions. Although this attitude toward nature is re-emerging even amongst non-Indigenous peoples, there are still Indians today who slaughter whales, eagles and all kinds of other nonhumans in the name of 'tradition'.

19th century Obijewa women traditionally harvesting wild rice
The American Aboriginal Portfolio, by Mrs. Mary H. Eastman, 1853
Illustrated by S. Eastman. Philadelphia: Lippincott, Grambo & Co.
via Wikimedia Commons

Wild rice, manomin to the Ojibwa, was a staple food for more than a thousand years. Manomin is a grass that grows only in water. At one time wild rice grew over a large portion of the continent. The natural habitat of the manomin was made much smaller with the influx of European settlers because they unwittingly disturbed the seed beds near the lake shores. For detailed information:
http://www.native-art-in-canada.com/wildrice.html

Obijwe/Cree artist Kerry Redwood Atjecoutay describes himself as 'antispeciesist, Earth First, Animal Liberation, Indigenous Peoples Liberation. anti-civilization. wilderness survival and bush craft, wild gardening, Green Anarchy and martial artist'. He lists his reasons for abstaining from eating animals as

> *not just for my health, but for the health of the planet, animals domesticated and free-living (wild), and the tribal*

peoples who are still struggling to hang on the their ancient ways… It is obvious by now, that someone like me, who is a descendant of the buffalo hunters of the Great Plains… can survive and live a very comfortable life on a vegan diet.

1908 Ojibwe woman tapping for maple syrup.
Photo by Roland Reed

Atjecoutay emphasizes the notion of adaptation.

Adaptation of the past, before colonization, was adaptation to the changes of nature. There is an old Telling of a band of Ojibwa who left the forest for the Great Plains. Because they did not know the region they didn't know what to eat, but over time they adapted, not just by experimentation, but by two Contraries already living in the Black Mountains and also through dreams. Dreams were extremely important to the people. Through dreams the people learned to adapt. Adaptability dictates our relationship with the Earth, with other animals, with each other. Millions of Native Americans adapting to and adopting contemporary way of life as their own has altered their world view.[15]

Cheyenne shamans *"used their spiritual power to heal animals and animals' diseases and to protect species against hunters of their own human community."*[16] If shamans had power to protect animals from the hunt, and mythologies shape-shift with shifting conditions, then if the ancient spirituality is revitalized, can they protect animals from the human hunt now? As humans have never been obligate carnivores, exploiting animals is a choice, not intrinsic.

After migrating Europeans colonized into Salish First People land, what once was a free lifeway devolved into stripped 'rights', which Natives in modernity strive to regain, often motivated by reconnecting with their heritage. Traditional hunting rights are diminished, and battled to this day. In her novel *Daughters of Copper Woman* inspired by northwest coast Nootka whaling peoples' mythology and culture, Anne Cameron's wrote on customs of the hunt.

> *No woman would kill a whale. Whales give birth to living young, they don't lay eggs like fish. They feed their babies with milk from their breasts, like women, and we never killed them. The man who killed the whale never tasted whale meat from the time of his first kill until after he'd retired as a whaler. And neither did his wife, because he had to be purified and linked to the whale by way of the woman's blood and woman's milk. No one linked to them will eat of them. It is a promise.*[17]

Through an ecofeminist lens this taboo is interpreted as a rationalizing device to cope with killing anxiety passed through generations of customs. A Salish tribe that previously battles with animal rights activists over hunting a whale is again seeking permission from government authority to hunt another whale on the grounds of tradition and treaty rights. The tribe has great mainstream public support.

The tribe traditionally used wooly dogs as sheep for weaving blankets and clothing.[18] The dogs' breeding was controlled, preventing them from breeding if they chose sex with hunting dogs. This retained humans' resource exploitation of the dogs' long shaggy hair, shorn by knife, in the end for manufacture and commercial trade. Wooly dogs went extinct after the blankets made of their fur were outcompeted with cheaper ones. If tribal people decided to breed the wooly dog into existence again to keep their heritage alive, would they receive the same level of popular support as killing a whale? The difference may reflect compassion dissonance based on eco-patriarchal valuation in using others as objects.

Mbendjele forest hunter-gatherers' beliefs are instilled through taboos of *ekila* on practices such as hunting, eating, sex and menstruation, but based in an ethos of sharing.[19] Anthropologists may interpret these taboos as allowing the group to have a sense of autonomy by shifting the locus of the rules' authority to others, in this case the forest. From an ecofeminist lens the *ekila* taboo on hunting may be more than a social organization device, as it intertwines with rationalized coping with anxiety of the kill.

Despite contemporary and likely ancient social pressure for native people to comply with culture, some native plant eaters report basing their decisions not within their heritage but on human relations with other animals. Native guests, callers and commenters on the podcast *Native American Calling*[20] discussing veganism report a variety of motives.

> *The only one that convinced me to become vegan was my soul and the animals. After 29 years i got to a point i knew i had to put my foot down. An unforgettable day where I was enjoying an elk burger at a town tavern while right in front of me was a couple of deer heads mounted on the wall. Something about the experience just didn't feel right. What I experienced physically and mentally afterwards for days was a clear indication that I didn't need meat and it wasn't doing me any favors.*

Another caller reports that he and his wife went vegan to be a part of ending speciesism within their culture and the world. *"When we teach our children... to adopt a plant diet we're teaching them compassion and love early on."* The guest Tina Archuletta, owner *of Itality : Plant Based Wellness* ended the show leaving listeners with *"Plant based eating is for our Earth, for our Mother"* It may be universal both across cultures and through times that some people who eat plants for liberation of animals and earth hold individual motives overriding culture.

Indigenous people detached from heritage may have idiosyncratic struggles with veganism related to their idiosyncratic longing to reattach. The government took C's grandmother away from her tribal community and boarded her in a school, forever disconnecting her from her people. From the time C was little they had an instinctive affinity for animals. As a teenager, listening to lyrics of bands like Gather inspired them to question why humans eat other animals, and make connections between liberation for humans and liberation for other animals – that no one was free until everyone was free. Living in a food desert was one challenge. Gaining support from their mother and grandmother has been unrelated to issues of tribal tradition.

Traveling from age 18 and meeting other vegans was eye opening. C grew to affiliate as straight edge vegan. In social media, leftist anarchists put forth that veganism is racist because it is white-centric. When C reveals their native born identity, they are accused of being colonized. Indigenous people too accuse C of adopting western ideology. C feels stuck in the accusations and doesn't know how to respond. They get support simply meeting and sharing food with other vegans, particularly indigenous vegans, and opting for individualism over conforming to restrictions of traditions.[21]

Illuminating diverse perspectives and realities demonstrates that broad spectrum beliefs portray native peoples as a fixed monolithic block, overlooking differences between the multitude of tribes, bands and individuals, and their changes over time. In the U.S. a common phenomenon is citing an archetype of a monolithic Native American indigenous people hunting for survival to support the claim that human hunting is 'necessary' or 'natural'. Here Aztec Emily Victoria responds to such a case:

> *There's nothing ethical about killing animals, nor is it 'respectful' to 'honor' an animal whose life was taken from them. It's time to evolve and stop trying to live by outdated traditions simply because it was done for years or because ancestors did it. We don't need to wear the skins of animals and we certainly don't need to eat them either. This is not something our survival depends on. And what bothers me even more is when non-natives speak on this subject by trying to erase indigenous vegans. 1. Animals don't 'serve purposes'. They exist with us, on the same planet. We share this world together, so respecting nature is respecting other animals. 2. Saying that vegans target indigenous people when a lot of vegan indigenous people exist is INVALIDATING and ERASING indigenous vegan people. I have dedicated the last two years of my life to veganism and animal liberation. 3. Tradition and culture is not a justification for animal use and abuse.* [22]

When the topic of indigenous veganism is brought up in anti-civ or anarcho-primitivist circles, there is a knee-jerk charge of indigenous people being enculturated into moralism and/or consumerism. But the inspirational basis for indigenous people adopting a vegan lifeway ranges from innate feelings of compassion to mythical to ethical. Meanwhile, the basis for nonindigenous people coopting hunting rationale tends to be linked to indigenous ethics selected to support a pro-hunting narrative. In particular

> *deep ecologists are most notably involved in this kind of overgeneralization, borrowing here and there from Native American and Eastern cultures the pieces that fit into their*

theory, while ignoring other aspects of those cultures. This type of conceptualization is cultural cannibalism."[23]
For example, deep ecologists have cited tribal justifications of hunting for subsistence. But even on impoverished reservations where wild tending indigenous plants is insufficient, today it is rare that hunting is out of need to subsist. Most hunting is largely for habit within a heritage justified in an assortment of ethics. Generally, the position that killing animals is justified if needed for survival applies to a low rate of humans' animal killings.

If indigenous people were cannibalizing for subsistence, would nonindigenous people coopt cannibalism? Co-opting pieces of their narratives and lifeways to validate eco-patriarchal actions of other cultures, with their own eco-patriarchy issues, is disrespectful and self-serving. Colonizer guilt gives widespread sympathy to indigenous people, so why not give them back their land instead of stealing their customs too? Beneath the social politics, humans - indigenous and nonindigenous alike - are responding to changing social and environmental circumstances, as humans always have, but under dominion of eco-patriarchy.

Even still, by far and until recently, plants have generally provided the staple of the human diet from origins on. While early human plant remains are challenging to find, evidence suggests weaning babies into plant foods in the late Paleolithic and later Pleistocene. Food remains in infant feces were found to be soft vegetable food, such as club-rush and chamomile, nearby a grinding stone for crushing plants into mush.[24] Despite mainstream Western culture belief in heavy meat eating early humans, nutritional ecology research into Neanderthal diet finds that an exclusive meat eating diet would have killed a pregnant Neanderthal and the unborn baby.[25]

Paleontologist study of prehistoric tooth plaque reveals an earliest humans' diet to be plant parts such as bark, fruit and leaves. The most recent *Australopithecus* discovery, *sediba*, shared a mix of features of earlier australopithecines, modern humans and chimpanzees. Remnant minerals of fruit, leaves and woody tissues were found on the teeth. Nearby sediment samples and fossilized feces found plants, grains, grasses, and pollen of savannah and fruits, leaves and woody fragments of woodland, pointing to a plant diet responsive to the savannah/woodland mixed environment.[26]

Even with most contemporary indigenous people living freely, plants are commonly the staple. While they live amongst abundant meat opportunities and refer to themselves as 'hunters', most of the Hazda diet is wild plants.[27] When hunting is involved, relationships between control of resources, inequality, and eco-patriarchal social practices emerge. Even the most relatively egalitarian Hadza have a religious stratagem, the *epeme*, where on occasions animals are hunted, choice parts of the largest game animals are reserved only for adult men. Anthropologist Frank Marlowe writes:

> When a male is in his early 20s and kills a big-game animal, he becomes an epeme or fully adult man. Certain parts of all larger game animals can be eaten by the epeme men only. Not only can females and sub-adult males not eat the meat, they cannot even see the men eat this meat or, it is said, they could die or get ill or suffer any number of misfortunes.[28]

This is an example of eco-patriarchy emerging in the hunt, and its resultant taboos.

The Western mind is so indoctrinated with 'man the hunter', it blinds itself to realities of wild food gathering lifeway. *"Why should I learn to farm,"* asked the !Kung San man, *"when there are so many mongongo nuts in the world?"* Half of !Kung calories are derived from mongongo nut and two thirds of their diet is plant-based - baobab seeds, palm tree seeds, wild oranges, plums, mangoes, berries, and a variety of roots.[29]

Gathering mongongo nut, !Kung foraging and preparing food.

Some Australian aborigines subsisted seasonally on seeds and fruit.[30] Acorns were the primary food of native peoples in what is now California, harvesting from at least ten species of oaks. Throughout most of the North American continent wapato, otherwise known as Indian potato, was the main staple.

Foraged tubers from wapato, *Sagittaria latifolia* –
Wapato is easily cultivated in shallow water. In the fall they can be detached
with feet or a stick, often floating to the surface. Ripe tubers can even be found
floating freely with no digging. They can be eaten raw or cooked, tasting like
potatoes or chestnuts, and can be prepared in the same fashions: roasting, frying,
boiling, or sliced and dried to prepare a flour. Buds and fruit are also edible.

Generally, the overall constancy of seeds, nuts, fruits and other plant parts and ease of gathering them gives humans subsisting in nature the stability to thrive. Contrary to the meat-gorging caveman image programmed into today's human mind, evidence of some meat eating by some earlier humans has neither implication for meat as the ideal diet, nor signaled that the human species has genetically or anatomically evolved to require meat.[31] A behavioral decision to eat meat has not changed human biology from herbivore to omnivore, but biology is distinct from psychology.

Art by Elizabeth Peterschmidt

Anthropologists Richard Washburn and Chet Lancaster spoke of humans' *"carnivorous psychology"* as being fully developed by the Middle Pleistocene.[32] A social psychologist reports on the neurological link between sex and man's desire to hunt, the two utilizing the same brain region.[33] Is this science bias, or has the hunt overtaken men to that degree? In the field of abnormal psychology, infliction of pain on an animal or another person inciting sexual excitement is an indicator of sadism. Prominent psychiatrist Dr. Karl Menninger wrote widely on the Erotic

Sadistic Motivation Theory of hunting, the socially acceptable outlet for cruel, sadistic energies. Psychologists theorize hunting may indicate psychosexual inadequacy, some theorizing hunting is a means of seeking reassurance of their sexuality. The feeling of power that hunting brings temporarily relieves sexual inferiority, subconsciously. While many hunters claim to hunt for sustenance, often hunting investments don't economically bear out that claim. In modern civilization desire to hunt is a seed that has been planted in the brain and given life by encultured norms repressing innate feelings and lifeways of human origins.

Australopithecines foraging wetland tubers.

Biological anthropologist Gabriele Macho studied whether a diet of tiger-nuts, edible bulbous tubers of the sedge *Cyperus esculentus* , would provide nutritional needs for the early hominin *Paranthropus boisei*. She determined that it would have contained sufficiently high amounts of minerals, vitamins, and of particular importance, fat for the hominin brain. Hominins selectively gathered parts of grasses and sedges, such as bulbs and grass blade bases, for their diet mainstay. Abrasive tiger-nuts, rich in starches, were also digested by chewing for a sufficient time, up to 3 hours for 80% daily calorie intake, corroborating fossil cranial anatomy. Large primates typically forage 5-6 hours a day. This is how 'nutcracker man' earned his moniker, surviving for around one million years because they could successfully forage nuts through shifting climatic conditions.[34]

Australopithecus boisei thrived on tiger-nuts *Cyperus esculentus*

According to the sciences of evolution, anatomy, and physiology humans are herbivores, designed to thrive from a plant-based diet. As put by professor of physical anthropology Katharine Milton,

> There is general agreement that the ancestral line (Hominoidea) giving rise to humans was strongly herbivorous... In hominoids, features such as nutrient requirements and digestive physiology appear to be genetically conservative and probably were little affected by the hunter-gatherer phase of human existence.[35]

While early human diets varied greatly, largely in relation to season, landscape and tool use, at its core the *Homo* biology remains facultative herbivore. Their body is anatomically and physiologically adapted to a plant diet, able to digest but not reliant upon meat. For example, folio herbivore gorillas optionally supplement their leaf foraging with invertebrates like ants, termites, grubs, caterpillars and larvae, or only eat plants.

That *Homo* is not biological hunter is simply evidenced in a look at one's own flat fingernails and short, blunted teeth.

> Comparative anatomy teaches us that man resembles frugivorous animals in every thing, and carnivorous in nothing; he has neither claws wherewith to seize his prey, nor distinct and pointed teeth to tear the living fibre... It is only by softening and disguising, dead flesh by culinary preparation, that it is rendered susceptible of mastication or digestion; and that the sight of its bloody juices and raw horror, does not excite intolerable loathing and disgust. Let the advocate of animal food, force himself to a decisive experiment on its fitness, and as Plutarch recommends, tear a living lamb with his teeth, and plunging his head into its vitals, slake his thirst with the steaming blood; when fresh from the deed of horror let him revert to the irresistible instincts of nature that would rise in judgment against it, and say, Nature formed me for such work as this.[36]

Even though humans' closest DNA kin chimpanzees occasionally hunt, their long canine is designed to capture and kill. Humans retain diminutive canine teeth, comparable to their earliest Australopithecine ancestors, before humans controlled fire and cooked.

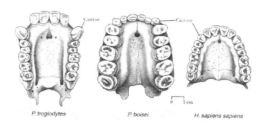

Chimpazee   Australopithecine   Homo

Human weaponry shapes culture, and culture may shape biology, but weaponry is not biology. That human teeth are herbivorous becomes clear when envisioning herbivorous teeth on a true carnivore. Despite canine size, to some extent dietway and lifeway

#humansareapesnotlions

are a choice. While not a scientist, responding to scientific studies raw foodist TJ Long summarizes and reflects on sociality differences between *Homo* genetic relatives chimpanzee and bonobos

> *Socially chimpanzees are patriarchal and bonobos are matriarchal/egalitarian. Chimpanzees rape and murder, and are generally more aggressive and dominant. Bonobos are more harmonious… it's an incredible comparison, observing such vast differences between two similar species who are our closest animal relatives.*[37]

Homo's dietway and lifeway is not set in stone, but a patchwork of adaptations to local environments paired with individual decisions. *Homo* is has always been in adaptive, pointing to potential for humans to relinquish domination and re-embed with wild.

Chenchu Digging Stick Culture
by Pakideadithya 8 January 2018
The main stay of chenchu economic life is the digging stick.
Following prehistorians custom of naming a whole culture after one type of artifact, the chenchus would be known as a digging stick culture. With the sharp point she loosens the roots and tubers like chenchugadda , varragedda, javaragedda, nulagedda, chedagedda, bhuchakragedda, etc. which form their staple diet. Creative Commons

Plant ecologist, Potawatomi and restoration ecologist Robin Wall Kimmerer apprised, *"In some Native languages the term for plants translates to 'those who take care of us.'"*[38] The human herbivore reveals its truth too in diseases caused by meat and prevented and sometimes cured by plants. Long-term vegetarians have a better coronary heart disease risk profile than do humans eating as omnivores.[39] Examination of plaque on and isotopes in ancient teeth, and fossilized fecal waste shows humans 10,000 years ago ate about 10 times more fiber than humans today.

Cholesterol is made from fat, something of which most plants have little. Herbivore bodies produce adequate cholesterol from a low-fat diet, holding onto and recycling fat and cholesterol. When herbivores eat meat, excessive fat and cholesterol cause the formation of atherosclerotic plaques in artery walls. Biological carnivores and omnivores do not get atherosclerosis. Still, if

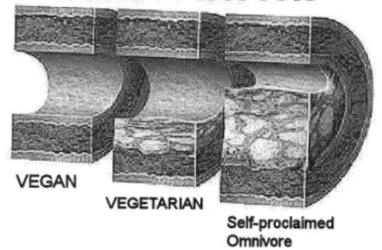

How accurate is this vegan propaganda?

87

biologically carnivore giant pandas, with their short carnivore digestive tracts, thrive off bamboo almost exclusively, then even without humans' folio-frugivore digestive tract, a vegan diet may not be 'unnatural'. What is unnatural is for humans to think themselves as lions, conforming to a modern ecosystem harming dietway, 'fitting in' to mainstream culture's spiral of death.

As humans worldwide are consuming more meat, heart disease, linked to fats and cholesterol, is the leading cause of death in the world and in the U.S. An article by seventeen doctors evaluating the history of atherosclerosis states *"Although commonly assumed to be a modern disease, atherosclerosis was common in preindustrial populations including preagricultural hunter-gatherers."*[40] Modern science has determined that plant foods prevent and heal atherosclerosis caused by meat.[41, 42, 43, 44, 45, 46, 47] Remnant nutritional science misconceptions, such as those made by Shepard in his writing *The Vegetarians* are easily refuted.[48] Mainstream nutrition mythology on veganism not only touts Orwellian notions centered on consumerism, but assumes rewilding vegans only obtain food from stores, oblivious to more nutritious foraging opportunities.[49]

DNA analysis shows that forest gathering Neanderthals found in a cave in Spain drew their food and medicine from plants, mushrooms, pine nuts, and moss.[50] It's interesting to note that some pre-civ humans subsisted wholly on plants and mushrooms like these Neanderthals, challenging civilization's romanticized 'man the hunter' image and pro-meat bias.[51] Ethos based on narratives such as Raymond Dart's are long lasting, with profound implications, as reflected in interpretations of other animals, which rationalize human's endless exploits.

> *We have doomed the wolf not for what it is, but for what we deliberately and mistakenly perceive it to be –the mythologized epitome of a savage ruthless killer – which is, in reality, no more than a reflected image of ourself.*[52]

Ranchers 'defending' cattle.

News from anthropology, biology, nutrition and other sciences keeps rolling in challenging what has become a man-the-hunter profiteering propaganda machine.[53] One would hope that unfettered awareness will reconnect humans with their earliest lifeways, drawing upon a more regenerative wild past to renew thriving.

Tasmanian tiger wiped out by human hunting in 1936.
Sadly, the Tasmanian tiger is just one animal in a long list of species recently
wiped out directly or almost directly by the hands of humans.
Other disheartening examples include
woolly mammoth, dodo bird, passenger pigeon, and western black rhino.
via Wikimedia Commons

4 HUNTING'S CIVILIZED WRATH

Gathering: Germanic *gath,* "bring together"
Hunting: Old English *hentan,* "to try to seize"
Dictionary of Word Origins

Australopithecus afarensis walking close to birds.
Based on diorama set in Laetoli depicting three Australopithecus afarensis walking on ashes leaving footprints, Federigo Federighi The University of Pisa's Natural History

Human hunting has seized upon all, estranging humans from others. As put by Washburn and Lancaster:

> *The human notion that it is normal for animals to flee, the whole concept of animals being wild, is the result of man's habit of hunting...*
>
> *Prior to hunting, the relations of our ancestors to other animals must have been very much like those of the other noncarnivores. They could have moved close among the other species, fed beside them, and shared the same waterholes. But with the origin of human hunting, the peaceful relationship was destroyed, and for at least half a million years man has been the enemy of even the largest mammals.*[1]

What came after hunting and intensified with agriculture is The Great Forgetting that is still now. Contemporary hunters use civilization's institutions to rationalize their tyranny, such as the North American Model of Wildlife Conservation, written by three hunters. Tenet ethos includes that: wildlife is a human resource, not autonomous beings with their own interests; exploiting over protecting is the value; killing for reasons of fur, meat, trophies, fun, and to rid the of 'vermin' are all acceptable; hunting to reduce carnivores and increase ungulates (inventing more 'surplus' reasons to hunt) is the aim; hunting using 'advanced technology' is 'fair chase'; unquestioned cognitive dissonance of hunters 'loving' animals that they kill is undisputed, and transparent; managing wildlife to ensure maximum numbers of preferred species to continue hunting is the goal; and keeping farmers and ranchers, profiteers of domesticates, happy is fundamental support.[2]

In applying contemporary concerns to eco-patriarchy, human hunting was origins of specialization and division of labor.[3] Hunting by the human ape incited powerful human-human bonding in coordinating and cooperating on the kill, creating and producing weapons, and was the first step toward social separation divisions, one being in the form of eco-patriarchal constructed family units.

Neanderthal family approximately 60,000 years ago. by Randii Oliver
via Wikimedia Commons

Homo neanderthalensis, Neanderthal Man,
by Maurice Wilson, 1950
National History Museum, Image reference: 001983

Eco-patriarchal social separation norms likely left human's longing for freer life. For humans, origins of hunting were a stepping stone not only toward self-suppression, but instigating the ecological catastrophe wrought by their ensuing colonization and mass civilization. The hunting ape spread across the world as a parasite, at first stealthily, then after initial incursions receding in impact. As progressively 'civilized' cultures formed in quickening pace, ravaging animals, plants and habitats correspondingly increased in pace. Parasitic relationships can be long and drawn out, and can be fatal, for the death of the host cannot but result in the death of the parasite by which it has been killed. The Neolithic top ape form instigated a disembodiment of any organic lifeway. Eco-patriarchal dynamics intensified in human-human and human-nonhuman relationships. Hunting forms carried over through generations, then withered, channeling into more socially acceptable domesticated customs.

Neanderthals driving Ibex over a chasm.
Zdenek Burian, 1951

While the question of whether some Neanderthals drove animals over cliffs as a hunting strategy is still unsettled, the archeological study *Shoot First, Ask Questions Later: Interpretative Narratives of Neanderthal Hunting*[4] found Neanderthal kill sites, with evidence of herding large herbivores like reindeer, horses, rhinos and bison, into areas for easy indiscriminate ambush, then selective butchering. The implication is that Neanderthals became adept at selecting geographic niches where other animals could be vulnerable to attack - cul-de-sacs, bottlenecks, depressions, blind corners. Triggering herds' instinctive flight behavior, they drove animals into places where they killed as many as they could. Using hunting strategies of surprise, forced panic, and coordinated planning gave Neanderthals the advantage over larger, faster and more dangerous animals. Still being discovered is evidence of this type of hunting strategy by other *Homo* species.[5]

Miles Lucas' reinterpretation of Buffalo 'Jumps' diorama at
The National Museum of Natural History, Native American Hall.
Smithsonian Institution Archives images 88-16885-88-16888

An extract from Mackenzie's Voyages: Wednesday May 29th 1805.
-Today we passed on the Stard. side the remains of a vast many mangled
carcases of Buffalow which had been driven over a precipice of 120 feet by the
Indians and perished... In this manner the Indians of the Missouri distroy vast
herds of buffaloe at a stroke; for this purpose one of the most active and fleet
young men is scelected and (being) disguised in a robe of buffaloe skin, having
also the skin of the buffaloe's head with the years and horns fastened on his
head in form of a cap, thus caparisoned he places himself at a convenient
distance between a herd of buffaloe and a precipice proper for the purpose,
which happens in many places on this river for miles together; the other indians
now surround the herd on the back and flanks and at a signal agreed on all
shew themselves at the same time moving forward towards the buffaloe; the
disguised indian or decoy has taken care to place himself sufficiently nigh the
buffaloe to be noticed by them when they take to flight and runing before them
they follow him in full speede to the precepice, the cattle behind driving those in
front over and seeing them go do not look or hesitate about following untill the
whole are precipitated down the precepice forming one common mass of dead
an mangled carcases; the (Indian) decoy in the mean time has taken care to
secure himself in some cranney or crivice of the clift which he had previously
prepared for that purpose.[6]

Step by step humans breached their relations with other animals. Chickasaw author Linda Hogan tells how her people *"broke (their) own treaty with life to participate in the hide trade, as so many others did. The beaver trade, for instance, with the Northern tribal nations."*[7] Charles Darwin noted the innate inter-species compassion, observing that the human mammal has instincts that *"consist of a feeling of love or benevolence… such active sympathy that the individual forgets itself, and aids and defends and acts for others at his own expense…"* Further, he observed mammalian inter-species selflessness as fundamental to social animals.[8] Each step away from human inter-species compassion was likely protested. For example, Cheyenne criticized the Blackfoot for their hunting practices, the running of the bison off a cliff, massacring hundreds of bison unnecessarily. Further, Cheyenne shamans at times felt it necessary to use *"their spiritual power to heal animals and animals' diseases and to protect species against hunters of their own human community."* [9]

American bison being chased off a cliff
as seen and painted by Alfred Jacob Miller, c. 1860.

Despite the resistance, the overarching movement away from wild interconnection continued. Alongside escalating detachment from wild were detachments between unwilding humans into identities, then placed into hierarchies of power. This manifested in role and value assignments empowering and disempowering, such as noted by editor of *Women in Human Evolution* Lori Hager: *"Many theorists have viewed females as passive recipients of evolutionary change, relegated to the bearing, nursing and transporting of young."*[10] Shepard exalted the benefits of hunting for men and boys, asserting that women are biologically drawn to gathering, while men are *"genetically programmed to pursue, attack and kill for food. To the extent that men do not do so they are not fully human."*[11] Contrary to Zerzan's condemning frontier expansion as *"male energy subduing female nature, one frontier after another,"*[12] Shepard's eco-patriarchy is aligned with masculine men mindset, expanding into 'virgin frontiers', bonding by bringing others under their control, oblivious to their obliteration of indigenous interconnected communities of life.

The Frontier is Essential for the American Project. By Walt Garlington
I write to say that we are the American generations for whom the frontier is the fact that there is no more frontier and who must somehow begin to decide how to deal with this... But take a step into the nominalism of the post-Schism West (whether Roman Catholic, Protestant, Cartesian, Newtonian, etc.), and this contentment is destroyed, and man is thrust onto the path of chasing frontier after frontier, boundary after boundary, in search of what will satisfy and give rest. The Puritan/Yankee City on a Hill will always need a frontier to forestall its inevitable collapse, proof that the American project is a diabolical fantasy. It is time for the peoples of the States to wake up from it. Hundreds of years of sleepwalking is more than enough.
https://www.geopolitica.ru/en/article/frontier-essential-american-project

Whereas the notion that men are biological hunters is sex eco-patriarchy, the notion that the human ape is a biological hunter is species eco-patriarchy.[13] Sexism and speciesism are both deep-rooted social constructs. That hunting is merely an elective culturally conditioned concept emasculates Shepard's belief schema.

When feminists expose patent patriarchy, they go largely ignored. A team member consolidating the 1968 volume *Man the Hunter* justified emphasizing the triumph of the male hunter thusly:

> *Hunting is so universal and so consistently a male activity that it must have been a basic part of the early cultural adaptation even if it provided only a modest proportion of the food supplies.*

On this, in her 1991 *The Paleolithic Glass Ceiling: Women in Human Evolution* Adrienne Zihlman explores the oppression of women and reviews suppression of women's stories.[14] Yet to this day, 'man the hunter' remains the prevailing myth.

FIGURE 6. Male Centrality among *Homo erectus*. Published in Josef Augusta and Zdeněk Burian, *Prehistoric Man* (London: Paul Hamlyn, 1960), plate 2, and entitled: "*Homo erectus* foraging in the wilderness of Java perhaps half a million years ago." Artist is Zdeněk Burian. Courtesy of Jiří Hochman.

Idolizing man-the-hunter eco-patriarchy has perilous consequences.

> *The practice of stalking and killing animals increased the propensity for violence among human hunters, and the status of men began to be associated largely with their skill and success at hunting other animals.*[15]

Generally, with hunting requiring higher energy output for unpredictable outcome, women took on additional responsibilities, gathering enough food for the entire group while men honed their skills in weaponry, stalking and killing animals.[16] Human hunting escalated both male violence and male social power with the effects playing out still today, and women and animals still carrying the burden.

Oppression and violence against animals and oppression and violence against other humans are entangled.[17] In *Animal Oppression & Human Violence* David Nibert begins his analysis from human origins. Earliest foragers were likely fairly communal, subsisting by sharing the fruits of gathering.[18] Plentiful food opportunities and the simplistic subsistence method - eat as you go - left time for a relaxed lifeway, aside from predator threats. When

humans attained a behavioral dietway of hunting animals, their disposition became increasingly violent. In this way, hunting set man in violence.[19, 20, 21] About 10,000 years ago domestication stratified and solidified inter- and intra-species social hierarchies, institutionalizing violence further.

Tapestry depicting a Florentine Wolf Hunt with Hunting Dogs
(c. 14th century), Uffizi Gallery, Florence, Italy

Social and economic mechanisms to reduce inequality brought on by hunting's separation between the sexes, like tradeoffs between mating and food sharing, may have entrenched eco-patriarchy further. Having lengthily lived with the Mbuti, Turnbull found the sexual division of labor without *"superordination or subordination."*[22] The generalizability of that notion is challenged in *The Origins and Future of Patriarchy: The Biological Background of Gender Politics.*[23] In *Nisa: the Life and Words of a !Kung Woman,* anthropologist Marjorie Shostak relays Nisa's story of how some men still try to dominate, and how a woman's brothers are called upon to rescue her from her husband. In clans without property where women are able to walk away, women still take on the extra burden of an unpaired woman providing for children.[24]

Other hunter-gatherer societies have cases of more severe inequality and violence, such as the Yanomamö of Venezuela and Brazil, popularized as being self-described 'fierce people'. While the interpretations are questioned, an anthropologist observed that some men inflict violence on their wives by beating with sticks, cutting with machetes, holding hot timbers against them, or firing barbed arrows into the buttocks.[25] Many Yanomamö women are covered with scars and bruises of violent beatings by seducers, rapists, and husbands. Men earn respect and fear through brutality toward women.[26]

In her book *The Harmless People,* Elizabeth Thompson describes actions of a man Gai, an ordinary event within a tribe renowned for their gentleness, Gikwe Bushmen of the Kalahari Desert. Gai set out to roast his infant son Nhwakwe's tortoise. With an unflinching pitilessness, Gai placed a burning stick on the tortoise's belly. The animal reflexively jerked her head and limbs and profusely urinated. The heat parted the two hard shell plates, which gave room for Gai to thrust his hand inside the struggling tortoise. He slit open her belly, pulled out her intestines, and flipped her beating heart onto the ground as she continued thrashing, while Nhwakwe came to sit and watch by his father.[27] How deep does humans' compassion 'cut off switch' track back?

Java Ape-Man Teasing a Giant Tortoise

After A. A. Jansson
COURTESY OF THE AMERICAN MUSEUM OF NATURAL HISTORY

Anthropologists are challenged to find shared power amongst hunter-gatherers deemed egalitarian. For example, attempts are made to locate female power beneath the realistic eternal image of Australian Aborigines,

> *(M)an the hunter strides along with spears and spear-thrower, and maybe a couple of boomerangs. Behind him comes woman the gatherer carrying a digging stick, a firestick, a food container or two... with perhaps a wooden dish half full of water balanced on her head, a child under one arm... and perhaps another at her feet – plus all her worldly possessions.*[28]

That stereotypical scene of gendered unbalanced division of labor is based in universal examples, like this field anthropologist's description of a Yanomamö on a community trek,

> *Each morning the men took off down the trail first. They would be there in the encampment and suddenly vanish silently into the forest. An hour or so later they'd stop hunting and gather together, squatting down on the trail to wait, talking about the game and examining each other's arrow points.*
>
> *Meanwhile the women moved slowly and leisurely, carrying huge baskets on their backs that looked as if they weighed more than the women themselves. Piled inside were hammocks, plantains, pots, gourds, wood ashes – every single thing a family owned. They even carried the roofing leaves that were used each night for the temporary shelter. Many of them also had little children on their hips, and some were thick-bodied and pregnant.*[29]

Feminists went through a phase of reinterpreting the early human experience as peaceful and matriarchal. *"Unfortunately, the evidence from excavated finds does not support the image of a peaceful past, although the levels of conflict were very varied across the broad range of prehistoric societies."*[30] When this became clear, feminists and male apologists sought to locate, reinterpret or theorize primitive women's equality, and have found some, or at least aspects of it. But *"in all hunting/gathering societies, no matter what women's economic and social status is, women are always subordinate to men in some respects."*[31]

Aggression and social consequences of division of labor hierarchy initiated by hunting cannot be ameliorated, compensated or construed into widespread egalitarianism.

Recalling his being positioned in the debate between ecofeminists and Deep Ecology, author of *An Unnatural Order: Roots of our Destruction of Nature* Jim Mason reports

> *I have taken a lot of flak from feminist and animal rights people over my use of Paul Shepard's ideas. I know where he's coming from, same place I came from, the southern Missouri Ozarks where hunting and fishing is a way of life. I cringed a lot when I read his views on hunting. Nevertheless, I think his most important idea, and the one that I tried to elaborate on in my book, is the importance of animals in the evolution of the human mind, speech, thought, and worldview: The ideas expressed in his early book, 'Thinking Animals'. I think it is very important to try to understand those ideas apart from his obsessions with hunting. To me it shows the importance of animals to the human mind and worldview, and then we can understand the devastation brought on by domestication and animal slavery.*[32]

Mason was not oblivious, tolerant or supportive of eco-patriarchy, but explored human-animal relations contextualized outside the confines of civilization's social justice movements. Shepard and Mason analyzed early humans' attentions and responses to other animals, and the impact on indigenous humans' lifeways and adaptations.

But from there on they diverge, with Mason retaining an intact innate empathy that he responds to with authentic compassion. Mason has no need to use romanticism with eco-patriarchy's rationalizing devise, such as Shepard.

> *A romantic removes the 'love object' from the reality of its being to the secret places of his mind and establishes a relationship of power/domination over it. There can be no reciprocity, no element of mutuality between the romantic lover and the 'love object'. The quest (chase) is all that*

matters as it provides a heightened sense of being through the exercise of power.[33]

Eco-patriarchy is a seizing upon others, as in how Shepard saw animals and women as the human apeman's plaything-prey.

Authentic Letters from Upper Canada:
With an Account of Canadian Field Sports, 1833
by Thomas Magrath and Thomas Radcliff. Dublin : W. Curry

I have had a pet one for years, (reared from a cub) that follows me about, and has often kept up with my horse, when at a round canter. This huge black bear, standing five feet high when upright, is of the fair sex. The name to which she answers: Mocaunse (in the Mississagua language, Young Bear). Her qualities, mildness and docility. She runs about the house like a dog, and is invited to the drawing-room, when any visitor arrives, who wishes to make her acquaintance—when my avocations led me to the woods in distant parts of the province, Mocaunse was the companion of my journey, and the nightly guardian of my tent—not asound or stir could be made, without a warning from her cautionary whine, or growl. It was amusing to observe with what gravity she took her seat each morning at the opposite side of the mat, upon which my breakfast was arranged, and the patience with which she waited for her share of the repast...

In the feminist animal rights book *The Pornography of Meat* Carol J. Adams illustrates how men similarly exclude both nonhuman animals and women from authentic care by normalizing objectifying them in similar language and images.[34] In the case of Shepardian Deep Ecology, both women and nonhuman animals are objectified through mystification centered on patriarchal perspective, an ethos making a game of seizing upon.

While eco-patriarchy's manifestations are sometimes tangible, they are rooted in intangible institutions, and institutions are incapable of care, for care is solely a human ability. Nonhuman animals and women, both lower in eco-patriarchy's pyramid, have lost freedom to live socially connected lives on their own terms. But so too have men. All are ensnared in eco-patriarchy's positioning. While it seems unfair to place the locus of control on those seized upon, to liberate, all must break free from fixed roles prescribing power relations.

Picking blueberries, Mesolithic
André Houot, colouring Jocelyne Charrance
Cantonal Museum of Archaeology and History,
Lausanne; Zion and Art Museum

In *Nature Ethics: An Ecofeminist Perspective* Marti Kheel discusses the indoctrination men undergo to disconnect them from their natural feelings, to take on an identity of dominance, to transcend nature.[35] In *Manhood in the Making: Cultural Concepts of Masculinity* anthropologist David Gilmore finds *culturally sanctioned stress on manliness—on toughness and aggressiveness, stoicism and sexuality—is almost universal, deeply ingrained in the consciousness of hunters and fishermen, workers and warriors, poets and peasants who have little else in common"*[36]

From primal cultures to today, males undergo formal and informal, premeditated and spontaneous initiations into virility, into manliness, into supremacy, through challenges to perform acts superseding nature, or of violence on nature, as devices of achieving eco-patriarchy power. The propagation of male violence has established collectively.

There is cross-culturally universal sex difference in human use of physical violence, whether it be fist fights or homicides, warfare or the slaughter of nonhuman animals.[37]

Under eco-patriarchy, humans are divided and tethered to socially coerced, self-vanishing roleplaying, to inauthentic, inorganic lives.

Hunting and trapping stories; a book for boys, 1903,
by J.P. Hyde, New York, McLoughlin

Text: All had to wait for a few minutes while the boy took the snow out of his eyes and got his second wind... the party came upon two sets of tracks, showing that there were a pair of moose ahead of them, and that they were moving swiftly. By-and-by a running stream was crossed and here the tracks ended. There were no foot-prints on the opposite bank and the boy was sure that this was the end of his moose hunt. The Indians separated at once, one going up and the other down the stream. In a few minutes the up-stream Indian found the trail and signaled to the other to follow. The boy was beginning to find out that hunting in the Northern woods was hard enough work. The tiny icicles on the branches hurt his eyes until he looked as though he had been crying and his heart thumped against his ribs as if it would break. After about a mile of straight running the tracks divided. Here a half...

Shere Hite's qualitative report on patriarchy includes boys' and men's self-reports on hunting in the chapter

Hunting: Learning to Be "Mean"

Hunting is another testing ground of toughness... boys are expected to dispense violence, pain and even death without flinching, not showing tenderness but pleasure.

Some boys object, but others develop a real taste for it and grow to enjoy it:

> *"One time a friend of mine and I trapped a wildcat and beat it to death with clubs. Even now my stomach turns when I think of it. I regretted doing it almost immediately."*

> *"Dissect animals? They are beautiful and fascinating-I did it in high school, but I did feel a bit guilty about it. There was some competition among the guys along the lines of seeing who could be the grossest."*

> *"I went hunting a few times with other men, with a .22 rifle when I was 18. It was, admittedly, a fun game, feeling the surge of power."*

> *"I grew up hunting and fishing. Most hunters pretend to hunt for something called 'sport'. But I know that what makes hunting game attractive is the killing of the animal. I like to kill things."*[38]

Shepard said he saw no difference between eating a vegetable and an animal.[39] Yet, he saw hunting as deeply spiritual:

> *Hunting is a holy occupation, framed in rules and courtesy, informed by the beauty of the physical being and the numinous presence of the spiritual life of animals.*[40]

For Shepard, it was essential that humans disconnect themselves from other animals,[41] while *"eating animals is a way to worship them."*[42]

> *(T)o be kindred... means... a sense of many connections and transformations – us into them, them into us, and them into each other from the beginning of time. To be kindred means to share consciously in the stream of life.*[43]

Shepard encouraged every man to hunt to recover

the ontogenetic movement; ...the value of the hunt is in a single leap forward into the heart-structure of the world, the "game" played to rules that reveal ourselves. What is important is to have hunted. It is like having babies.[44]

Shepard's words are reflective of those who hunt as a malformed means of connecting deeply with wildness, superseding the harm and disintegration of wild. In the widespread hunting book *Meditations on Hunting*, Jose Oretega y Gasset wrote *"Death is a sign of reality in hunting. One does not hunt in order to kill; on the contrary, one kills in order to have hunted."*[45] Is this the way of all animals, or are humans special this way?

Essayist Joy Williams replies *"This is the sort of intellectual blather that the "thinking" hunter holds dear."* Williams suggests that if wildlife managers, instead of monitoring hunted animals, would affix listening devices to hunters, actual attitudes would be revealed not as *'suffering as sacrament'* and *'spiritual experience blather'* and other *'specious arguments'* mindlessly accepted by hunting apologists, but something much more *'grisly'*. She continues on displaying evidence of how *'for hunters, hunting is fun... Hunters kill for play... They kill for the thrill of it, to make an animal'' theirs."*[46]

Shepard's thinking distinguishes from anarchy, primitivism and ecofeminism. Those who want to break free from the conditioned manly roles would concur with Andree Collard and Joyce Contrucci in *Rape of the Wild: Man's Violence against Animals and the Earth,* that

> *the efforts of modern man to rationalize the contradictions and delusions surrounding the hunt and the hunter extend to the romanticized images he fashions of primitive man as the archetypal hunter with the hunt as the sine qua non of his existence.*[47]

Contrary to Shepard's variety of Deep Ecology, anarcho-primitivism is liberation of the human and all dominated wildness. The rationalized, sexualized hunt is narcissistic suicide and ecocide of wildness, especially in contrast to ecofeminism's full being of intact sensual wild empathy, caring and belonging.

An ecofeminist critique of Shepard sees through the veil to dynamics of eco-patriarchy. Marti Kheel saw how Deep Ecology

> *employs ethical discourse as a means of shielding the hunter from the actual experience of the animal he kills... The focus of the hunter is on his own interior mental state. As long as his mental attitude is said to conform to a particular ethical code, his violent behavior is thought to be legitimized. The emphasis on the instinctual (sexual) nature of hunting functions to further remove the hunters' conduct from ethical reproach, since hunting is seen as a natural and elementary drive. The ethical discourse thus functions as a "decoy," focusing attention not on the state of the animal who is about to be killed, but rather on the hunter. What the holy hunters see as a "reciprocal" activity is, in reality, a unidirectional morality in which the hunter formulates and follows his own moral directives... the animal is reduced to an object, a symbol against which the hunter seeks to establish his masculine selfhood and moral worth.*

Hence Deep Ecology partakes in the *"quest to establish masculine identity in opposition to the natural world."*[48] The masculine savage ideal emphasizing primitive prowess over other traits deemed 'feminine', based in a primal spiritualism, is a socially constructed notion. Followers are programmed, obedient, trained, unfree.

> *Men must use their imaginations... to create a new masculinity. I hope that by gaining a broader, sociological view of themselves as gendered beings in a gendered society, men might see the caveman identity as an empty fiction... Manhood itself must morph into something new.*[49]

This 'something new' is not a restructuring of powers between man and woman while overlooking human domestication and exploitation of nonhuman animal. It is disbanding of civilization's eco-patriarchal construction that frees all.

Illustration du proverbe
"Triste maison que celle où le Coq se tait et où la Poule chante."
Grandville : Cent Proverbes
(Sad house where the rooster is silent and where the chicken sings.)
Granville (Jean-Ignace-Isidore Gérard) - H. Fournier Éditeur, Paris, 1845

Eco-patriarchy separates by many categories, widely today being sex. Discussing the divide risks running into identity politics rabbit holes. *Poor people need to hunt to eat. Now you're trying to take hunting away from indigenous people? Women hunt too.* Etcetera.

Women fighting a bear.
The Early Cave-Men, by Katharine Elizabeth Dopp, 1904

Ladies hunting in the 15th century.

The rationalizations of today's identity politics has intensified into a tool of social control through one-upmanship and exclusion. The most potent primal 'last resort' social power of banishment, in context of overpopulated modernity takes form too habitually in fervent shaming, marginalization and expulsion from a clique. Here is how identity politics dynamics was experienced by a queer bisexual person:

> *'Listen', responded the Activists (capital A – they presented themselves as The Only Authority). 'Listen and do as we say.'*
>
> *I learned all the Correct Language and the Correct Actions, so I would not be Problematic. I cringed and sucked through my teeth at all the Problematic People... I learned to be pure in thought, word, and action, so that I would not risk the ire of the Activists. There are certain things that must never be said, certain questions that must never be asked...*
>
> *...after my first altercation, (where I failed to recognize a latinx queer on sight and was roundly shouted down by the*

whole group) I became much quieter. I listened without speaking... I didn't realize until much later how much anxiety began to build in me whenever I entered these spaces, fearing that any misstep would result in my admonishment and potentially, my expulsion.

Still, I was unwilling to leave the Left behind. If this was justice, then I must submit myself, however uncomfortably, to the greater good.

Never mind my questions. Stuff them down deep.

... I questioned how, exactly, I was supposed to avoid speaking over... always 'stay in my lane'

... I self-flagellated over past... without ever really understanding what I had done wrong besides doing something I was forbidden from doing.

But I never dared to ask anyone else – least not the Activists.

... I began to meet people who had been 'called out'; people who had made transgressions so egregious that they had been banished from the circles of the Left...

The accused became a pariah. No defense, apology, or self-improvement is good enough when you are marked for life.

... When the veil was lifted, it became clear to me that the left was infested with wolves in sheep's' clothing, manipulating the good will and efforts of earnest, well-meaning people.

Or, maybe we were all a little wolfish – although I had fancied myself a pure, earnest person...

I just wasn't interested in it anymore. I wasn't interested in helping to create a society of unquestionable rigid social mores. I wasn't interested in silently tallying each 'problematic' misstep of every individual around me – or quietly policing my own speech in constant fear that someone was doing the same to me. And I wasn't interested in perpetuating the socially assigned identities that fed the hierarchies I wanted so badly to tear down.[50]

Oppressed groups are disillusioned with struggle for equal power, risking joining and becoming the abuser.

Few women have confronted how closely they mirror patriarchal oppressors when they too participate in other species' denigration. Women who avoid acknowledging that they are animals closely resemble men who prefer to ignore that women are human. "[51]

An all too common knee-jerk dynamic of oppressed people is to attempt to free themselves from eco-patriarchy by adopting the ways of their oppressors, only walking deeper into the quicksand, ensnaring themselves farther into the trap.[52, 53]

With women largely exempt from machismo indoctrination, their liberation struggle is to focus on refusing the dominant paradigm as a whole.

Human superiority is as much a lie as male superiority... Other individual worlds are only as wide as our empathy... Animal encompasses human. When we finally cross the species boundary that keeps other animals oppressed, we will have crossed the boundary that circumscribes our lives.[54]

"The world turned upside down" (gender-role reversal)
Israhel van Meckenem - eingescannt aus: Alois Niederstätter: 1400 - 1522:das Jahrhundert der Mitte: an der Wende vom Mittelalter zur Neuzeit, aus der Reihe Österreichische Geschichte, Wien 1996, ISBN 3-8000-3532-4

Pressure to conform takes place early, first in the institution of the family, then in the institution of the school, working away at young minds with bodies bound to desks pointed toward teachers, graduating into The Final Institution as worker/consumer. The *Brave New World* inches closer. Young minds are vulnerable to the ever present, all surrounding Leviathan, and even blamed for their own conversion, detailed in a novel by Olga Tokarczuk:

> *That's why I only liked the smaller children. The older ones, over the age of ten, say, were even more loathsome than adults. At that age the children lost their individuality. I could see them ossifying as they inevitably entered adolescence, which gradually forced them to be hooked on being the same as others. In a few cases there was a bit of an inner struggle as they wrestled with this new state of being but almost all of them ended up capitulating.*[55]

The aim is not to share in eco-patriarchy's power, but to liberate from eco-patriarchy, recovering compassionate, free lifeway of wildness.

While in recent decades ecofeminists have criticized *"exploits and destructiveness of hegemonic masculinity"* and met resistance, the *"ecological feminist discourse has grown and diversified... pressing the edges of gendered identities as some of the necessary ingredients of Earthcare."*[56] The blame does not rest with straight, white, heterosexual 'first world' men, but the structures and sovereignties seeded into place by human hunting's omnipotence that placed all into eco-patriarchy's positioning. *"It's not human*

nature that makes us engage in this blind destruction of our world and ourselves... it is the nature of civilization, an emergent social structure in which our species is presently trapped."[57] Shifting energies of victimhood identity politics into energies liberating and rewilding self through liberating, defending and rewilding Earth is a resistance strategy that dissolves civilization's cultural eco-patriarchal structures, both overt and covert.

Today two grippingly linked yet opposing undercurrents are ecological reconnection and civilizations' collapse. In her novella *Liminal*,[58] Natasha Alvarez merges these provoking themes. In a soothing yet unsettling setting, Alvarez reminds humans how feral love energizes courage to ultimately stand for wildness. As the reader's ethical mind scurries through dilemmas and principles, the plot pulses along with Earth beckoning in the background. *Liminal* speaks the purest truth that Earth calls compassionate humans to act on, not more experiments with yet another form of a gentler civilized future, but next steps required for any feasible flourishing future. While the story doesn't redress human subordination of other wild animals in the immediate lifeway of the characters, it is fearless in taking the next step feared by indoctrinated humans latching tight to their domestication.

Humans' return to herbivore lifeway is an essential part of caring for Earth, recovering thriving wild community through liberation of domesticated and wild life. Flower Bomb disputes that liberation is consistent with civilization being that it *"requires large-scale exploitation of natural resources, subsequently destroying and wiping out entire eco-systems."*[59] And with modernity's infrastructures strung across the planet, where will liberation take place?

> *Capitalism requires the expansion of technological industrialization to accommodate the demands of mass society. Mass society requires the ever-expanding displacement of wildlife to house the growing human population. Civilization is rooted by agriculture which is predicated on the basic formula of taking more from the land than putting back. This results in irreversible damage to all ecosystems that directly affect non-human animals.*[60]

A return of land for rewilding requires a substantial decrease in the escalating human population. While humans' hunting may have triggered rise in violence, if its resultant overpopulated civilization appears to decrease violence, it is only so via shifting violence to institutions of states in exchange for freedom lost to the state. Individual separation from violence hardens compassion's 'cut off switch' for all. Still, humans are voluntarily having fewer or no children based on many factors, including innate Earth care ethos. Capitalism and industrialism, built on models of infinite growth from exploited natural 'resources', prompting people to view animals as 'products', wildlife habitat as mining fields, and bred-into-existence pets as profit potential, are the antithesis of a free world. But capitalism, industrialism and agriculture are only the most recent manifestations of eco-patriarchy. These manifestations sprung from colonization, conquering habitat of others, which sprung from ethos of the human ape hunting.

In "Addendum to Gardening in Eden" anthropologist Helga Vierich pulls together recent research demonstrating that archaic hominins like *H. erectus, H. floresiensis, H. neanderthalienesis,* Densisovans and archaic African hominins spread out of Africa before being overcome and absorbed by swifter expanding *Homo sapiens sapiens.* Series of absorptions and reabsorptions *"demanded of every human individual increasing cognitive capacity to fit into, not just a cognitive niche, but a COLLECTIVE cognitive niche."*[61] Not only did this Pleistocene collective culture pass on hegemonies of engineering ecosystem vegetation to control food, soil fertility and water retention, but too normalized and honed hunting. The early expanding universal human culture perfected distance hunting strategies with hafted weaponry such as spears, throwers, and bows & arrows, making hunting safer and increasing calories to expand and colonize farther and further.

> *Especially men... ceased to be so often injured, maimed, and even killed when grappling at close quarters with large, frightened, and injured animals. Hunting from a safer distance and relative silence also changed the behavior of game: flight distances reduced, as the animals did not necessarily connect the human glimpsed at a distance with the sudden start of the animal struck by a*

hurled spear. It was especially effective to hunt with small arrows, tipped with a slow acting poison... these gains let our ancestors increase their numbers and expand their range.[62]

The new weaponized physical separation from the kill also separated humans emotionally from whom they killed, diminishing grappling with compassion through rationalizing. Folio-frugivore human primates became enveloped into a massive colonizing generalist hunt-gather culture species.

The occupation of the planet...was a long precarious application of a novel adaptive strategy – one that shaped intergenerational transmission of behaviour largely through cultural patterns... all through the Pleistocene we continued to evolve cognition/behaviour systems finely tuned to cultural adaptations.

Over and over again our species was hit with profound crises where our very survival was at stake, and we made it. We made it because we ultimately learned to be the gardeners of eden... we learned how to manage – to engineer – the ecosystems of our planet to preserve species diversity... – against formidable odds. All modern hunter-gatherers do this: even in the arctic, they replant favoured wild species of vegetation, maintain very accurate assessments of wild game numbers and reproductive rates, and tend to prey switch when numbers are down.

This integration of the ecological engineering model appears to have happened in bits and pieces, appearing and disappearing during the Middle Stone Age: as scattered camping parties of high mobile hunter-gatherers met and exchanged ideas, technologies, stories, and occasional personnel, and as all sorts of memes, insights, stories, songs, dances. Ideas, like material objects, wafted effortlessly via six or seven degrees of separation across linguistic and demographic overlaps to span entire continents.[63]

Hence, eco-patriarchy's early cultural seeding dissolved wild's limits of the wild human habitat range, instigating movement into habitats of others, followed by a colonization and domination, later intensified with overpopulation, supplanting wildlife habitats worldwide with human engineered habitats as eco-patriarchy rooted in the human mind spread. But the more humans disconnect from lifeways embedded in wildness, the more they long for a return to it.

Exploring pre-colonization past points a path to life free with others – with an ethos of belonging together replacing the cannibalistic, failed ethos of colonization and domestication. For modern humans to expand their circle of compassion to all is challenging while still feeling dependent on the domesticated world to exist. Fear spreads with awareness of domestication's tangible and intangible foundations weakening, bound for collapse. Even after the advent of civilization, scatterings of humans have always resisted, opting to live life freely as possible, instinctively sensing how to live on their own terms, based on an intuitive sense of fairness with others.[64] Too, scatterings of humans have always compassionately defended wild animals and wild earth.[65, 66] Pains of eco-patriarchy drive pangs for return.

"Like Gold to Us"
Native American Nations Struggle to Protect Wild Rice

https://www.boreal.org/2019/08/26/271458/-like-gold-to-us-native-american-nations-struggle-to-protect-wild-rice?fbclid=IwAR2iLhrT642m6pqSdmPfTZsq821FdctjCddPMDv8TRV39yK3fEFiikRrMTE

Compassione, December 31, 1602, Cesare Ripa
Allégorie de la Compassion
Iconologia.jpg

Rewild: Restore to uncultivated state.

5 REWILD ETHOS TO REWILD EARTH

Primal remorse is buried with conformity implanting historical justifications into the subconscious. Once this barrier is breeched, another emerges. Unlike other forms of anarchy, anarcho-primitivism is not an ideology seeking a fairer civilization, carving out power within the synthetic system, but a desire for organic freedom for all, for wild symbiosis with one another and bioscapes, through liberated actions and ways of being, both interconnection and resistance. While civilization continues colonizing, to what state of nature can humans and earth be un-colonized? Chickasaw poet, historical fiction novelist and artist Linda Hogan shares stories of a human degraded earth, yet too inspiration.

> *Traditionalist and activist Dennis Martinez, tells of a nation of indigenous people in South America who make the sounds of each species that is gone in order to keep a place within the ecosystem for that bird or animal to return. This is how significant we take each species to be.*
> *The compassion we offer to animals is the same measure of love we are capable of offering other human beings. The suffering and pain of one is universal. When there is a wound in our world, we must do our best to heal it, and yet we live in a culture of wounding that could just as easily become one of healing for animals and humans.*[1]

Humans attached with wild habitats long for their protection and return, for both self-interest and interest of other animals. Margaret Robinson, two-spirit Eski'kewaq, Lennox Island First Nation, declares, *"It's important to make sure we preserve the territories where traditional foods grow... the more the federal government chips away at Indian land base, the less we're going to have access."*[2] Too, entire villages in India have relocated to return habitat back to wildlife without modern human presence.[3] Primal remediation remains alive.

Cultivator of 'defiant compassion for an uncertain future' Benjamin Voigt asks,

> *How do we overcome our evolutionary-based animal brains that yell at us to compete and fight for survival by subduing the world and others – or rearranging it for our use... How do we find a better balance as a species that wants to interfere and must interfere? When do we hold back and when do we rush in? When do we love and when do we let go as an act of greater love"*[4]

Professor of Environmental Studies and Director of the Animal Studies Initiative Dale Jamieson points out how modern cultures are lacking in *"positive images of how to relate to animals and nature... When asked to provide a positive vision many people turn to the past, to their conception of what life is like for indigenous peoples, or what it is to be "natural." None of this will do."*[5]

Modern humans can draw from primal past, but the wild-degraded modern context requires more than adoption of an ideal, even from the same place but in a faraway time.

Of all the mammals on Earth, 96% are livestock and humans, only 4% are wild mammals

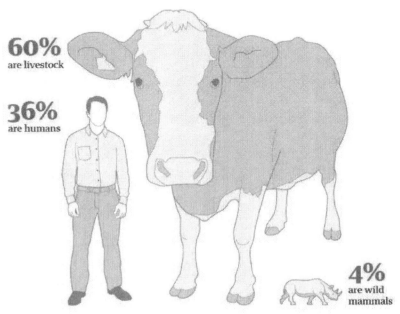

60%
are livestock

36%
are humans

4%
are wild
mammals

The 2018 report "The Biomass Distribution on Earth"
Proceedings of the National Academy of Sciences USA (PNAS)
at https://www.pnas.org/content/115/25/6506

Homo's gradual early colonization of the planet in time climaxed with traumatic impact on the biosphere's animal and plant populations and communities. *"Over the relatively short span of human history, major innovations, such as the domestication of livestock, adoption of an agricultural lifestyle, and the Industrial Revolution, have increased the human population dramatically and have had radical ecological effects."*[6] Today's biomass of humans and the pets, work and food animals humans bred into existence far surpass that of wildlife. Further, plant biomass has halved.

Humans have demonstrated resilient adaptability. Now conditions call for a shift from human as eco-patriarchal parasite to human as compassionate healer playing an ecologically beneficial role. Effective, lasting changes are rooted in clear understanding of problem origins. Comparative anthropologist Layla AbdelRahim posits that the early humans' transition into predating upon other animals instigated a shift in humans' ecological role from symbiotic seed spreader to parasitic predator. This was human's disconnection from lifeway embedded within wild community with others.

> *The key issue in wilderness is that reliance on co-operation and mutual aid accentuates one's perception of interconnectedness with the world and, in turn, formulates one's knowledge of the world as being contingent on respecting the wildness of others and letting them be.*[7]

Hall too sees liberation as simple respect for other animals living life on their own terms without human domination and control.[8] Sociologist Corey Wrenn contends after liberation humans have a responsibility to ally in amending the harm, such as restoring wildlife habitats

> *...repairing Nonhuman Animal communities devastated by human colonialism and imperialism. The project of human supremacy has subsumed Nonhuman Animals into systems of oppression that would continue to cause suffering and harm even in post-liberation vegan world. Therefore, a policy of noninterference is not recommended. Oppressive relationships with Nonhuman Animals... should cease, but a major component of dismantling oppression is the engagement of restorative work... by dismantling human supremacist structural conditions.*[9]

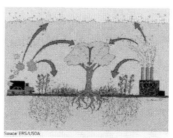

Source: ERS/USDA

Calling for liberation through restoring ecology is manifesting in projects worldwide. The function of such efforts can shift from human-centric to returning the world to wildness on its own terms.

In 1967 zoologist Desmond Morris writing in *The Naked Ape* was forthright in his human supremacist declaration of control and use of all wildlife.

> *...we all have an emotional need for animals that can serve as rarity symbols... There are, in addition, perfectly valid scientific and aesthetic reasons why we should wish to give aid to unsuccessful species... If we allow them to vanish, we shall have simplified our environment in a most unfortunate way. Being an intensely investigatory species, we can ill afford to lose such a valuable source of material... It is pointed out that intelligent protection and controlled cropping of wild species can assist the protein-starved populations in certain parts... No matter how valuable they are to us symbolically, scientifically or aesthetically, the economics of the situation will shift against them. The blunt fact is that when our own species density reaches a certain pitch, there will be no space left for other animals. The argument that they constitute an essential source of food does not, unhappily, stand up to close scrutiny. It is more efficient to eat plant food direct, than to convert it into animal flesh and then eat the animals... Unless we can colonize other planets on a massive scale and spread the load... we shall have to remove all other forms of life from the earth.*[10]

For a scientist, even then, to seriously put forth the possibility of a cosmic evolution and the human species survival without other life forms, demonstrates the severity of science and humans' mind disconnect from wildness. But perhaps the most alarming feature to Morris' statement is his absolute void of authentic interspecies compassion. Lack of compassion and disconnect from wild seem to be correlational.

Many humans still act on capacities rooted in compassion to assist in recovering free living habitats, based in a deep calling to adeptly attempt to undo what they can of the damage their species has done. Earth's communities thrive in wild mutual aid. For human allies to shift their lifeway from exploiting and dominating to supporting habitat recovery is the wildest of mutual aids.

Mushrooms are the fruit of mycorrhizal network fungus,
exchanging nutrients with and connecting trees through their mycelium.

Efforts toward the shift have been there all along, like in the story *Texas Hunter-Turned-Vegan Is Now Protecting 900 Acres for Wildlife.*[11] Humans liberating themselves and reconnecting with wild tends to happen collaterally with directly defending and rewilding Earth. These humans re-engage in wild's network. But to fully re-engage, awareness of the nature and origins of the problem is required.

Can humans face this story of their species? Eco-patriarchy was born in the survival misstep of human hunting. Hunting incited the human primate into a Pleistocene expand-and-conquer frenzy, turning Earth into 'the planet of the Top Ape'. Conquest was won with more than weapons and skills. An ethos of 'top predator' infiltrated the human species, ensnaring all, including themselves.

Bechuana hunting the lion, 1841
William Cornwallis Harris, Sir - New York Public Library, from The wild sports of Southern Africa : being the narrative of an expedition from the Cape of Good Hope, through the territories of the chief Moselekatse, to the tropic of Capricorn

In the hunt, early humans progressively normalized violence against their own bodies and their own human group. Pleistocene humans suffered injuries and death in close hunting with stronger, fiercer animals. In time humans turned eco-patriarchal violence on themselves. Jebel Sahaba, in Sudan, may be the oldest setting of a human massacre, 13,000 years ago. Bones of more than sixty children, women, and men have wounds seemingly from arrows. What incited the massacre? The reason can only be speculated. But neither *people kill people* nor *people kill animals* is inevitable.

Arrow head marks on skeletons, suggest victims were killed by enemy archers.
British Museum

As outlined in the *Parable of the Tribes*, humans everywhere had limited choices as the violent human ethos spread and colonized: voluntarily join it, be involuntarily encapsulated into it, be sidelined by it, or be killed by it.[12] Moore posits that frugivore primal people embedded in wildness were *"subjugated by marauding bands of hierarchical patriarchal militarists."*[13] The question is how to break the cycle. From earliest human origins, long before humans' advent of hunting, foraging plants likely inflicting little to no self-harm.[14] This dietway could be again. But that is only an outward manifestation of a feasible way forward. Less violent foodways of gathering may have been allowed to persist because they too fed eco-patriarchy's Top Ape.

The story of humans' relationship with others is heartbreaking. As to the motivations that sparked and drove human hunting and colonizing Hall asserts

> *our devastation of natural habitats and their free-roaming residents is rooted in deep fears, ancient struggles for survival. We're primates. Biologically speaking, we're the age-old prey of large carnivores.*[15]

For example, paleontologists sometimes find evidence of early human prey to giant hyenas and big cats.

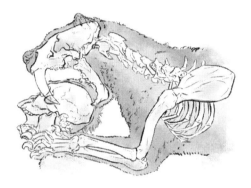

Danger Under the Moon
Prehistoric Man, the Great Adventurer
Illustrated and authored by Charles R. Knight, 1949

Environmental changes combined with early human terror and inventiveness sparked changes to survive. These adaptations turned humans' predators into humans' prey, paving a path of blood as humans expanded over the planet.

Recent research has bolstered the Pleistocene Overkill from hypothesis into theory. Elephant-dwarfing wooly mammoths, elephant-sized ground sloths and various saber-toothed cats highlighted the array of massive mammals roaming Earth between 2.6 million and 12,000 years ago. Studies estimate that large

Mammoths walking near Somme River in France.
by Charles R. Knight, 1916
The American Museum of Natural History.

mammal extinctions started at least 125,000 years ago in Africa just after *Homo sapiens* came on the scene. Then as humans migrated out of Africa, large mammal extinctions followed in regions and on timelines coinciding with known human migration pattern. The magnitude and scale of these extinctions surpassed any other recorded during the last 66 million years.

Humans hunting a woolly mammoth.

Further, there is little support for the idea that climate change affected the extinctions, as large and small mammals seem equally vulnerable to temperature shifts, and only large mammals were impacted. Restructuring animal makeup from large to small mammals had *'profound implications'* for the world's ecosystems. Large mammals tend to be herbivores, devouring large quantities of vegetation and effectively transporting the associated nutrients around an ecosystem. When they disappear, the small mammals are poor substitutes for important ecological functions.[16] The human species began patterning adapting *to* an environment, then adapting *on* that environment.

Hunting Extinctions, Heinrich Harder, 1919
Glyptodons were hunted to extinction after humans' arrival to South America

A study of global data reveals that humans have adapted into a *'unique super-predator'* with ruthless hunting practices and heavy ecological impacts.[17] Humans overhunt at unsustainable rates, exploiting wild animals with imbalanced advantages like no other predator. As tools advance into technically destructive weapons, from bullets to hooks to nets to traps, there is little cost or risk to the hunting humans. Land animals are too often left injured, and habitats left failing to thrive.[18] Hunting larger fish is leaving superfluous smaller fish, disrupting the food chain. In addition to how humans hunt, eco-patriarchy has wrought human overpopulation with a culture that preys upon wild animals and their habitats at increasing rates. Human overdevelopment preys upon itself as well, with eco-patriarchy binding women into reproductive vessels within constricted family units that together produce the mechanisms of civilization's machinery.

Civilization will always lead to overpopulation by its nature. It can never get enough, can never take enough through its human vessels. Anti-natalism is vital resistance to civilization. Human breeding during human driven ecocide is abuse of the child, Earth & all wild life, feeding civilization more worker-consumers, killers of wildness. And breeding with a plan to train children to fight civilization and/or to live feral is idealism turned eco-fascism, putting rejection of culture above the individual, under a friendly, well-intended form of family dictatorship. Being that the intensity of civilization correlates to human population rate, the bottleneck will likely reverse as humans reconnect with wild and de-civilize.

Giant Moa, 1896
From Extinct Monsters: A popular account of some of the larger forms of ancient animal life, by Rev. H.N. Hutchinson: When Polynesian settlers called the Maori landed on the islands of New Zealand around 1280, they encountered several endemic species of moas: large, wingless cousins of the ostrich. Confined to islands, and never knowing humans, the moas were easy prey for the Maori. Even the topographically and ecologically diverse landscape of New Zealand couldn't curb the hunters' excess success. Radiocarbon dating shows all species of moa were hunted to extinction within 200 years of Maori arrival. Not a single species in the moa genus survived the 15th century, not even these 12-foot-tall giants.

From early to modern times, humans have unequivocally had a vast variety of relationships in habitat, from predation to domestication to co-existence to interconnection. But overall as a species, outcomes of the inventive human ape's shift to hunting – specialization, division of labor, colonization, and domination – have disconnected humans from and wrought destruction on robust, co-adapted wild communities.

> (R)elinquishment of domination is the final frontier – the greatest risk the human spirit could take. For we are primates. In some regions of the planet we're still the lion's prey. Maybe it's no surprise that we'd fashion weapons, and set out to vanquish and tame. That we'd reformulate food chains; invent, subscribe to, and jump to the top of hierarchies, and then justify oppressions – from the "man the hunter" identity... to everyday bullying. To be sure, we know how to project hierarchy... Meanwhile, the planet's communities of free-living animals are dying.[19]

Modern humans have two potential paths. Either ride their perpetual apocalypse into annihilation, or step down from their role as Earth's Top Ape and recover thriving life in wild habitat. Release the free living and join them in freedom. Return the lands and return to liberated lands. Or we all continue this catastrophic march toward mass extinction. With wildlife communities everywhere disintegrating and disappearing, is this not the time to release hold of eco-patriarchy, for all Earth to finally be free again?

Punch Magazine's "Mr. Briggs" cartoons illustrated issues over fox hunting 1850s.
JohnLeechBriggsPleasuresHunt.jpg

Compassion adapted and passed on from early human ancestors can energize rewilding action. On the back of Jane Doe's *Anarchist Farm*, a spinoff of Orwell's *Animal Farm*, Utah Phillips wrote,

> *Anarchy holds out the best hope for a world that requires, not a change of system, but a change of heart. 'Anarchist Farm' goes to the heart. Here we have an intelligent, quirky, funny and often ironic parable of how that change of heart can grow from dream, through action, to reality.*[20]

Anarcho-primitivism is intuitive, constructive action locating, supporting and growing the organic. In *Two Cheers for Anarchism*, James C. Scott points out that mammals spontaneously engage in seemingly purposeless play.

> *...it is through the apparent chaos of play, including rough-and-tumble carousing, that (children) develop their physical coordination and capacities, their emotional regulation, their capacity for socialization, adaptability, their sense of belonging and social signaling, trust, and experimentation. Play's importance is revealed above all in the catastrophic effects of eliminating play from the repertoire of mammals...*[21]

The modern mind devalues play because it is rooted in ecological wildness from which contemporary humans have detached. Wild play is essential for the health of a wild heart, nourishing rewild action.

There are superfluous silenced examples of children, pre-enculturation, compassionately and intrinsically resisting eco-patriarchy.

> *From a young age, I would rage against the injustices committed against the trees felled behind our house, the mice killed in the snap traps, the insects caught by the glue paper, the deer shot by the hunters. "It's not fair!" was a mantra oft screamed from my tiny mouth, and as I grew, it hardly changed.*[22]

Adults are aware of the heartedness of children. This is why children's literature tends to hide harsh realities of human harm onto other animals, saving the hard life lesson for later years.

When the topic of human harm is allowed to surface, the story often spins a happy ending, like Charlotte's Web.[23] An excerpt of the classic Laura Ingalls Wilder series beginning back in 1932 was adapted into a preschool book in 1995, *Deer in the Wood*.[24]

> *"Last night I went into the woods and climbed up into a big oak tree to watch for a deer," Pa said.*
>
> *"Soon the big round moon rose, and I could see a deer with great big horns that stood out from his head.*
>
> *"He looked so strong and free and wild that I couldn't shoot him. I sat and looked at him until he ran off into the Big Woods.*
>
> *"Then I remembered that Ma and my girls were waiting for me to bring home some meat for supper. So I made up my mind that the next time I saw a deer, I would shoot.*
>
> *"After a long while a mother deer and her baby fawn stepped into the moonlight. They stood there together, looking out into the woods. Their large eyes were shining and soft.*

"I just sat there looking at them until they walked away among the shadows. Then I climbed down out of the tree and came home."

Laura whispered in his ear, "I'm glad you didn't shoot them!"

And Mary said, "We can eat bread and butter."

Pa hugged both of them together and said, "You're my good girls."

This story shields children, enabling their compassion for other animals to remain whole, at least for the moment. The man too soothed his broken compassion, even if only provisionally.

"Poison ivy likes to climb hunting stands, just use gloves when planting. clover is commonly planted in clearings to attract deer, usually placed in a clear firing lane from the stand, buttercup flowers, outcompete the clover and repel deer. Don't just focus on the hunting stand, look at how the habitat around it has been altered. Is there a native that can be used in place of buttercup to achieve the same effect in your area? Sabbing a hunt isn't just about going after the hunter or being present during the hunt, it is about interfering with how humans alter the landscape to make the destruction of wildlife a hobby."[25]

Combined with taking a stand defending the wild, preserving and restoring wild draws from restoration ecology. Renewed biodiversity culminates with return of recently extirpated wild plants and animals. To begin recovery of a place, a Paleolithic through Holocene history of the site is considered. For example, Marcel van der Merwe bases African cape restoration in response to the impacts of the habitat's history of increasing human impacts.[26]

Inside cover of
Rewilding The Lost Wilderness: Green Heritage of the Forgotten Cape.
May 30, 2014 photograph by the book's author.

Allying with wild life, drawing from times of wild thriving past, intimates paths for return of wild life autonomy. Yes species assemblages and ranges are always shape-shifting motion. Further, all animals shape vegetation, just as vegetation shapes animals. They co-adapt. But colonizing humans have wrought too speedy changes, interfering with long stewing wild community co-adaptation dynamics.

> *With the annihilation of the animal populations, whole galaxies of natural checks and balances are altered forever, some abstrusely and some so directly that the effect is almost instant. The hundred-year war against wolves and coyotes, bears and bobcats, badgers and lions, has already*

had a marked impact... In Arizona, where the stately saguaro cactus has long characterized the beauty of the desert, the destruction of predators has had complicated results, not the least of which seems to be the gradual demise of the saguaro... the cactus no longer seems to be reproducing itself. Rodents, once kept in sharp check by predators, are multiplying out of all proportion, and they gobble up the seeds and root systems of the saguaro before they can get started. The lesson seems clear: predators play many roles in the whole biological spectrum, and man is highly uncertain of what these roles are.[27]

In Kollibri Terre Sonnenblume's explorations into wild tending, Jayesh Bear speaks to humans moving plants in and out of their indigenous habitats. *"I would imagine that there was some sort of discernment - knowing the characteristics and the spirit of the plant, what it's going to do to the ecosystem and what to put where, I can't imagine that it was done without any thought given to it."*[28] Shuffling flora and fauna out of their habitat and into habitat of others makes humans, borrowing Fredy Perlman's words, *"rapists of the Biosphere."*[29] Slowing changes by restoring toward recent indigenous homeostasis effectively assists recovery and tenderly invites return of wildness.

Indigenous woman gathering huckleberries.
Photo taken in the Gifford Pinchot National Forest. U.S. Forest Service photo #281584.
Original Collection: Gerald W. Williams Collection
Item Number: WilliamsG:USFS281584

Imagine a land filled with wild flowers as far as you can see... Underneath them a ground filled with native edible perennial roots. Lilies, onions, garlic, breadroots, sweet wild carrots, potatoes, and sweet ground nuts... surrounded by wild trees loaded with fruits and nuts available throughout the succession of seasons, and underneath these wild orchards dozens of different varieties of berries, herbs and greens... feeding an abundance of wild life all throughout the land. All maintained without irrigation or domesticated agricultural systems. This is how it once was and will be again! That is why we gather seed and plant.
~Conrad Justice Kiczenski

In rewilding earth,[30, 31] humans hone wild connections, such as in indigenous wild tending,[32, 33] a dietway and lifeway re-surging in practice of many forms worldwide. Beware that wild tending itself has evolved toward domination. Wild tending's beginnings were first as incidental, involuntary animalistic foraging interactions shaping and co-adapting with vegetation. As human domination ethos rose, wild tending increasingly leaned toward cognizant nature management, such as permaculture. Management and control of animals and plants creates an ethos and psychology of systemic management and control over others. Communities of life are interconnected and flourish when their individuals live subliminally within wildness, interacting organically and spontaneously. The transition toward wild dietways can slowly revert from conscious control to visceral living. A foraging guidebook begins the transition, including mutual nurturing, giving back to the wild when taking from it.

> *This book... speaks directly to how you, as the plant harvester, can help foster the growth of food plants in wild settings. Every plant entry in this book is accompanied by a "Future Harvests" section, in which I offer basic guidance on how to avoid local overharvesting and increase the natural availability of wild plants through the use of simple enhancement methods.*[34]

Dominion over women, animals and men too can be countered with a compassionate diet. Behind the rationalizations such as *Plants feel pain too,* there is human beings' innate empathy for animals that connects us.

> *The appeal of vegan foods flows at once from an urge to resist patriarchal forms of dominance and control, and*

from positive feelings of empathy and care for the other animals with whom we share the earth.[35]

Yes, consumerist vegans today partake in earth degrading agriculture[36] too, which is a prime exploiter of wildlands. But a local, organic plant diet reduces harm,

and requires substantially less agriculture within civilization's infrastructures. Vitally, as the world rewilds, foraging plants resets humans power imbalance with other animals, reviving core origins before eco-patriarchy. Sociologist Bob Torres spoke to veganism as a resistance to domination challenging civilization's hierarchies. Using the metaphor of veganism being a *"wrench in the mental machinery of carnism, veganism has perhaps its greatest impact as a form of inducing cognitive dissonance."*[37]

Modern humans' shift from eco-patriarchal exploitation to compassionately giving back has been intuitively happening for a long while in the forms of caring foodway and tending to nature on nature's terms. One autonomous example of modern humans rewilding earth as wild allies is sisters Joan and Eileen Bradley in Australia with their strategy outlined in *Bringing Back the Bush*. Theirs is simply a gentle, gradual removal of colonizing human introduced invasive plants allowing nearby indigenous vegetation to recover lost ground on their own time and in their own way. This method has proven successful in the bush and other continents as well,[38] despite and through climate change's impacts.

Where today's social media confirms one's convictions, Jonathan Franzen says literature *"invites you to ask whether you might be somewhat wrong, maybe even entirely wrong, and to imagine why someone else might hate you."* Literature increasingly portrays resistance visions of earth being liberated from dominating human control. Over a century ago feminist Charlotte Perkins Gilman wrote the underappreciated novella *Herland*,[39] a futuristic matriarchal utopian, or techno-dystopian, all-woman and girls 'paradise' omitting violence, excess, superiority, misery, and possessiveness. The females functioned as one interconnected clan, all respected and cared for, and included nonhuman animals. Yet being anti-'savage', the women held on to technology and education, domestication devices of the failed era of civilization, a radically engineered ecology. In 1962 Aldous Huxley's ecotopian novel *Island*[40] also offered a restrained civilization of more respectful co-existence with other animals, but based in a blending of modern science and the gentler religion of Buddhism. Like all gentler human societies, human supremacy remains a founding principle. In *The Overstory*[41] Richard Powers emotionally overlays stories resisting human 'development', bringing to life the primordial wisdom of trees. Despite his blunt chauvinism, Edward Abbey shows how to deconstruct civilization in defense of earth, both individually[42] and in a group.[43]

The torment driving some anti-civ fiction plotlines is self-hypocrisy of humanity allowing human honed brutality to nonhuman animals to carry on. Without the hypocritical shield, hunters would know and sense the torment they inflict. So they engage in self-deception, thinking themselves virtuous. In Olga Tokarczuk's dark comedic, anarchic ecofeminist treatise *Drive Your Plow Over the Bones of the Dead*[44] the narrator sees behind civilization's veil. Hunting is justified as tradition, while exploiting nature is justified as progress. Destruction of anything wild is promoted as a supreme role which humanity has an obligation to honor. As the protagonist Janina Duszejko, bridge engineer turned hunt saboteur, English teacher, and translator of William Blake knows, *"The whole, complex human psyche has evolved to prevent Man from understanding what he is really seeing."* Janina wants revenge - mainly against local hunters who kill animals with whom she has affinity. She is unable to break through the wall of institutional cronyism the hunters erected to protect themselves. The town frightens when the elite, the police, the state forestry people, and even the Church, i.e. the principal hunters, are under attack, one after another turning up dead. She frames the murders as revenge by wild animals in vengeance on hunters, advocating that the animals not be punished but forgiven as a matter of natural justice.

Tania James' *The Tusk that did the Damage*[45] has a South Indian elephant narrator powerfully telling stories of those involved in elephant poaching, revealing humans' compassion 'cut off switch' from the elephant's perspective. In another century old feminist novel *Gone to Earth*[46] made into a film in 1950, the human protagonist adopts the perspective of the hunted animal. The anti-hunting activist and author Mary Webb's main character, Hazel, reflects her own childhood simply wanting to live connected with nature. In a country landscape invaded with man's tradition of fox hunting, Hazel empathizes and bonds with a fox, Foxy. She *"identified herself with Foxy, and so with all things hunted and snared and destroyed"*. Together they live in a state of vigilance, fearing and hiding from humanity's dark side, men who needlessly prey for the sake of preying. Confused by love, she fights her hunting husband's brutality to animals:

> *Reddin pulled and wrenched until at last the hedgehog screamed- a thin, piercing wail, most ghastly and pitiful and old, ancient... Centuries of pain were in it, the ago-*

long terror of weakness bound and helpless beneath the knife, and that something vindictive and terrifying that looks up at the hunter from the eyes of trapped animals...

Before the cry had ceased... she had flung herself at Reddin, a pattern of womanly obedience no longer, but a desperate creature fighting in that most intoxicating of all crusades, the succoring of weakness.

On Reddin's head... on his face... rained the blows of Hazel's hard little fists. Her blows were by no means so negligible as most women's, for her hands were muscular and strong from digging and climbing, and in her heart was the root of pity which nerves the most trembling hands to do might deeds.

In the end Hazel chooses love for a hunted animal over all else. Webb connects the brutality of hunting with generalized human cruelty. A death pack *"hunts at all hours, light and dark; it is no pale phantom of dreams..."* consisting not of monsters, but of *"our fellows, all that have strength without pity... mankind's lack of pity, mankind's fatal propensity for torture, that is the nightmare."* For Hazel, *"the earth's all bloody"* and *"the world's nought but a snare."*[47] Brutality is a human infection, with any living being a potential target to humans' compassion switch, on or off.

In Octavia Butler's *Xenogenesis* trilogy's first book *Dawn*,[48] Oankali aliens save humankind after a nuclear war. Their aim is to recover planetary ecology. In the context of a changing ecosystem, issues of hierarchies and human nature are explored. Breeze Harper's essay "The Absence of Meat in Oankali Dietary Philosophy: An Ecofeminist-Vegan Analysis of Octavia Butler's *Dawn*" interprets that Oankali have a vegan lifeway in accordance with environmental harmony, that the aliens *"connect a society's consumption philosophies to either perpetuating or destroying physical and emotional harmony of the human body and spirit as well as the ecology of the earth."*[49] Cara Williams extends the notion of consumption, to an all-consuming ethos.

The nuclear war that brings down humanity before Dawn even opens was not a suicidal final solution, but rather a ravenous feast of self-consumption in an attempt to feed our voracious and never-ending hunger... Oankali then

function as the anti-humans, looking at existence as an
exchanging of goods rather than a food chain. The Oankali
would never and could never hurt another living being for
consumption. To do so would not only mean pain for
themselves, as the social behavior of the Oankali is
extremely empathic, but it would be like severing and
eating their own arm; it would be cannibalism.[50]

Butler suggests the first step in adapting out of modern humans'
cannibal nature is by transitioning toward an ecofeminist exchange
relationship with other animals, not exploiting and consuming
them.

South-African novelist J. M. Coetzee's novel *Elizabeth
Costello*[51] creates an interesting twist in the field of animal rights.[52]
Through Costello, an Australian writer delivering controversial
lectures, issues are presented on humans' cruelty to nonhuman
animals as framed in academic and cultural worlds. Her analysis of
philosophical and scientific perspectives invites the reader to
critique modern politics and academia considerations of animals.
While making no outright arguments for veganism, in the fictional
setting of an academic conference she compares factory farms to
Nazi concentration camps. In assessing animal rights movements,
she discusses how the social conformity nature of humans leads to
violence condemning other animals. Through allegories the author
incites an ethic of empathy, not rationality, in human relation with
animals.

In the olden days the voice of man, raised in reason, was
confronted by the roar of the lion, the bellow of the bull.
Man went to war with the lion and the bull, and after many
generations won that war definitively. Today these

creatures have no more power. Animals have only their silence left with which to confront us.[53]

She denounces civilization's pro-meat propaganda appealing to dominance, especially being aware of suffering humans cause other animals and environments. For Costello, refraining from eating animals is an easy act of compassion. Through the character's persistent confrontations the author calls the readers to act on civilization's atrociousness by broadening the community of compassion to nonhuman animals and earth's ecology.[54] Connecting *Elizabeth Costello* to animal and woman liberation, Laura Wright proceeds with a discourse of ecology being within embodied life.[55]

Civilization overflows with true stories of organized human apes hunting humans. Historical fiction too portrays scenes of civilization's man-on-man disposition, sometimes using their domesticated animals to assist the predation. The hunted are often civilization's most enslaved, such as in historical fiction's *Uncle Tom's Cabin.*

"Well, he was a powerful, gigantic fellow,--a native-born African; and he appeared to have the rude instinct of freedom in him to an uncommon degree. He was a regular African lion. They called him Scipio. Nobody could do anything with him; and he was sold round from overseer to

overseer, till at last Alfred bought him, because he thought he could manage him. Well, one day he knocked down the overseer, and was fairly off into the swamps... Alfred was greatly exasperated; but I told him that it was his own fault, and laid him any wager that I could break the man; and finally it was agreed that, if I caught him, I should have him to experiment on. So they mustered out a party of some six or seven, with guns and dogs, for the hunt. People, you know, can get up as much enthusiasm in hunting a man as a deer, if it is only customary; in fact, I got a little excited myself, though I had only put in as a sort of mediator, in case he was caught.

"Well, the dogs bayed and howled, and we rode and scampered, and finally we started him. He ran and bounded like a buck, and kept us well in the rear for some time; but at last he got caught in an impenetrable thicket of cane; then he turned to bay, and I tell you he fought the dogs right gallantly. He dashed them to right and left, and actually killed three of them with only his naked fists, when a shot from a gun brought him down, and he fell, wounded and bleeding, almost at my feet. The poor fellow looked up at me with manhood and despair both in his eye. I kept back the dogs and the party, as they came pressing up, and claimed him as my prisoner. It was all I could do to keep them from shooting him, in the flush of success; but I persisted in my bargain, and Alfred sold him to me. Well, I took him in hand, and in one fortnight I had him tamed down as submissive and tractable as heart could desire."

"What in the world did you do to him?" said Marie.

"Well, it was quite a simple process. I took him to my own room, had a good bed made for him, dressed his wounds, and tended him myself, until he got fairly on his feet again. And, in process of time, I had free papers made out for him, and told him he might go where he liked."

"And did he go?" said Miss Ophelia.

"No. The foolish fellow tore the paper in two, and absolutely refused to leave me. I never had a braver, better fellow,--trusty and true as steel. He embraced Christianity afterwards, and became as gentle as a child. He used to *oversee my place on the lake, and did it capitally, too. I lost him the first cholera season. In fact, he laid down his life for me. For I was sick, almost to death; and when, through the panic, everybody else fled, Scipio worked for me like a giant, and actually brought me back into life again. But, poor fellow! He was taken, right after, and there was no saving him. I never felt anybody's loss more."*[56]

This dominator-dominated relationship reveals the twisted form of unfree love in civilization. Eco-patriarchy is directed by humans toward targets in all directions.

Natalie Babbitt's young adult novel *Tuck Everlasting* is a family otherized by their immortality, forever hiding from being found, trapped living life timelessly in woods, like many other animals in civilization. Their home is set afire. They too are stalked and hunted down by men on horses with dogs and weapons. *"Don't be afraid of death. Be afraid of unlived life."*[57]

Hunters with American black bear with dogs.
Great Smoky Mountains, 1916

Eco-patriarchal *Homo* has become a colonizing, domesticating human, turning human apes upon selves, other animals, and other animals upon other animals, removing and transferring species from and into bioregions, fragmenting interconnected life assemblages. For liberating humans, this has left many hard decisions on how to halt their species' overpowering impact and revive a lifeway embedded in the struggling remnant wild. For example, earliest humans like all animals found their food and medicines through instincts and primal senses.[58] Science diminishes this kind of primitive awareness in lieu of a manipulation by supreme institutions. If the only ecofeminist way for humans to live wild is located at wild tending or earlier, how will humans undo what they can of domestication's impact on wild habitats during transition away from eco-patriarchy? How can humans shift the locus of control back to wild as they adapt into ecology contributors?

Humans across the wild-civilized spectrum on some level intuit intensifying globalization pressures lunging toward a boiling point. Indigenous biodiversity loss is, by some estimates, a greater problem than climate change. After humans dominated animals and spread across the world, they domesticated plants and animals with agriculture to 'settle' lands.[59] While a plant or animal behavior change from introduction to invasion can be delayed, once introduced into homeostatic habitats nonindigenous species can outcompete, eat, infect and hybridize with indigenous species, exponentially impacting flora and fauna. This harm is often compounded by overarching dynamics such as climate change.[60] Even with civilization's science confirming ecosystems everywhere are collapsing under various human linked invasions, the indoctrinated human kingdom cannot begin to envision renouncing its terra-conqueror thrown.

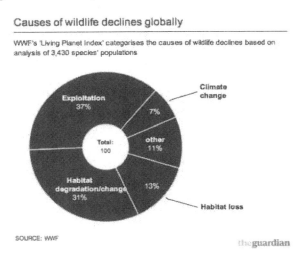

Causes of wildlife declines globally

WWF's 'Living Planet Index' categorises the causes of wildlife declines based on analysis of 3,430 species' populations

Exploitation 37%

Climate change 7%

other 11%

Total: 100

Habitat degradation/change 31%

13%

Habitat loss

SOURCE: WWF

theguardian

There are endless unintended consequences of domesticated humans rearranging species about on domestication's terms. Introduced, domesticated and wild species are all puppets and victims of colonizing, predatory human folly. With palpable ignorance of primal ways, the best domesticated humans can do is attempt to undo what they can of the most recent harm domestication has done. Domesticated humans liberate themselves and others by re-engaging with wild in a recompensing liberation ethos. De-colonizing restoration, such as returning indigenous plants co-adapted to a place, frees all to naturally evolve over time.

> *If we garden with native plants that form living communities... we begin to cross-pollinate again. We begin to learn to speak languages we've forgotten. We mend. We bind.*[61]

With ecological dynamics, recovering species will reestablish their niches and spread seed until they settle into spots with others they remember and prefer, rekindling thriving resilience.[62]

147

On a final note on rewilding earth, three suggestions. First, many people rewilding patches of earth come to realize the impact all domesticated beings have on habitat. From humans to farmed animals to pets, the domesticated reveal their unwildness in their actions in homes of thriving wild beings. In domesticating others, humans have unwilded them from their ancestral form. Many human domesticates are unable to go feral, and even those that can do so at the cost of harming wild habitat of surviving wild beings in their shriveling wild homes. Human disconnection with and impact on wild animals, plants, soil, air and water are perceptible, especially to wild animals. Wild lives are unquestionably struggling under civilization. Innate sense of fairness calls for end to interference in wild thriving, which means protecting wild from domesticates. In a major collapse a predictable scenario is overpopulated, domesticated humans running to the hills, exploiting remaining wild food and shelter 'resources.' Even humans exploring going feral tend to also exploit wild 'resources' with lack of intimate awareness from deep connection with wild communities. The first step in rejoining wild is a lengthy period of reacquainting. And without dogs. The harm both dogs and cats do to indigenous beings and their homes is distressing.[63]

Second, in sitting with a wild place, capture wildness with wonder; let it arouse senses and sensitivities. Be prepared to emote, to sense and grieve the losses and cherish life anew, for those who let compassion touch reality, sadness can be overwhelming.

> *Sorrow, I felt great sorrow, an endless sense of mourning for every dead Animal. One period of grief is followed by another, so I am in constant mourning. This is my natural state… sorrow is an important word for defining the world. It lies at the foundations of everything, it is the fifth element, the quintessence.*[64]

For those interested in reading up on resistance, the books *Liberate: Stories & Lesson's on Animal Liberation Above the Law*, by Peter Young, Dave Foreman and Bill Haywood's *Ecodefense: a Field Guide to Monkeywrenching*, and Susan Zakin's *Coyotes and Town Dogs: Earth First! and the Environmental Movement*[65] detail much inspiration, techniques and lessons learned. Letting compassion have its outlet in the form of channeled rage can be healing to self and others.

> *Anger makes the mind clear and incisive, able to see more. It sweeps up the other emotions and takes control of the body. Without a doubt Anger is the source of all wisdom, for Anger has the power to exceed any limits...anyone who feels Anger, and does not take action, merely spreads the infection.*[66]

Lastly, before intervening in remaining wild homes of wild others, to shift from domesticated Takers to feral Givers, humans shift from conscientious toward intuitiveness. Use caution to avoid assigning human supremacist value or function to an ecosystem. Bioregions are autonomous, with autonomous communities and individuals. Go slow, observe, wonder, sense the habitat, and listen to their calling. Human intervention is at best restorative toward thriving indigenous diversity, at worst colonizing, unwittingly damaging the home of indigenous others. Gradually restorers re-embed, even rediscover their own native foodway in a wild mutualistic lifeway. Through handing back control, letting wildness decide how to respond to humans' devastations, humans revive their wildness too.

Especially with the next chapter, if you are uncomfortable with the notion of anti-civilization but are interested in exploring it further, psychologist and self-described civilization heretic Mark Seely put out three illuminating books: *Born Expecting the Pleistocene: Psychology and the Problem of Civilization, Anarchist by Design: Technology and Human Nature*, and *Civilization Heresies*.

Given the existence of biocidal totalitarianism, life itself can be preserved only through global renewal, in the dual sense of resurgency and reintegration... The best of the present culture – a culture in the pathological sense only – points beyond itself toward the recovery of primate lifeways. ~John Moore

Modern day self-castaway Masafumi Nagasaki.
*"stopped eating meat and fish and refused to eat the vast number of turtle eggs
left by its maternal visitors,
saying 'I've seen those baby turtles being born and crawling towards the sea. I
get goosebumps every time I see that. It makes me think how wonderful life is.'"*
*Source: 'Naked hermit' who lived on deserted island for thirty years 'captured',
brought back to civilization. www.news.com.au*

6. RESURGENT SAVAGERY

*The innate sensual acuity of human infants steadily atrophies as they grow and
develop in interaction with a symbolic culture that continues to infiltrate and
monopolize most aspects of our lives. A few remnants of the unmediated, the
direct still survive. Lovemaking, close relationships, immersion in wild nature,
and the experience of birth and death awaken our senses and our intelligence,
stimulating an unaccustomed hunger. We long for something other than the
meager, artificial world of representation, with its second-hand pallor.*[1]

~ John Zerzan, anarcho-primitivist eco-philosopher

Perhaps humans indoctrinated into civilization don't think they can rewild themselves, infused with human supremacist lifeway to the point of total enmeshment. As portrayed in a scene by Olga Tokarczuk,

> *"There's nothing natural about nature anymore," he said, and at that point I saw who this forester really was: just another official. "It's too late. The natural processes have gone wrong, and now we must keep it all in control to make sure there's no catastrophe... Don't get so upset about things. Don't take the whole world on your shoulders. It'll all be fine."*[2]

Yet all life today senses no, it won't 'all be fine' anymore, what humans have done to Earth's wild homeostasis. Even the 'apex' ape senses it, if buried inside.

Being authoritatively construed as the civilized essence, hunting's eco-patriarchy permeates as the basis for modern *Homo* lifeway.

> *Hunting is the modus operandi of patriarchal societies on all levels of life – to support one level is to support them all. However innocuous the language may sound – we hunt everything from houses to jobs to heads – it reveals a cultural mentality so accustomed to predation that it horrifies only when it threatens to kill us all.*[3]

But humans are at a liminal point of their final frontier, one way or another, the return to wild belonging. To rewild, that is, to nurture wildness, is the highest form of aliveness in community with others. Unschooling and detaching from indoctrinated ideologies is essential to rewilding. Humans still clinging to notions that humans can fix civilization's ecocide problem with gentler civilization or more advances in technology are sharing in hallucinated ideology en masse, for they *"assume that technology is an adequate replacement for natural restorative processes, further widening the disconnection between humanity and the real world."*[4] While animality negates ideology, conformity with all-consuming technology is cannibalism.

> *Snowmobiles aren't the only non-firearms tools hunters can employ to destroy these carnivores; lobos, coyotes and their young offspring can be felled with poison, flattened by*

151

ATVs, snared, and incinerated live by pouring gas or dynamite into their dens and then lightning a match—acts that most would consider barbaric. If a person doesn't want to do the killing himself, he can summon gunners employed by a federal agency called Wildlife Services, a division within the U.S. Department of Agriculture, to shoot wolves and coyotes from the sky using aircraft.[5]

Parks Victoria's deer control trial in the Alpine National Park since 2014. The trial is in sensitive alpine communities, susceptible to damage from deer. In 2016, the deer control work undertaken by contractors complemented the work undertaken by volunteers, which will continue.
The aim of the trial was to demonstrate the technique, and to assess its effectiveness, efficiency and cost
https://www.parks.vic.gov.au/about-us/news/alpine-deer-aerial-shooting-trial-

Whom shall we persecute, for whom feel pity?
It is all a matter of the moment's mores,
Of words on wood pulp, of radios roaring...[6]

Every year, thousands of animals are killed for fun (and often, cash prizes) in wildlife killing contests. Participants at these events are given free rein to kill as many animals as possible of a single species in a fixed period of time—or, as is the case in many "varmint" killing contests, several species... In some places, state wildlife agencies even support wildlife killing contests under the guise of managing species, although this contradicts the latest science.[7]

The species culturally deemed 'varmints' in this case include coyotes, foxes, bobcats, wolves, woodchucks, marmots, prairie dogs, crows, rattlesnakes, and sharks.

A behavior once sensed as disgusting, under certain conditions, can become preferred and even defended. Add in the power of mass social norms, and suddenly humankind is routinely engaged in mass slaughter to have fun, or make meals of animal tissues and organs, silencing and suppressing primal compassion. A theme of Adorno's essay "Culture Industry Reconsidered"[8] is that the power of 'culture industry' in its obliviously embraced ideology compels conformity, subordinates consciousness. Social pressures and cultural beliefs under the overarching spell of domination are powerful forces to overcome. Eco-patriarchy's conformist ideology evolved in 'man the hunter' stalking animals for kill as stalking women for sex.[9, 10] is neither the wild way of the human primate, nor a sufficient metaphor for conceptualizing what it means to be human, wild or not.

Yet at least some are still not so disconnected from their innate wild. Some go feral reviving their dormant organic senses. Again, examples of total primal immersion in wildness are waning conversely with domestication's growth. Turning to stories to hold a rewilded vision in the heart and mind may be beneficial. But indigenous storytelling is fading and coopted or commercialized, and liberation literature, such as *Ecotopia*[11] and others previously discussed, remain utopian and/or within human constructed boundaries of artificial technologies subordinating others, side-stepping ecology authenticity.

In her book *Feminism and the Technological Fix*, Carol Stabile asserts *"a rejection of technology is fundamentally identical to a rejection of patriarchy."*[12] The thought of living without technology may make rewilding Earth seem easier to achieve than rewilding self. To begin reviving the human ecological being, if she is to remain on the scene, she must deconstruct eco-patriarchy built in to inventing and using technology that has impacted human relations with other animals.

"Manner in which Natives of the East Coast strike turtle" Cooktown, Australia.
From Phillip Parker King's Survey. 1818.
Sidney Parker King's Journal http://freeread.com.au/ebooks/e00027.html

Time and time again domesticated humans build a strong, logical anti-civilization case but cannot let it blossom into its consistent conclusion in the end. Crossing the bridge to wild may simply not seem conceivable for a human stuck in the progress trap[13] even though they suffer within it, especially if they lack a lush human primate habitat nearby. For evolutionary biologist Stephen Jay Gould, even the concept of progress is *"a noxious, culturally embedded, untestable, nonoperational, intractable idea that must be replaced..."*, and evolution is a drive not up a progress ladder of complexity, but toward diversity inclusive of simplicity.[14] For those who have the option and nerve, whether out of necessity or pure will, the journey to rewild may at first seem adventurous yet impossible. But during the cross the lucidity of animality resurges making barriers easier to overcome, ambling on with increasing flow and ease. Why then as the systems collapses are starting, do almost all humans cling harder to Leviathan? Nevertheless, there have always been some along the margins who sense the calling to resist, who in the throes of ecological desolation choose release.

The true telling of the life of Carol Ruckdeschel, *Untamed: the Wildest Woman in America and the Fight for Cumberland Island*[15] serves as an archetype of modern human rewilded as adaptive creature connected in and contributing to wild community. Carol's actions in kindred shared life with nonhuman others are in sync with restoration ecology, but immersing her entire being, and importantly, with her only aim being for wildness. Her feral being is at home in wild communal life as a pauper sustaining herself on a biologically diverse barrier island. But the wild community is under civilization's attack. Fortuitously, being a self-taught published scientist gives her standing to leverage the eminence of science and politics to draw bureaucratic support officializing her conservation efforts (though she's most willing to take Edward Abbeyesque action for some quick and fun results). Driven by her primal purpose, she performs washed-ashore sea turtle necropsies, connects with a blind gator, befriends vultures, grieves for human introduced wild horse castaways failing to thrive outside their habitat, and serves witness to a wild mourning ritual. Her intertwined civilized personal life tragedies do not deter her fight for a true wild family, protecting it from commercial development and exploitation. But even she clings to civilization in ideology.

To be anti-civ comes from primal pain of deep losses and resolve for restoration. *Untamed* Carol is a wild warrior whose personal story is the story of wildness under siege, and a plea for humans to let go of civilization's primacies, to become deeply aware of life around them, to take action assisting wild recovery. To be rewilding human in transition times is to trust instincts to find sustenance in the moment. Accepting wild fate is the cost of free living, a low price considering the alternative - deluding oneself into reassurance that civilization escapes fate. To rewild away from eco-patriarchy is to rejoin the primal force through action based on innate empathy, tending to wildness not for human dominion but simply for wild.

Still, there's a lucidity that sometimes comes in that moment when you find yourself looking at the world through your tears, as if those tears served as a lens to clarify what it is you're looking at.[16]

Do humans need to learn and practice survival skills in preparation for major collapse before it happens? Are humans braced to cope emotionally for events following cataclysmic systems failure? In Jean Hegland's *Into the Forest* two sisters absorbed in civilization are suddenly immersed in widespread collapse. The story centers on the paced, evolving relationship between Eva and Nell as the technologically dependent society they were born into crumbles, testing them to survive alone in lush second growth redwood forest. Fiery newfangled feelings charge relationship intensities while acquiring abilities to survive on the fly, motivated by sheer need. Through a series of losses and adversities met by grief and adaptations, they tackle the transition in jagged bursts, moving from strong attachments to civilized culture to, in the end embracing a wild lifeway.

The film adaptation of *Into the Forest*[17] starring Ellen Page and Evan Rachel Wood replaces Nell's edifying inner thinking with enlivening sights and sounds. Modern society trickles to a halt. Eva and Nell's instincts wake as permanency of this new reality sets in. They retreat from the now disappearing and dangerous town community into their isolated steadily failing house structure in the forest. The story ends with Eva and Nell's full step into wildness with rudimentary forest skills balanced with resolve to live life, not just deter death.

While on the surface a post-apocalyptic, dystopia-to-utopianish fiction, from start to finish this story is a study on the raw emotional and attachment shift from culture of artificiality providing synthetic novelty, safety, shelter and food, transplanted into organic wildness. *"When amnesia continues for an extended period of time, the amnesiac occasionally begins a new life entirely unrelated to its previous condition. This response is called a "fugue state."* In the story's beginning there is a foretelling of taking on a 'fugue state' identity, which by the story's end is revealed to be civilization itself, and the return being to the original indigenous being. Eva and Nell's transition to forest women reveals how loss of wild lifeway can be found again, drawing on inactive yet intact instincts, reverting to animality.

In critique, the film had potential to inspire more action if it had explored the practical survival strategies, foraging and gathering details more in depth as in the book, e.g. how they prepared acorns as their staple food. There are mistaken details that make a difference in reforming human-other animal relations, e.g. civilization bias with the B12 myth. [Despite the modern belief that B12 can only be acquired by eating animals, it is byproduct of a bacteria. The sisters killed a wild boar for B12, but only ruminant animal digestive systems have the bacteria in their gut. Farmed pigs are supplemented B12. Early humans may have derived B12 from both plants and drinking free flowing water. Recent cellular biology research[18] indicates B12 available in plants such as garden cress, a traditional medicinal food in places today known as India and Ethiopia. Research findings also indicate bio-available B12 in duckweeds including *Lemma* and *Wolffia* species, apparently as a naturally occurring symbiotic relationship with bacteria inside plants' biomass.[19, 20] Another study shows the likely availability of B12 in other varied ancient plants such as sea buckthorn, wheatgrass and the sunflower horse yellowhead.[21] Research suggests humans 45,000 years ago likely had plentiful B12 in water.[22] The research into B12 availability today and especially in pre-history is young, but the findings are promising.]

Into the Forest is a believable fiction that feels like the first in a trilogy. The second might shift away from relying on guidance from books and rationality toward intuitive awareness and deeper awakening of their animal instincts, reawakening awareness of other wild life forms, and repositioning humans' role from Takers to mutualistic Givers. They might join other feral humans in wild tending the bioregion toward diversity of interspecies co-adaptations. The final piece in the trilogy might be the completion of humans' total return to primal life. Inspiration could be drawn from *Julie of the Wolves*, a naturalist's story of an indigenous girl rewilding her primitive animal being, envisioning the possibility and path of humans adapting to living wild as earlier human animals.

Jean Craighead George's *Julie of the Wolves*[23] is a realistic detailed account of the survival of a young teen 'Eskimo' girl

Miyax lost, alone, and famished in far north tundra. With a wolf pack nearby, she draws insight from a tale her father told long ago of a despairing winter when he asked a wolf for help and was fed.

5th-century BC Etruscan Art

Inspired and informed by it, from a comfortable distance she observes the wolves' communication signals with each other, their social dynamics, and experiments with initiating contact to gain their trust and assistance. Step by step she deciphers and hones enough of their ways to secure acceptance by the pack. Once fed, Miyax continues tapping her intuitiveness and her nearly-lost ancestral wisdom to interpret the seasons, sky, land, plants and animals, in addition to ancestral simple sewing, foraging, cooking, navigating and sheltering to thrive in the harsh environment.

From there the story flashes back to her early childhood with her father in a seal camp, where hunters measured richness of spirit by intelligence, fearlessness and love compared to the way 'gussaks' measured richness with money and property. At age nine Miyax is sent away to live with her aunt in an Arctic settlement. She learns English and math, writes with a pen pal in San Francisco, and takes a nonindigenous name, Julie. At thirteen she decides to follow "Eskimo" tradition of arranged marriage with the teen son of her father's close friend. When her new husband attacks and tries to rape her, she suddenly escapes, setting out to live with her pen pal in San Fransisco. It is as she sets out that she becomes lost in the tundra with the wolves and becomes Miyax again.

After acceptance by the pack, humans' modern lifeway encroaches in the wilderness when a man shoots two wolves from an airplane, killing the pack leader Amaroq.

In that instant she saw great cities, bridges, radios, school books... long highways, TV sets, telephones, and electric lights. Black exhaust enveloped her, and civilization became this monster that snarled across the sky.[24]
In the aftershock of the assault on the pack, she takes her turn to nourish and heal her new pack companions, now using her indigenous human ways to assist them, as her loathing of civilization stews. Dropping her plans to journey to San Francisco, she sets out to find her father whose wisdom had kept her alive. Upon arrival, she is stunned to see how far he too has crossed into the trappings of civilization's dominion, and worse still, that he is

the one who evidently shot the wolf Amaroq from a plane to protect his musk-oxen herd. She instantly leaves him, then pauses to reflect on her life choice as the story ends.

Most mistakenly interpret this story's conflict as civilization vs indigenous cultures. From an ecofeminist perspective, this story suggests nuanced conflict between not two, but three lifeways. While Miyax-Julie appeared content in the security of her first home, events led both the civilized and indigenous cultures askew for her. When she first ran into the wilderness, confinements of customs old and new vanished. Wolves revealed a third choice: wildness. But could humans with wild callings, such as Miyax, hold on to a wild lifeway today, as what remains of the wild warps and vanishes at the hands of their own kind? Sadly, Craighead George does not seem to notice that third choice. The story's ending is a contradiction of a too-common over-simplified choice, one that plays out in the sequel with a toxic blended culture against wild life, leading remnant indigenous culture further and further away from raw wildness.

The third choice drew from original ways of knowing, enlivening dormant senses and instincts, to resuscitate whole belonging in habitat. Even if one's decision is to remain in the trenches of civilization to fight it internally, civilization's hangers-on tend to blind themselves to a rewilded human possibility. In these times, choosing a wild lifeway appears on the surface to be choosing the losing side in a predestined battle. But isn't the clearest calling of all life to live your truth to the extent that you can, even if it's bittersweet with little hope as the world around you is being destroyed? Rather that, than join the slaughterers in an anti-natural life? Isn't that why the caged bird still sings, and the wounded wolf pack still howls?

Whether or not humans somehow collectively decide to end their eco-patriarchy, when civilization can no longer support the burdensome Leviathan of the supremacist humanway, it will implode making humans' only choice rewild or die. Julie and *Into the Wild*'s Eva and Nell show that humans can still adapt to conditions. Focus on survival prep while waiting for tipping point collapse distrusts the here and now. Situational need, ability to emotionally cope and openness to adapt are the greatest how-to teachers on liberation from civilization. Great remembering through great release sparks a vitality of humanway as re-thriving primal belonging in re-thriving communities of wild life.

Rewilding self means rewilding dietway too, adjusting from domesticated to wild foods. The transition is a reconsidering of wild tastes, challenging indoctrinated domesticated diet by returning to a wild palette. A study of human diet 780,000 years ago at the ancient site of Gesher Benot Ya'aqov shows a staple dietway of at least 55 species of plants, including nuts, fruits, seeds, vegetables, and tubers. These findings change previous notions of 'paleo diet' and shed light on hominin abilities to adjust to new environmental flora. Some of the plants were foraged heavily, but the plant variety was broad based, some still eaten today, like water chestnuts, *Trapa natans,* and olives. Plants that grew in lakes include dense patches of a water lily, *Euryale ferox,* for white seeds, and bulrush, *Typha,* for rhizomes. Thistle, *Silybum marianum,* seeds provide a good source of oils.

Acorns, probably roasted, had to be collected quickly before wild boar and rodents got to them first. Many plants no longer recognized as food were eaten during the last few centuries somewhere in the world.[25]

Beginning before *Homo sapiens*, humans set fire onto earth's landscape gradually transforming biota into a designed niche human constructed foodscape, in time worldwide. Before bows and arrows, fire was used to drive large mammals off precipices and into hole or boggy traps for easy slaughter. Later, to increase food from hunting, early humans managed fire to create forest openings and sight lines, to facilitate growth of plant fodder luring in unsuspecting browsing animals, and to cook carcasses making them digestible to humans' herbivore bodies.

> *Fire was the key to humankind's growing sway over the natural world - a species monopoly and trump card, worldwide... Armed with fire to sculpt the environment and able to eat so much more of it, early man could both stay closer to the hearth and, at the same time, establish new hearths in previously forbidden environments... Fire largely accounts for our reproductive success as the world's most successful "invasive."* Yet, *"we have adapted so massively to fire that our species would have no future*

without it... we are utterly dependent on fire. It has in a real sense domesticated us. "[26]

Homo used hunting's power over animals to make food closer, abundant and predictable by becoming disturbance ecologists, fire domesticators of others and self. Humans used fire not only as a tool, but a weapon to bring all others under supreme reign, assisting ecological volatilities of invasion, colonization and overpopulation of humans and their wild tagalong opportunists and domesticates, monopolizing Earth.

The impact of humans' fire landscaping transitioning fauna and flora toward 'productive' species is evidenced in the marked decline in CO_2 during Native American genocide, 56 million deaths between 1492 and 1600 Forest managing humans were directly and indirectly massacred en masse and land once forested essentially went feral.[27] One idea during initial rewilding is for humans to continue intentional burns to sustain fire-dependent species, while returning the role of the predator to others. Forest liberation from human hands will in time require shifting away from hyper-engineered fire regime adapted vegetation, which may not appeal in the mind of today's eco-patriarchy ideal, as humans relocate their habitat.

While uncooked, raw wild foods is the human primal dietway, raw foodist TJ Long envisions rewilding transition.

> *It has taken us so long to get to where we are (lost), and it's going to take a while to find our way back. Living in (a colder region), if I were living outside of civilization, I'd surely manipulate fire! But I recognize that I'm not really supposed to be living here in the first place. (E)liminating fire would be one of the last steps, as many people would still need fire to have basic needs met.*[28]

Dave Mayton grounds original diet in relation to ecological events:

> *Recorded history told us that man consumed animal flesh long before he mastered fire, but archaeology, paleontology, physics, anatomy and biology tell us otherwise in so many ways it's ridiculous...*
> *We are tropical frugivore primates who, with our exceptional capabilities, should have long ago created a*

proverbial Garden of Eden across much of the planet with 20,000+ edible plant species.

There is no such thing as renewable in nature. There is only regenerative.

When some men mastered fire (only about 6000 generations ago) they could then consume the flesh of animals without getting sick or dying. This was the beginning of the fall of man. This eventually created a subsequent need for a concept called property rights and over time moved men to the hierarchical constructs.... Our primary needs (i.e. truly clean air and water, high nutrient species specific diet, sunlight) have been traded for cheap knockoffs. Because of this litany of events we now have far more subsequent needs than primary needs and suffering has increased. How much more can we convert the life systems of the planet into trinkets? How much more can wild life (AKA natural creatures) take from the roads, fences, habitat destruction and many other man-made dangers? In the last 34 years the flying insect population has decreased by nearly 75%. The plankton in the oceans, which create over 90% of the oxygen we breathe, have been decimated. How do you 'manufacture' one of those?[29]

For TJ Long, first steps in rewilding would be denouncing agriculture and rejecting technology while reconnecting with wildness.

If early hunting weapons are not technology, could they have sparked the ascent of technology? While that may be less clear, the control of fire seems certain to have lit technology's flame. Fire empowered planet-wide human colonization, a force exponentially growing, dominating, and conquering all. What is technology? Most may agree with this definition - machinery and/or abilities stemming from knowledge. But much more, technology powers the Leviathan civilitopia. Technology shapes the modern ape's ethos, which working in tandem, technology and ethos, become a self-driving force engineering the world on their terms. Technology's (artificial) life invents dependence on its functions, eroding free will and wildness with 'unforeseen', 'unintended' consequences.

Could Jacques Ellul's[30] characteristics of technology apply much farther back than he intended, to origins of human control of fire? Turn to journalist Andrew Nikiforuk's analysis of Ellul's critique on technology.[31] *"The world of (technology) imposes a rational and mechanical order on all things. It embraces artificiality and seeks to replace all natural systems with engineered ones."* Imagine the high calorie mechanical efficiency of cooking, and the artificial power of fire used as weapon to unnaturally evoke fear in primate humans' predators. *"(Technology) automatically reduces actions to the 'one best way.' Technical progress is also self-augmenting: it is irreversible."* In time the intentional engineering of land through controlled burns over 100,000 years ago invented vast new habitats with plants and animals reliant upon systematic burns. Fire is the only method to maintain hegemonic habitats, there is no other way and no going back. *"Technology is indivisible and universal because everywhere it goes it shows the same deterministic face with the same consequences. And it is autonomous."* Control of fire rather quickly became a locus of control over organized human lifeway, spreading 'like fire', with human dependence on fire eliciting systematic social dynamics since early in *Homo sapiens'* origins. As humans use fire for cooking food, protection from predators, shaping tools and weapons, fire uses humans. Who gathers the ever needed supply of wood, who sparks the flame, who stays up all night to keep it burning, who carries the embers when traveling to keep it alive? Fire compels human labor and labor's specializations and divisions. Fire may have been the first form of taxation – in order to participate in the group, there is a compelled pressure to pay dues to keep fire running like a machine for the benefit of everyone in the group. If fire may not be organically alive, may not actually be autonomous, but at least resembles a human parasite. Can humans truly rewild without abandoning the juggernaut of controlled fire, or is the relationship so far gone that releasing control of fire would kill the parasite's host?

Urban Scout's *Rewild or Die: Revolution and Renaissance at the End of Civilization* philosophizes on the

> *emerging rewilding renaissance… Rewilding is the process of un-doing this domestication, and restoring healthy,*

> *biologically diverse communities... thinking, feeling and most importantly living wild is the only way to reach true sustainability.*[32]

The movement of wilderness connection programs and schools excels in rewilding the human animal – basic survival skills, ethnobotany, reawakening senses, natural body movements. But they retain Deep Ecology ethos of mysticism and employing rationalization in dominating and exploitative relations with other animals. Ecofeminism challenges rewilding programs deeper than the social justice critiques suffered by one of their inspirations, Tom Brown Jr. When asked about healing the harm civilized humans have caused habitats, the line they tend to tow is that when humans rewild themselves they gain an ethic of earth care. Perhaps they are careful to not harm the places in which they rewild themselves, but their approach seems human-centric while the wild biomes of diversities of species is diminishing under eco-patriarchal siege worldwide.

Some rewilding programs are picking up the practice of permaculture, a form of agriculture architecting human-centric foodscapes on land, rife with introducing nonindigenous species that sometimes becoming invasive[33] and exploiting domesticated animals. Despite any airs otherwise, permaculture treats wild like wild is a shop and it is the owner. All belongs to it, under its control. Permaculture may plant whatever its nonindigenous heart or mind desires, but at its core it's a pure pillager of wildness. Domestication and permaculture are intentional rearrangings of wild biota and abiota in a way intended to increase food opportunities within reign of the domesticator, for permaculture especially aesthetically pleasing arrangements, as opposed to a primitive co-adaptive lifeway.

Arrangement breaks past ways of wild, enabling domesticators to spread into and settle ranges outside their species' habitat. Moving into habitats of others without effective wild defenses to humans, wild symbiotic relationships transform through opportunistic usury, colonizing swaths of wild homes of others. With *Homo* shifting foraging and gathering foodway to hunting, even killing off and controlling their wild predators, *Homo* has perhaps become wild's most destructive parasitic colonizer. Humans who sense the need to rewild without understanding the deep catalyst origins of human domestication are spinning their wheels thinking like they are going somewhere while in reality they're stuck in civilization's muck.

With most humans today living far away from conditions of a wild human habitat range, many rewilders strive to increase their food opportunities with a central focus on hunting. Some include scavenging 'road kill'.

...I won't fool myself into thinking scavenging from this rabbit would be a 'wild' way for civilization's humans to live, or to 'rewild'. The wildest act I could take would be one of reintegration, to bring the rabbit into the forest for wildness to have its way. My being knows the wild human does not hunger for roadkill, but the death of 'progress' that causes roadkill.[34]

If a human was killed by a car, would rewilders instinctively scavenge that 'road kill'? There's hardly discernable biological difference between eating human and eating deer. The difference between scavenging deer and scavenging human is the dissonance of humanity's fragmented compassion inciting rationalized anxiety - speciesism. An ecologically mutualistic act, or act of innate fairness, might be for the colonizing human ape who is rewilding to move the killed animal into an area safer for omnivore and carnivore animals, most struggling under human rule, to have nourishment.

Artist: Elizabeth Peterschmidt

Where empathy has been blocked by eco-patriarchy, the challenge is to shed ideological rationalizations legitimizing ingrained disconnecting lifeways. Liberation comes from replacing civilized ways of being with inner and outer animality, sensory awareness driving intuition. Here is an actual experience as portrayed in *Original Wisdom-*

> *The jungle was suddenly dense with sounds, smells, little puffs of air here and there. I became aware of things I had largely ignored before... I could smell things I had no name for. I heard little sounds that could be anything at all. I saw a leaf shivering. I saw a line of insects crawling up a tree...*
> *"Drink?" he asked.*
> *... I looked at him, thinking he would find a water vine... Suddenly a new thought burst in on me: maybe I could sense water...*
> *"Do not think. Water inside heart," I knew he meant I should sense inside – not with my mind, but from the inside.*
> *As soon as I stopped thinking, planning, deciding, analyzing – using my mind, I felt as if I was pushed in a*

certain direction. I walked a few steps and immediately saw
a big leaf with perhaps half a cup of water in it.
...My perception opened further. I no longer saw water-
what I felt with my whole being was a leaf-with-water-in-it,
attached to a plant that grew in soil surrounded by
uncounted other plants... And nothing was separate; all
was one, the same thing: water-leaf-plant-trees-soil-
animals-earth-air-sunlight and little wisps of wind. The all-
ness was everywhere, and I was part of it.[35]

Elizabeth Costello sees that human fullness of being involves *"feeling (one's) way towards a different kind of being-in-the-world,"*[36] a kinetic consciousness. But how does wild aliveness effect compassion? Does it instinctively lead to action protecting and recovering wildlife and wild habitats?

Many modern time earth-embedded hunter-gatherers reveal the prehistoric disconnect with compassion, their ability to turn off its 'switch'. In the Kalahari Ju/'hoan hunter /I!ae embodied tracking as *"constant physical dialogue with the environment and ultimately an ability to project oneself into the animals that left the track"* experienced through an *"intimate knowledge."*[37]

/I!ae experienced the desert as a vast interactive canvas
animated by the stories its many creatures inscribed into
the sand. He insisted that if you walk through this part of
the Kalahari looking only ahead of you "like people in the
town do," it is a dead place, a home only to birds, flies,
livestock, and the dung beetles that followed them. As he
walked, his eyes would dart back and forth across the
ground, picking out interesting stories from the cacophony
of narratives etched.[38]

Tracking has deep roots in humanity, possibly as the first expression of symbolic 'mind reading' and 'emotion reading'.

This kind of empathy arises out of the performance of the
hunt and, for the Ju/'hoansi, found its most graceful
expression through the art of tracking, arguably one of the
earliest and most enigmatic forms of reading.[39]

Ju/'hoansi consider nonhuman animals they kill as people because *they too lived and thought… each species of animal had its own distinctive physical forms, customs, habits, and ways of experiencing and interacting with the world.*[40]

Trackers use cognitive empathy to take on their prey's perspective of thoughts and feelings.

Tracking is more than physical tracks, sensed with more than sight or touch, even more than intuition.[41]

Trackers empathize without sympathy because it would deter the hunt. The author James Suzman justifies /I!ae's difficulties in describing how other animals saw the world and his apparent indifference toward the animals killed, because his sense is experienced bodily.

It was something that was felt and so could not be easily translated into words. When he discovered fresh tracks of something he wished to hunt, he shivered briefly, as if tickled by this trace of the animal's presence. It was a sensation, he explained, that he felt in the back of his neck and sometimes his armpits…[42]

This empathy is based in biology, solely to advantage his killing. Compassion is buried deep to cope with killing. For /I!ae, hunting is *"hypersensory,"*[43] human *"bodies and senses progressively merge with those of their prey up to and beyond the moment that the fatal spear thrust is delivered.*[44] This is the breaking point from human with whole compassion to human with eco-patriarchy. [For me, all this hits too close to home, my compassion searches for how my brother experienced the end of his life as he lay dying with his killer looking down at him:] *"the animal usually will offer no response to the hunters, its sensory universe reduced to a haze of poison-induced pain, paralysis, and trauma."*[45] [My compassion is stunned straining to connect with my brother and the billions of animals killed by human hands. Knowing my brother's killer well, I know that what seems like a void of compassion is essentially compassion battered into a suppressed nothingness.]

> *...a hunter and his prey are linked by the poison; hunters describe feeling shadow pains, often in the corresponding part of their bodies where the arrow struck their prey... But these sensations are neither overwhelming nor particularly distracting. They have form and presence yet no substance.*[46]

/I!ae's rationalization strategies suppressing his compassion are bountiful. He

> *considered the animals he hunted to be both companions and adversaries. They knew he was a hunter and were 'right' to fear him, just as he was 'right to try to outwit and kill them. "*[47]
>
> *To Ju/'hoansi, adopting the perspective of animals did not mean feeling compassion or sympathy for them so much as understanding that - in the broader scheme of existence - happiness, death, and suffering were simply part of how the cosmos was ordered. And in this cosmic order all animals accepted their roles. Many were meat. Others were hunters. And a few, like humans... were both meat and hunters, depending on circumstances.*[48]

If primitive humans accept their 'role', that they are both predator and prey, then why have they attempted to kill off, many times to extinction, all their predators?

On occasions when the hunter entering the human village incites an anxiety that something may go wrong, to keep the empathetic bond with his prey the hunter avoids eating meat of others' kills and avoids women, who can break the empathetic bond because they are "like meat."[49] Then the author joins in the rationalizing, expressing the form of eco-patriarchy embraced by Deep Ecology:

> *For Ju/'hoan hunters the moment of the kill is one of neither elation nor sadness. When I asked one man what he felt when he cut an animal's throat, he replied that it felt no different from cutting bread. But this is understandable. It is hard to feel anything at all when overwhelmed by the*

almost postcoital sensory void that marks the end of a successful hunt.[50]

His life story ending sadly is also immersed in eco-patriarchy's violence inflicted on his own species and himself. The tracker-hunter-predator /I!ae, the man with a *"portal into places where he felt alive and at ease, where he could dissolve into the world around him and, if he was lucky, merge his being with that of the quarry he stalked,"*[51] had been enculturated to suppress compassion. He finished his life by choking his wife to death in a drunken rage and running off. After being released from jail having served sentence for the murder, he raped and beat a young woman. This time instead of returning to jail, he hung himself on a tree.[52]

Artistic rendition of whale hunters harpooning a whale.
Wiki Commons from the Wellcome Library, London

Eco-patriarchy of an individual spans out into all aspects of his life, whether explicit or suppressed. Eco-patriarchy of a people spans into and is advanced by other people. Deconstructing eco-patriarchy offers more than lessons. Features can be reformed, making them adoptable to a wilded ecofeminism. /I!ae's life offers ecofeminism abilities and inspiration. /I!ae experienced tracking as something more than killing and eating. He seemed to understand, as put in the novel by Olga Tokarczuk:

It is the feet that all knowledge of Mankind lies hidden; the body sends them a weighty sense of who we really are and how we related to the earth. It's in the touch of the earth, at its point of contact with the body that the whole mystery is located...[53]

The whole idea of compassion is based on a keen awareness of the interdependence of all these living beings, which are all part of one another, and all involved in one another. ~Thomas Merton

Tracking itself is not eco-patriarchal when used to be aware of comings and goings of other species and individuals, to exist and interact within community, to heighten a sense of togetherness.[54] Even if ground beings camouflage to hide their presence, the changing elements will catch up with them, whether it be rain's mud marking actions, wind fallen leaves revealing movements, or snow on all surfaces ground level and above chronicling almost all until melt. *"...prints in the snow documented every move. Nothing could escape this register"*[55] Not always to all, but life in wild communities has a longing to know and to be known, to have presence and mingle. To know the story of a place heightens a sense of security, of belonging.

> *...it was the tracks of warthogs, kudu, oryx, and steenbok that excited /I!ae most. Out of a seemingly insignificant set of indistinct prints, scuffs, and twisted grass stems he would conjure detailed descriptions of their movements and motivations. He'd explain where they were going and why, what they were doing, and where they had been. He'd also tell me their gender, their size, and whether they were healthy, hungry, nervous, or agitated.*[56]

This way of knowing is /I!ae's gift when no longer used for eco-patriarchy's hunt. Reading tracks is an ecofeminist ecology in its active listening to others, a force that draws beings together in aliveness and belonging. Leaving and reading tracks on earth's surface is a wildscape's compassion, for compassion is wild belonging. /I!ae lived and died where he sensed belonging.

A field anthropologist speaks to the true appeal of the hunt:

> *I had to plunge into jungle life, going hunting every chance I got until I had a good feeling for what was going on. In essence, I learned, the Indians had no elaborate hunting techniques or strategies, but they were minute observes and deadly trackers. I'd try to stay behind because I was so noisy. But they didn't seem to mind, and soon I found that I enjoyed the hunt. It was communal. I'd be out in the woods with a few of the men; we'd go out together, and we'd come back together. Not much talking but that was okay... In a way hunting was an escape from the village, and I found out later that the Yanomamö think of it that way themselves.*[57]

The love of the hunt can be contagious, not so much for the provisions, but simply the sociality, a sense of togetherness, belonging within the wild. This differs from other animal predators.

Cat expert Paul Leyhausen's experiments on domestic and wild cat behavior found that cats continue chasing, catching and killing prey whether or not they are hungry. *"Note that what the cat likes best: most of all to chase, then to catch, next to kill, least of all to eat.* "[58] As with humans who hunt, they enjoy the stalk and the catch, some may enjoy the kill, *"but most hunters would claim that they do not enjoy the suffering of the pheasant or the deer."* [59] Perhaps carnivores like cats engage in hunting 'play' as practice.

But for the human ape, hunting has too often become a contest, with feelings like pride, chauvinism, and sexual prowess, and a malformed identity rooted in power and control, too often extending into other aspects of their lives. In adopting the way of the natural born predator, *Homo* has honed compassion's cut off switch. For the human species, to be predator is a choice. Wild cats cannot live without the hunt, humans can. The question is whether humans can be incited by compassion to act on caring, or at least to embrace ecological mutualism in wild community, to let go of an eco-patriarchal predatory lifeway, before they devour wild life to death.

ALF Streiter der Nacht

Dialectic on Tracking as Symbolic 'Reading':

In the case of a lion stalking a gazelle using varying degrees of sight, hearing, and smell, etc. the focus is directly on the gazelle. How would the lion's ability to take cues from indirect sources, like movement of a branch, compare to symbolic thinking of humans 'reading' animal tracks?

Birds of prey's vision is sharp to focus on attacking prey through direct spotting in land, water or air, depending on the species.

Birds like falcons flying over open land can see in the ultraviolet light range, making it possible to track small mammals who leave urine trails that glow in ultraviolet.[60] They can also use indirect sight cues, such as moving forest floor debris. How do these forms of 'reading' distinguish from human's tracking?

Would symbolic thinking-tracking via visual cues be equivalent to tracking using olfactory cues? Other animals like elephants whose noses are closer to the ground, use their sense of smell to investigate tracks, interpreting their meanings. Most predatory vertebrates rely on their sense of smell first, then on hearing and sight as they move closer. If big cats encroached by civilization had the visual ability to recognize human tracks, but they rely so much on their nose that they get more information from human's scent, would that be symbolic, olfactory 'reading'?

Animals also learn by association, which seems to be symbolic. In certain seasons just before dusk, I go to the shore and wait for a certain osprey to fly in from the south with a few crows trailing the wing, but with no warning calls. The crows can predict which of the osprey's dives will be successful, as even before the speedy osprey hits the water, the crows fly to their sit spot in a Doug fir. The osprey carries her resisting catch in her relentless talons up to her customary branch hanging out horizontally above the waiting crows. As the osprey tears flesh from the fish, small parts fall that the crows dive to and catch midair. What has become an interspecies habit started with learning an association, but deeper. Not just knowing osprey's hunting mode, but pre-determining or intuiting particulars of the upcoming act between the osprey and the fish. Would this type of association be a symbolic symbiosis?

Animals have incitable senses - smell, sight, sound, and ample more of which modern humans have likely grown unaware. They use senses in combination, following incitements in the direction the stronger sensation leads them. There is a point that instincts meld into a bodily intuition, similar to how muscle memory is built into the being. When a raccoon backtracks in her own footprints, is she cognitively making herself harder to track, or is that instinct passed through generations based on senses or intuition that man-the-hunter is near? It is commonly said that animals sense fear. What other emotions are sensed?

Even if humans are the only animal that can follow tracks, would that necessarily be due to symbolic cognitive ability? Do tracks require more cognitive perceptive analysis, with mental pictures as opposed to bodily acuity, such as in determining the track's species? For example, a hunter may wonder: *Can I hunt this species, and this particular individual? How long ago was this track made, how fast was the individual going, and how much energy would I need to exert to catch up? Might there be other individuals where this individual is heading?* Do different animals track more instinctually with less 'critical thinking', based on the intensity and form of their sensory ability? Do trans-cognitive channels aid interpretation of scat, urine, fur, marks left behind, traces from feeding upon or movement in vegetation, habitat map, herd social behavior, etc.?

How does an animal decide when to hunt - biological sensations, social expectations, habit of routine? Do they simply wander around likely areas until they hear, see or smell prey? How do they sense or know 'likely areas'? Do they have 'historical' body memory? How do they pass knowledge through generations? Are humans unique in how they mentally or viscerally 'time travel' when tracking? Indigenous trackers travel back to the moment the track was made, and meld their mind or spirit with the mind or spirit of that animal. They follow after the sensory signs fade by predicting how the animal would have behaved in the past. Do other animals make such predictions?

At what point did early hominins begin recognizing that footprints indicate the presence or passage of animals? Primates have strong vision. How does primates in canopy habitat reaction to tracks compare to that of primates on the ground? Was there a time when humans used tracking simple to know their community, based on more than defense but in forming alliances of belonging? Could tracking have played a role as humans were adapting both hunting and more intense compassion? Did tracking play a role in humans adapting 'big brains'? Did humans develop the form of 'intelligence' they have today because their senses were not strong enough to thrive on their own within wildscape changes? Would humans have started hunting without tracking 'intelligence'? Would they have made tools, weapons, and fire? Would humans and others be thriving today if early humans had remained within their intelligence range of using senses for a foraging lifeway?

While the human species feels static in the moment, life itself is a process of ever change.

He remembered with amusement that in 1989 he taught a seminar to forty young biologists, half of them women. When he remarked casually that like most of them, he had become a wildlife biologist because he liked to hunt and fish, he was met with a chorus of boos. Surprised, Thomas asked how many participated in these sports. Less than a third had ever hunted, less than half had ever fished. "They come into it from a totally different direction than the old-timers," he said.[61]

This is a true experience. Life itself is oblivious to most changes while happening, yet awareness is central in shifting toward rewilding, or all out going feral.

Eco-patriarchy perceptibly and imperceptibly disconnects organic attachments, supplanting them with connections to the synthetic, while ecofeminism disconnects from the artificial and connects, or reconnects, wild attachments. Modern efforts to reattach wildness are twisted with contradictory actions, feelings and powers, like hunting. Can sensual animality of hunting be adapted to rewilding without the hunt?

... all emotions and all instincts depend for their working on the senses. Emotions and instincts are usually aroused, and arousal is a sensual activity whereby the organism integrates with the environment, especially with other organisms. So, in a way, the senses are more "basic" than the instincts and emotions.[62]

While anthropologist Peter Wilson applies his thoughts above to neither hunting nor rewilding, the collective unconscious experience of human hunting is a disintegrating force, while rewilding integrates. Wilson expects that humankind had two major environmental breaks disconnecting their senses. The most recent was settlement into domestication through domesticating plants and animals. Another romantic tale.

Fig 207.—The Cultivation of Gardens during the Bronze Epoch.
Primitive Man, by Louis Figuier, Chapman and Hall, London, 1870

The first was during human origins' shift from arboreal to savannah habitat. Rewilding earth is the first step in reintegrating. Reviving unmediated senses that arouse wild compassion reconnects humans with a home ecology, a rewilding habitat. In the words of Frank Cook, *flow happens through connection.* Connection is the longing of ecology, despite eco-patriarchy's romanticized taint. In the words of Collard and Contrucci,

> *Participation in nature is in diametric opposition to the romantic appetite for nature epitomized in the hunt, an appetite which consumes the object of its love and which is insatiable because it is based upon a neurotic need for power and control. Participation in nature is based upon a recognition of the reality that nature exists of, for, and by herself; that she is ordered by principles and forces which defy manipulation and harnessing; and that understanding of nature flows from the experience of her and not from the experiment upon her, from being with, not being over her. Participation in nature joins the lover and the loved in regenerative, mutually sustaining cycles of living and dying.*[63]

Eco-patriarchy of the hunt into eco-patriarchy of colonization into eco-patriarchy of civilization. Ecofeminism of defending humans' brutalized from origins to now, into ecofeminism of rewilding earth into ecofeminism of rewilding self.

Here at the end, I feel a bit guilty for being a bit rough on Deep Ecology. All apologies. Well, some apologies. Eco-patriarchy creeps into even the most compassionate places. Ecofeminism could use a good dose of your (Deep Ecology's) earth ethos paired with action. Your unrelenting action for biodiverse co-adapted wild communities makes real differences for many, and is inspirational. Your shift from anthropocentric to biocentric is heavenly, but your embrace of patriarchal religion rationalizing hunting is not so divine. I've been inspired by my friend G.H. Yeah, you're the reason I got that pang of guilt that brought on this apology of sorts. Your efforts do more for wildlife than any Starhawkian pseudo-ecofeminist, with their herbalism and such. Hell, they slipped away from FAR into discombobulation on whether eating animals is incongruous with ecofeminism.

I should write a sequel criticizing today's brand of ecofeminism and feminism. *"Feminist philosophers and activists from all over the world have called for a new ethic for both women and men based on 'feminine' values like nonviolence and caring.*"[64] But do those 'nonviolent' feminists resist participation in violence against caged and free living animals and their wild homes? Do they instinctively sense that if they have children, they will pass on participation in civilization's earth-exploiting dominion? Hmmm, continued reading, landed on this feminist declaration... *"The modern rebellions of women and men against a dominator society have come along with great technological advances."*[65] Look feminists, it's a hard reality, but there's no way around it. Feminism is as incongruous with civilization as veganism is. Did I hit 'em hard enough, G.H.? Would you accept a challenge to experiment with going all the way feral in your ethos of protection and restoration of wild? Feel free to critique my critique. I'm updating this in about a year.

At the risk of theatrics, a thought experiment: What's realistically going to happen when eco-patriarchy's colonization of the planet and resulting overpopulation inevitably collapse? Ya know what's happened before in collapses, like when a Neanderthal population collapsed due to climate shifts and food shortages in the Upper Pleistocene, they resorted to cannibalism.[66] I hear vegan cannibalism is a thing, right Peter? To what extent will today's eco-patriarchal populace resort in the big collapse?

Cannibals with their victims.
Samara province, Volga region, Russia, 1921
copy of photo images published in the book
"Russia 1904-1924. The Revolutionary Years" by Eric Baschet

And what will happen when the eco-patriarch's ammunition runs out and they are left in their bare beings?

How much money can civilization make from a tree? It depends how many it cuts down – and it's not just the money from the wood, for that is a pittance compared to the money civilization could make form an absence of trees. The teeth of the chain cut into the arboreal flesh one last time, leaving a glorious space for – what do you want? A new parking lot, an out-of-town retail park, a blockade of oil palms, a herd of grazing cattle, thousands of acres of soybeans, an open pit coal mine, a toxic sludge lake; a city or two...[67]

Or, true story: *"The trees had to be cut to pay for construction of the logging road that had to be built to take out the trees."*[68]

May rational thoughts of eco-patriarchy... fade forever away.
May emotional senses of ecofeminism incite com-passion action -
for forests, for every wild life.

The sun, moon and the stars do not wait;
they bomb the sky with their presence.
A tsunami does not hesitate;
it announces a death rattle of destruction before dissipating.
So why should I wait?
...this reality, however dismal,
motivates my desire to make my life,
through fierce revolt,
as joyful and fulfilling as possible!
My hopelessness does not paralyze me with fear or depression;
I celebrate it with hysterical laughter and ecstasy
in spite of civilization's death march.
I arm my desires with the urgency to live...
against the social order of monotony and peaceful enslavement,
to sleep beneath the stars,
to feel sunshine and a breeze with every hair on my body,
to listen to the latenight conversations of the insects,
to become wild...

~ Flower Bomb 2019 [69]

Hunters' self-serving arguments and lies are becoming more preposterous, as nonhunters awake from their long, albeit troubled, sleep... Hunters are persecutors of nature who should be prosecuted. They wield a disruptive power out of all proportion... It's time to stop being conned and cowed by hunters, time to stop pampering and coddling them... it's time to stop thinking of wild animals as "resources" and "game," and start thinking of them as sentient beings that deserve our wonder and respect... Hunters make wildlife dead, dead, dead... As for hunters, it's long past check-out time. ~Joy Williams

LATER THAT NIGHT
I HELD AN ATLAS IN MY LAP
RAN MY FINGERS ACROSS THE WHOLE WORLD

AND WHISPERED

WHERE DOES IT HURT?

IT ANSWERED
EVERYWHERE
EVERYWHERE
EVERYWHERE

WARSAN SHIRE

CHRIS RIDDELL

Do you have any regrets?

I will let the burden of guilt and regret fall on the bloodthirsty killers of the world.

~Peter Young[70]

We have never been so empowered- and the ecological stakes have never been so high.[1] ~Entomologist Douglas W. Tallamy

As we ourselves prosper in unseemly numbers they (animals) vanish, and in the end our prosperity may amount to nothing without them.[2] ~Paul Shepard

Plants and animals domesticated by humans remain outside the primal order and because they have no access to hematasoomao (immortal spirit) they are only physical... The same applies to the great mass of global human population today. In Tsistsistas (Cheyenne) thought, the self-domestication of ethnic groups to civilizations and to a condition of exploiting the world has led to a withdrawal of hematasoomao.[3] ~Karl H. Schlesier

We Can Restore Ourselves to this Land
Our truths come from tenure on this land. The animals known by ancestors meet us still in some way, despite the passing of histories. I remember when the buffalo were returned to Lakota land. Long grasses not seen in years by the elders returned and grew. The mere weight of the animals' hooves on the earth brought water to the surface. Creeks and streams came back. These returned the insects and the birds. A great restoration of the land began after the reintroduction of the bison. Several years later the tribe released a herd of wild horses. The bison stood quietly on the top of a ridge and watched the horses come out of the trailer and begin their run toward freedom.[4] ~Linda Hogan

Animal liberation... is a refusal to be tamed into supporting anthropocentrism... By reasserting and expanding our... compassion for animals, we are in the position of feral animals, formerly domesticated but now occupying a semiwild state on the boundaries of hierarchical civilization... Animal liberation enhances our agency in two ways: through our increased autonomy, and through our development as caring beings.[5]
~Brian Luke

By shedding light on the root causes of social problems, ecofeminism can help us to deepen our capacity for empathy for all living beings, thereby helping to bring about a world of peace and respect for all living beings... We have to end this war against the natural world, we have to call an amnesty.[6] ~Marti Kheel

Mr. David Watts

Hello. Would you consider doing an interview on Free Radical Radio to challenge their perspectives on eating nonhumans is essential to live in an anarchoprimitivist world? I understand John Zerzan is also of the same opinions as Rydra and Bellamy who were both vegan but no longer. Thanks David

Hi David – Sorry I picked this up so late. Rydra & Bellamy would slaughter me in a debate, even if my perspective were the winning one, just because they articulate so well. I'd be reluctant to do more damage to folio-frugivorism than has already been done with ex-vegans like them spewing anti-veganism. You need a good debater. I wonder if Layla AbdelRahim would be interested. I'd love to hear her & John discuss this – he adores her so much, yet they avoid the one topic on which they disagree most. Feel free to call me XXX. Peace, Ria

Ria, Yes, it is interesting that John and Layla never discuss veganism. John often mentions two catalysts: domestication, approx 10000 years ago and the industrial revolution. I think there may be a third catalyst which Jim Mason writes about in *An Unnatural Order:* humans hunting and wearing nonhuman skins. This enabled humans to populate areas which were low in plant based foods, nuts, seeds etc by surviving on grass feeding nonhumans and where the climate would have killed us due to being too cold (we used their skins to keep warm). John and Ian Smith who john has had on his show never mention veganism either… I read Ian's blog too and how he is conflicted by veganism as the moral baseline based in the techno mass society and anarcho-primitivism based on the use of nonhumans for food and clothing. Regards David

David, John said this a few months ago:

…Q: What do you think about eating animal products? JZ: I'm still trying to improve my personal approach to that. I don't eat red meat at all, but I'm not exactly a vegan either, though I have a huge respect for that perspective. I guess also part of it for me is the historical thing. As homo species, we started cooking meat almost two million years ago, and I'm always wondering: "Do vegans think that humans were completely wrong or evil because they were eating meat?" It's one thing to attack the slavery of domesticated animals, of course, but I don't know if that will rule out any kind of hunting, for one thing. That's what we were doing for millions of years. They don't like to look at that as an historical question, I think. But I'm not an expert on this. I'm intrigued by the vegan point of view, I can at least say that, though I'm not a vegan. I think it's very good to go in that direction, away from animal products. We don't need that now, and maybe we won't need it in the future either. But I don't know…

{ https://archive.org/details/ZerzanIntDec2015/mode/2up}

Hi Ria, I've had emails from john pretty much saying what he says below. however, i never hear these would-be 'hunters' ever mention eating humans if they are so into their meat? i never hear rydra, bellamy, john and others talk about eating human meat which is interesting. also, i never hear them talk about themselves being food for others be that human and nonhuman. layla and john would be ideal to go into greater detail. i've asked john to get ian smith and/or layla on his show or do a podcast because this issue is gaining greater interest as people think through the mess that has been created... layla, in her presentations etc, looks at the historical question so i don't understand why john would say that. layla discusses humans were vegans which may have included some scavenging and eating insects. generally, people are conflicted about eating flesh and they rely on history. yes, humans can survive on flesh and not many would refuse if that was all there was. if there was a strict choice between a vegan techno mass industrial global society or anarcho-primitivism with scavenging or even minimal hunting, which would you err towards? that's an interesting question? i would argue the first ain't gonna last long as the cost of that infrastructure and of maintaining it, is a killer.

John says vegans do not like to look at the history! If John is so OK with the history as he sees it, then why does he no longer eat red meat as historically, homo (according to what John is saying) ate red meat? Regarding Jim Mason's book, there is a chapter *"Before Agriculture: A World Alive and Ensouled"* which provides a historical reading of how and why hominid and homo came to be: geographically and dietary. The controlled use of fire is cited a major catalyst which enabled us to spread out. He claims that, initially, we ate very little, if anything, by way of flesh, all that came much later. Any flesh that was eaten was scavenged and not hunted. Hunting came later. Indeed, the book claims that *homo sapiens sapiens* did not originally hunt as an organised activity. He states *homo sapiens sapiens* was here around 45000 years ago and organised hunting appears widespread around 25000 years ago. So, arguably, technological improvements provided the killing apparatus and indeed, a change in thinking? Initially, we had digging sticks to get at roots. John would not class spears as technology. These things were designed to kill though, just as a gun is designed to kill. John argues that a spear doesn't require specialised (alienating) labour and a gun does. OK. But a spear is still a killing tool. Historically, we didn't need to kill for food nor see the need to kill for food. So, fire was the first catalyst and that *homo* were becoming more and more social with each other and aware of each other. Then came hunting, following the herds, eating meat and wearing skins. The whole book is well worth reading if you haven't read it. The book claims (page 84*) "The year round hunting of large animals would have given us greater mobility and range than before. On a plant-based diet, they probably would have stayed in a familiar ecosystem with familiar plant species, moving about with the seasons but never moving very far from the home range. As specialised herd hunters, they could travel as far as the herd ranged, even into unfamiliar ecosystems, and never be far from food and materials. They could also survive in cold climates, where plant food is scarce during much of the year."* The book talks about the huge over exaggeration of eating meat/hunting. This is a male ego thing: the big hunter. The book discusses us as not seeing ourselves as any different from other mammals (pre-symbolic?) and then becoming increasingly symbolic and separated. The book is very accessible and is basically about the rise of domination. To finish, as John says, we maybe do not now need to eat flesh as dietary knowledge has increased. We don't need to eat flesh or dairy or eggs or honey unless there is no other choice. We know that now. Right now, John doesn't need to eat animal products, he doesn't live in food desert. He chooses to. Simple. I hope this helps

R – It would be so good to see a comprehensive essay on vegan primitivism exposing & addressing the questions & conflicts, the possible past catalysts and future possibilities. Do you know anyone who'd be interested?

D – Date: Wed, 27 Apr 2016 18:43:02 -0700 From: ecofeminist@riseup.net To: mrdXXX@hotmail.com Subject: Re: FW: John said this a few months ago… Can't wait to read that book. Reading through your email brought a couple questions to mind. Exactly what is the anarcho-primitive purpose of understanding *homo* history?

JZ says the purpose, perhaps "a" purpose, maybe general purpose (unsure about "exact" purpose as John isn't dogmatic in my opinion, he is more of a 'question raiser'), would be to claim that pre-symbolic *homo* lived for a long long time supposedly in nature. Mason goes into this too.

R – How does our past inform us in our present and future?

D – humans do "use" the past/their past as a guide. What that tells us is the stuff of debate. John v those who maintain faith in civilisation would be a crude example.

R – To what extent can we use the past as a reference point of a way humans have lived 'in balance' to help us return to that kind of relationship with Earth life?

D – I put a similar question to John way back: is it not out of human control, that we are where we are because human is doing what human does and has done, only now, the technology aspect is such, that we are accelerating what we do/who we are? He said that we have choices as a species and he cited, as an example, Kropotkin's Mutual Aid.

R – How far back do we go?

D – *Homo sapiens sapiens* is supposedly who we are today and have been, according to Mason, for the last 45000 years. However, as you say, and I have brought this up to on Ian's blog, that there is an argument for controlled used of fire to be included as a civilising agent which takes the path of domination much further back. I think John would argue against that.

R – Were we 'living in balance' when we were hunting, even into extinction, and even one another? Were we more or less 'in balance' when settled into a much smaller habitat, or when we were nomadically spreading into many ecosystems? Is living more as prey than predator a corollary to living 'in balance'? What is the correlation between life 'in balance' and pre-symbolic life?

D – Balance is based on shifting sands, possibly. Daniel Quinn's *Ismael* and *Story of B* come to mind regarding balance. There is, perhaps, a lag, before an imbalance is noticed. That lag has now quickened and so we notice. Plus, the irony of technology, allows to us to witness that imbalance. Mason talks about, band stand-offs and bands moving on to avoid fights. Mason discusses how the human changed through greater social interaction. No one knows why we changed. However, out of all life, I think we are the only one who uses controlled use of fire? There are others (nonhumans) who eat flesh and/or are social, or who eat plants and/or social. Prey and predator which are human concepts as Layla point outs. We assume a relationship between a lion and a gazelle is one of predator/prey but that's just a guess. Mason argues that pre-symbolic life (human) lived in balance as we didn't differentiate, we had no superiority complex. We just existed with few questions asked so to speak. We didn't need to question. Of course that changed very very gradually over time because we now question like fuck. Indeed, Mason claims that we began to see nonhumans as superior to us and we "killed" them in order to ingest their superior qualities: their speed, their strength etc. So, it is debatable whether we hunted for food but for other reasons (page 251). I have read that where human have eaten human, it was also for reasons other than food, often for the perceived superior qualities of the human killed.

R – If you go by John's definition of 'technology', then neither a root digging stick nor a spear are technology, so what is the essence of the difference between them? John seems to embrace controlled fire, but is this not part of the 'logic in domination'?

D – Yes, John sees a digging stick and spear as something an individual can make and so is a tool. John would have technology as a process which involves division of labour and the fall out of that. I would agree that fire could be part of domination. Like I said before, John comes across as human-centric as he never posits himself as being the hunted, being taken out in the prime of life, and eaten. He is the one doing the hunting. Control! None of the AP anti-civ material that I have read ever consider themselves as not being in control. They talk about the prospect of being eaten, only that their body will be returned to "cycle of life" at some point, though not through being eaten. Have you ever *seen The Road*? It is a dystopian near-future collapse where humans are being bred for food in a cellar. This is the bit that gets people who watch it: imagine that happening, knowingly being farmed!

...I asked Layla if her position was humans are vegans anarchistic and primitive and so, they should have (in the past) and ought to (in the future) live in places where the plants grows etc and where it is warm enough not to require wearing nonhuman skin. I didn't mention the controlled use of fire which would be a useful discussion point too.

R – there will come a time when this whole issue is going to explode. have you ever considering writing an article on it or anything? if you have time & inclination, what is your background?

D – My background has always been that of a critical on-looker: why are we here kind of stuff. Specifically, the controlling aspect of 'society.' The Big Lie as I call it and Death by Convenience is another term I use for conspicuous consumer culture. I did loads of reading, thinking, long walks talking to myself, trying to find that elusive answer as to why it is so fucked up. I went through the mainsteam stuff, Greenpeace etc and discovered that they are basically corporate entities, same with the welfarist organisations which Francione articulates so eruditely. I just kept digging. Read John's stuff re-read him and thought the idea made some sense. Whether they are achievable is another matter. We are symbolic after all. We are where we are. John is often misrepresented. He is about discussion. I understand why he doesn't get the exposure that even Chomsky does. Zerzan's ideas require people to do something: namely give something (significant) up: animal 'products' (which ironically John uses his historical perspective to cling to, ha ha) and Zerzan is asking people to give up the charade of civilisation which, at first thought, seems ridiculous until people delve in and unravel the roots of possibly why we are where we are. I agree with John, there is more and more realisation that it's fucked or nearly fucked… and is it necessary to be fucked, was it inevitable that it would get fucked?: extinction rates, climate change, human migration, human population growth, increasing inequality, atomisation, surveillance, increased militarism, nuclear weapons, pollution, representative democracy is now the joke it always was, the reaction to the Arctic melting is one of sick opportunism for the deranged megalomaniacs etc. John's ideas make people face all that and more. But he ain't given the chance. He's up for it. All he wants is the chance to get his ideas across, have the discussion. What chance has he got when even the red anarchists shoot him down? All they appear to offer is similar to what we have now only in the control of "the people!" I put the hypothetical question as just that: to get a response. I'm not advocating either/ or. I don't know if you heard John's show last week with the green syndicalist caller but it is well worth listening to. The discussion was about the possibility of a green syndicalist/anarchist federated approach to reducing reducing reducing the size of where we are. John has said many times, nothing will happen unless people decide they have had enough or are forced to as any collapse comes a knocking. How people then react (when it's too late so to speak) is obvious: fights over "resources." All this may be the inevitable course of "time." Let's face it, if humans suffered a mass die off, life will go on. Species would appear and disappear. Existentially, does any of it matter? Was I ever here before? Is my life the total extent of my presence? When I die, is that it? Consciousness. Morality, it is purely a human construct? Are other animals as conflicted as we are? Does any of it matter? If so, why? why not? And what about the future generations of life? Do we not have an obligation to them all? Were we happy to discover that the world we were born into (without our consent I may add) was not /is not the world we were born into. As we questioned, we learned of the lies we were told. Now what? Would we not want a "better" world to have been born into? Do we have to symbolic think to know? We are here now. We need clean air. We need clean water. We need clean food. We need others. We want more!!! We want as much as we can get, until there is no more. Then, we know we've had all there was to have! Domination and colonisation. Do we really have a choice? John thinks we do: Kropotkin for example.

Yep, another email from yours truly. I got reading and then I got thinking and finally ended up wondering. Here goes, and this will be short. I am currently reading *Black and Green Review 2*. I know number 3 is out but number 2 has only just arrived in the UK. I don't know if you have it or not but that is besides my point. Anyway, there are loads of references in it (and not only from Kevin Tucker who seems obsessed with the NEED to hunt) to hunter/gatherers. No one in B&GR ever refer to nomadic living, past or present or future, as gatherer/hunter or gatherer/scavenger and God forbid....vegan. No, it is ALWAYS printed as hunter/gatherer. So, I know you are into (more than me anyway) social media and you will have registered with some of them including Facebook and so, how about you contacting Layla and asking her if she would write a piece for *Black and Green Review* and to even put a piece on her website regarding the possibilities of a vegan anarchistic primitive (or vegan green anarchy) and challenge Kevin Tucker and others. Perhaps you could submit a piece too as the publication is loaded with views from males. You write eloquently so don't be afraid of them. I know Kevin Tucker can be brash. I did read somewhere, ages ago now, him going on about being vegan fucked up his health blah di blah. He fetishises primitivism in my opinion or he gets damn close to it.

I think it would be useful for Layla to go beyond abstraction and put forward how she believes humans can/should exist as vegans. Does Layla believe that fire is to be done away with? The wheel too? I have watched, listened and read most of her stuff and I don't hear much beyond abstraction? Does Layla believe that there is a human habitat and if so, what is that?

Then there is the usual questions of how does she suggest we manage nuclear waste and all the oil capped oil wells that need maintaining? What do we do about health, medicine as natural remedies as often too weak to "fight" human domesticated illness? I know John will turn the question on its head claiming it is not necessarily his responsibility as a primitivist to "justify" any solution as he didn't want all the domestication and industry in the first place. He would add that those that brought this stuff into the world have the responsibility of dealing with it but how does that get us anywhere? Critiquing civilisation is one thing: naming all the problems etc but to then not provide any tangible way out of it is, arguably, a cop out. John is very good at putting such questions back to the people who pose them to him. I get that. I really do. I just think if he is willing to put himself out there (as he has done) and tear up civilisation with his writings etc, then why not put himself out there and pose the questions about what to do with the pollution, infrastructure etc. Layla needs to be, in my opinion, way more detailed in the nittygritty. How? How do we do it Layla? What is to be done as she says? We must rewild ourselves she says. How? But she leaves it at that because that is the anarchist way: not to impose solutions!!! It's a great cop out used by many a so-called anarchist. I say, put one's suggestions on the line for the purposes of getting the ball rolling. I remember a caller into John's show regarding nuclear waste: https://www.youtube.com/watch?v=w5Ny6sAdD50 I am not convinced by John's response on this. There has to be something much more concrete and by him saying "…the ball is their court" doesn't get us anywhere. I don't know the answer either.

For me both Layla and John could put scenarios forward as to how we "solve" the mess we have created and not just be abstract about it.

I'm in buoyant mood. Fuck knows why. Ride the wave til it crashes I guess. Anyway, check this out: http://www.rewildingbritain.org.uk/about/our-people Go on stick this on your blog with the title: "Britain is Safe/Is Britain Safe?"

Here we go again: White Professionals etc etc. I'm gonna be massively judgmental here: can you realistically see any of these re-wilding themselves? But what about tea and cakes they cry? Ha ha ha.

I gotta go. Gotta get my meds. The red ones look great too. Yum Yum, my favourite. They make me feel so much better. No, not the ones from the professional doctor. No silly, the ones from the street doctor. Seriously, I'm off to the hills to sit by a bubbling brook and maybe see a kite. I was in a local church yard yesterday being very still and very quiet with a big smile on my face as I watched 3 mice scampering about within two feet of me.

I took magic mushrooms years ago. I took them for a few seasons. That whole time has never left me. The people I took them with and the edges we found as we supported each other through our trips.

Anyway, with the Good White Ultra-Clean Nice People (in the link above) and their hobby/project of re-wilding Britain, I can sit at peace knowing all will be well in the world!!!!

George Monbiot wrote a book called *Feral*. Read it. It's all smoke and mirrors. He doesn't want to really change anything. He is well-spoken, the typical middle Englander accent, a journalist for the Left. The type Kaczynski despised. Monbiot wants to keep the mines and the infrastructure going.

Lastly, I shall leave with this question: What can be done: how can 8 billion humans get to a place where there is a human/non-human balance? Is it possible? What would your guide book contain? With the abstract, there must be the tangible. So, for example: reduce human numbers. Yes. How? Nuclear waste, how do we deal with it? Can nuclear waste be dealt with and descale human presence and infrastructure at the same time? Do we reduce inequality? Yes. Ok. How? Where? Who? I'm just throwing that out as an example. I know you are "working" on restoration. Is this for your own sanity and not necessarily for you to "achieve" anything more than that?

Horticulture? What about that with simple wooden tools?

If a global natural disaster struck, would humans help each other and fellow non-humans by doing what we would want them to do? Arguably, we are in a global disaster now I know. But, let's say a meteor hit the earth and something had to be done. Would people then react differently? As Jensen says, if aliens came and wanted to destroy the place and kill everything, would humans react differently and realise we need to live differently?

David

David,

Would you be interested in co-stewarding a wordpress with me to 'flesh out' some of these questions & possibilities? I took the liberty of setting up an email for us: XXX@yahoo.com (password: XXX), and a blog: primitivegan(password: XXX). If you're interested, we could change the email and site names if you prefer.

I started structuring it with some larger questions at the intersection of Vegan & Primitive. If you feel motivated, I'm fine with you leading this up, or tag teaming it, whatever you find inspiring. Feel free to edit or delete anything I post.

If we team up with this ether endeavor, after we get the site set up we could submit our writings and invite folks to submit to our site.

How does this sound to you?

{crickets…}

Raging Questions

Let me first disclose that I am a folio-frugivore (vegan) anarcho-primitivist, and may I add, thriving on healthful sustenance. Questions on the nature of rewilding for present-day 'hunter-gatherer' anarcho-primitivists burn inside me. In returning to primeval wild, how are primitivists preferential in selecting the bits of our past ways we strive to make future? As humans have been scavengers far longer than hunters, how does the label 'hunter-gatherer' proudly persist? Whenever archeological or anthropological evidence arises of cannibalism, oppression, humans as prey not predator, etc. why is the knee jerk reaction to rationalize it away as somehow not truly in our most natural nature? Why is evidence of hunting so straightaway accepted, lauded and proliferated?

Why is there such disdain for searching further back than industry and agriculture for human's wrong turn? What if there were ever earlier gradual catalysts like controlled fire, wearing clothes, hunting tools, and organized hunting that removed us from our habitat and allowed us to adapt and evolve our way into the invasive species that we have become today? Were we not living more 'in balance' when settled into our early human habitat than when we spread out into Earth's other ecosystems?

Why do primitivists have defensive reactions to evidence that hunter-gatherers have degraded biodiversity, and harmed animals and plants even to the point of extinction? Or when asked for their definition of the human habitat, as if we have innate superiority to freedom from boundaries of habitat as other animals have? When a primitivist is challenged to hunt and eat as all omnivorous animals hunt and eat, does his sense of outrage that his weapons and fire for cooking were 'taken away' not reflect his sense of dominion? How does a modern mind come to ponder the possibility that earliest bipeds might have been persistence hunters? Further, does the fact that humans have done a thing for a long time justify the necessity for its continuance in a primitive future?

Is bias found in mis-interpretations solidifying mis-beliefs? For example, primitivists point to Richard Wrangham's *Catching Fire: How Cooking Made Us Human* to conclude 'meat made us human'. But what if the point of the book is reflected in the title itself? What if it is cooking itself that allowed for rapid consumption of calories and nutrients by breaking down plant fibers that led to a larger brain? In his book Wrangham lays out that meat was unreliable and human's early diet was primarily plant-based. What if researchers proposed that cooked starches met the energy demands of an increasing brain size? What if our ancestors thrived without meat, just as we do today? Even if true, what is so much better about having a larger brain? What if cooking was a step down a path toward human dominion and Earth destruction?

Human Foraging Persists Human's foraging instinct still thrives today, as evidenced especially in innate actions of our young. I first began witnessing the natural state of human eating in the seconds after my son was born. His strong neck muscles propelled his heavy head, lining up his mouth into perfect suckle position, clasping my breast with his tiny fingers encouraging flow.

At 18 months he wandered outside in a new place, spied ripe grapes on a vine, walked up to them for closer inspection, intuitively plucked one off with primal foraging fingers, placed it in his mouth for an exploratory taste, decided it was good as he chewed it with pleasure and swallowed. He had never before seen a grape. This led me to ponder if the 'stage' young humans go through of 'putting everything in their mouth' is not a stage at all, but the beginning of learning to forage from all the food around in wild habitat. Whereas in this human domesticated world young are reprimanded until their foraging instinct is suppressed, in a wild world perhaps our young hone their foraging for berries, nuts, seeds, flowers, leaves, stems, tubers, grains, fruits, and mushrooms.

Even before the foraging instinct is suppressed, he still will not accept mouthing a living animal. Try to put a live cricket or worm in his mouth & he grimaces. He has to be conditioned to overcome his disgust. His only first reaction to animals, no matter how small, nonthreatening or 'tasty', is fear or curiosity or compassion. But he does generally accept and trust what humans put in his mouth, even pieces of charred animals tissues. When humans put animal tissues in their babies' mouths, is that the first indoctrination into and normalization of a myth that humans are intended to be hunters?

But…Paleo! Primitivism calls for an Earth devoid of artificial technology. Some say the only period that sustains that lifestyle is the Paleolithic which is characterized by hunter-gatherer. Many respect veganism's boycott of civilization's brutal animal farming, but don't see how hunter-gatherer bands could support veganism. Hence, the primitivist allure with the paleo diet.

Actual human diets during the 2.6 million yearlong Paleolithic era of vast migrations included a broadly flexible food list reflective of seasons and conditions. Despite popular belief, wild grains and legumes were very likely included, with some evidence of food processing, such as flour 30,000 years ago as well. While Paleo humans were flexible eaters, there is little evidence of that time to draw solid conclusions on nutrition. The most conclusive diet evidence of the Paleo era supports that diets based primarily on plant foods promoted increased health and longevity, at least during times of food abundance. Further, applying any version of a Paleo diet to today's food repertoire has the extra challenge that modern domesticated plants and animals differ considerably from those of Paleo times.

And then there is the unanswered question of how hunting shaped who we are intrinsically, especially in relation to a mindset conducive to hierarchy and civilization.

Life in balance with Earth The past seven years I've channeled virtually all my energies into ecology restoration. This has opened my mind and spirit to hard realities. Now as I walk in a neighborhood or natural area, I see which plant and animal species naturally belong in that place, which species come from which other places, and how the introduced 'alien' species degrade the place. I sense the urgency to reverse civilization's course, and chronic frustration with modern human's aloof, callous willful ignorance. To point the mirror at myself, some primitivists who lack my experience rewilding nature are quick to label me a 'native plant nazi'.

Primitivists are likely in agreement that we aim for an Earth with healthy ecosystems (biological communities of interacting life and their physical environment). An ecosystem is comprised of native species (indigenous to a bioregion, the result of natural processes such as co-adaptation, generally with no harmful colonizing human intervention). Modern ecosystems are threatened by introduced invasive species (nonnative life degrading habitat). A healthy ecosystem strives for increasing resilience through diversity of life in connection engaged in a process of co-adaptation.

Negative impacts of civilization on ecosystems are stark, with well-defined catalysts such as agriculture. To effectively change, we begin by understanding what led to human's fading nature connection resulting in harmful catalysts such as agriculture. Potential early nature connection catalysts such as hunting tools (perhaps humans first shift toward dominance, establishing hierarchy over the world), control of fire, biocultural adaptations such as clothing, need consideration. Though painting an accurate picture of early humans is generally a game of guess, it seems to be fairly accepted that before the migration out of Africa, earliest humans had a primarily plant based diet and were living native life embedded as a part of an ecosystem.

The main question becomes, *Did humans evolve into an invasive species when we expanded out of our habitat? What is the human habitat?* Every species has a habitat, with all its benefits and limitations. If a species spreads into a region where it begins co-adapting within that ecosystem, and then the conditions change, species unable to adapt move back or die off. If we are a part of the natural world, we need to accept that nature reality. A species can forgo co-adapting and 'overadapt' to the point that it becomes invasive. If we have the awareness that our invasive nature has now swollen to doing extensive damage to nature connections, including within our own species, do we also have the motivation and ability to evolve ourselves back out of our invasive nature, back into our natural habitat with more wild symbiotic relationships in lieu of our mega-dominating stance of today?

A Path Forward Is the transition from *Australopithecus* to *Homo* marked by scavenged meat eating? Did a transition toward eating meat correlate to a transition in habitat spread from tropical sub-tropical climates to seasonal climates of constant change? Could it be that humans' transition to hunting is a major factor shaping our physical and nature connection evolution, turning our species more predatory and invasive? How did and does human survival equate to being an invasive species, and what are potential paths to restoring our nativity? Until these questions are adequately addressed, perhaps the most Earth-connected past practice worth bringing into the future is simple foraging.

Our species has obviously radically impacted all habitats, ruining them not only for other species, but for our own as well. Virtually all species (that are not invasive like us) are struggling to find & keep their niche. Instead of forecasting the best path forward by constructing and recreating the past, primitivist energies would be well spent focusing on stopping civilization's destruction and undoing the damage civilization has done. Along the way in rewilding Earth we will instinctively and organically rewild ourselves into a species that reawakens connections and co-evolves, re rediscovering our habitat, our niche with Earth.

Ria

Black & Green Review & KT response with my reply to *Epiphany on the Hunter-Gatherer Myth, by Ria*

The coyote in me cannot be held down. She submitted *"Epiphany on the Hunter-Gatherer Myth, by Ria"* to *Black and Green Review* for consideration. {Ha! Good one, Coyote!} I previously submitted a piece and got no reply, so I was anticipating the same. Was a bit of an elated shock to get a response this time, especially being that *Epiphany* seems to strike right at the core of their man-the-hunter basis. Don't precisely remember, but I must have offered to expand on the piece if they found it lacking. Gotta give it to them for not just reading, but considering and responding with well thought out questions.

Interesting questions. Very telling of their pedagogy & methodology – rigid scientific with underlying vegan skepticism and blind acceptance of the mainstream meat norm – just doesn't blend with my more sensual, experiential free flow. So I just answered & returned, leaving it up to them to do as they may. Enough prelude, here's their response (bold) with my reply (italics):

You manage to squeeze a lot of a big question into something without feeling the need to ground it. As it stands, it's just a "what if" aimed at something you've made up ("hunter-gathererism") to promote something you made up ("folio-frugivore*" I'd love to take credit, but this one comes from paleo-anthropology readings on the earliest human diet, forget the exact* *sources).* **I have yet to see "primitivism" that goes beyond being vegan to be explicitly anti-hunter-gatherer.** *Just for the record, not all vegan anprims are absolute anti-hunter-gatherer.* **Obviously I'm not sympathetic at all.** *Understandably. You might just win the trophy for the toughest pro-hunting advocates of all times. Hence many vegan anprims have had moments of being silent & silenced on this matter. Thanks for being open to reading & replying earnestly.*

But if you want us to run and respond this in BAGR, then I'm going to have to take up your offer to expand. This circulated amongst the editors and what would be more printable and response worthy would be if you could answer and respond to the following points. If you want to promote "alternative" history and have others take it seriously, you need to support it. *Sounds like something the oppressor would say to the oppressed, but I'm game.* **The world is not social media**. *hmmm. 'social media' dis. I read this as a mechanism of discrediting. Perhaps one thing we can agree on (or maybe not) is the bias in stuff spit out 'professionally' by 'professionals' published in 'professional publications'. Authoritative crap. Why exclude so much of others' experiences revealed in the manner truest to them? Friendly warning: if B&GR limits itself to 'professionalism', emphasis on academic may end up being its downfall.*

For wildness, *For Wildness.*

KT

My answers to your questions based solely on my personal short-lived experience:

a. who are the Pemón? *Pemón simply means people. But more. My impression is Pemón are the Chinook of indigenous people of the Pacific Northwest US. They're a connection of loosely affiliated groups of people acting in mutual aid at a minimum through reciprocity. From a modern lens the word refers to people who live in a vast region in northeast South America (21,000 acres in Venezuela alone) left fairly wild with help from protective mountains. Pemón encompass many tribes speaking several distinct languages, with varying degrees of interaction between tribes, mainly revolving around trade, sometimes marriage. In my estimation each village is able to subsist independently if need be. I did not have a sense that they had reached the point of interdependence, rather 'interpreference'. Of the estimated 20,000 Pemón living in vast wildness, I mainly stayed in a Chirikayan village of about 50.* **What is their documented mode of subsistence**? *I don't know about 'documented'. There has been little* historical 'documentation' of Pemón in general, and I would be skeptical of bias and overgeneralizing any 'documentation' if for no other reason than inability to fully account for the multitude of variances. **Why do they have a 'chief'?** *I surmise for this village having a chief has been a long-standing way of facilitating matters and resolving conflict both within the group and between groups. There seemed to be no extra privileges given to the chief for holding the few responsibilities. He truly seemed to be humbly representing the interests of the people. He worked hard and sacrificed much, which probably earned him the chief crown.* **Provide general overview of culture and ecological adaptation.** *I was there during turbulent general elections. The whole country seemed to pause, from Caracas to the most remote indigenous villages the fervor was strongly felt. Even in the chief's home there were books on abstract political ideology, like by Chomsky. He tried to engage me nightly on issues of politics, but the language difference was too much of a barrier. He and his wife, parents of 5 young children, both voluntarily enlisted in the military, garbing up every weekend to serve while their children adeptly cared for themselves. Chirikayan were excited to keep the Socialist party in power for both high ideals and tangible benefits, such as the health care they now received. The morning of the election a pickup truck came, all the adults squeezed into the back to ride to the voting place one village away. They gave us their big socialist flag to wave as we drove through jungle and savannah. Point being, this was not a typical time for them or us, excitement ran high, and there were military with loaded assault weapons all about, even in this most remote region.*

Especially given the uniqueness of the moment, I don't feel comfortable trying to draw overarching conclusions on their culture. But the place. Ah the place. An anprim's dream. Along a forest edge filled with monkey hollers. A rolling savannah intersected with a sunny stream with a boulder in the middle, perfect spot for washing things like clothes and cookware and human bodies. A pond, for play of course. Across the savannah a half days' walk to the tepuis, flat top mountains, the source of much myth. Pemón wildness of spirit is connected to the wildness of this place, which makes me fear for the coming changes.

This time of fast change is a melding of deep wild roots with incursions of civilization. Little things, like a rooftop rain catchment system on the chief's stick built home, directing the afternoon's heavy rains into a metal barrel. Old things, like owning a diamond mine and working it to afford village 'improvements'. Older things, like slash & burn forest gardening. The plant I helped them harvest was cassava, a staple to both their diet and their trade, in the form of vegetable and bread. Newest things, like when I observed their first turning on of an artificial outdoor light. The level of my sadness matched the level of their delight.

Big things, like their traditional round white & yellow clay homes with thatched roofing, gradually being 'updated' with small solar power units providing each home with one outlet. When a unit is installed, each family is given the decision of what to plug in to their outlet, and the accompanying challenge of how to afford it. When I was there only a few homes had been given the socialist revolution's Bolivarian gift of solar power. The family headed by a young couple chose a music stereo system with cds. Another chose a television and vcr. The chief chose a refrigerator and stove. This 'progress' forever changed not only their traditional forms like singing, entertainment, food storage and cooking, but their relationships with their community. Each type of electric device makes each home, each family, a domesticated specialist.

Many traditional ways seem woven with encroaching domesticated reality. Newly electrified traditional clay homes remain open, with children freely running into any house. So much activity still naturally occurs outdoors that homes remain more of a shelter, a place to seek refuge from daily afternoon rains rolling in from the east tepuis, to sleep and sometimes eat.

Where trade was once in form of barter after long distance foot travel through people-less places, now the Santa Elena market funnels human activity into one spot with most exchanges in the form of cash. Once a week in the village as birds start their morning sing a pickup truck appears to drive a load full of humans and some wares, mainly cassava bread, through jungle to city. Santa Elena has become a hub of indigenous trading, each village bringing goods to booth manifesting a vibrant market. More rhythmically, intuitively than colonist 'farmer's markets', each booth offers a specialized part to collaboratively nourish the whole.

But with everything in civilization, there is an insidious cost. Goods wrapped in plastic from distant profiteers are making their way into the market. Plastic makes its way into unknowing hands, transported a jungle ride back into remote villages. After the consumable part of the good is consumed, Pemón do what they've always done with the nonconsumable portion – throw it on the ground for Earth's mystery to do its work. I wonder their surprise, then their frustration when they first noticed that plastic did not follow Earth's natural ways, and took the process into their own hands. Now the plastic is routinely left on the ground, then after it piles up, set afire.

Food is nothing special, nothing more than body sustenance. Hunting seems nonexistent, and if it happens it is unimportant. The only 'ceremony' was a birthday party for a child, they said it was a new thing they were doing. They had music from a solar powered stereo and had brought balloons from the weekly market. They asked us how to blow them up with air. We played with the kids hitting the balloons up into the air, diving and laughing until dark. The adults seemed to think it odd that we played with the children, both then and in the swimming hole. Is this not an acceptable form of adult fun? Children have much freer rein than adults. Different from worldly reports, they have a taboo against drinking alcohol or any other way of getting high.

I'm unsure of ecological adaptations, but I did see ritualized habit changes in response to increasing encounters with civilization, like those above, and attempts to form new habits that didn't work for them. When I first arrived, I asked the chief's wife, Where is the bathroom? She outstretched her arm and slowly gestured my eyes toward the low rolling ground of low vegetation. When you squat there's just enough cover for privacy. I couldn't find signs of bury. I looked around for signs of other excrement on the ground. None. I couldn't wait. After a nervous poop, I took a walk just to look for more signs. Nada. Soon this place's daily rhythm showed me. First the sky turned grey, then the wind picked up. Droplets tickled the skin. Everyone took shelter. Drops pounded on the roof as we watched the rain barrel overflow in deluge. Later I wondered what impact the hard rain had on my poop. I couldn't find the exact spot. It was so broken down into such tiny pieces that it just disappeared to the human eye. But days later, even with such an easy and beneficial natural poop dispersal system, I discovered where they had hauled in a plywood outhouse, set it straight on the ground without digging a hole, and abandoned it saying it 'didn't work'.

b. for the people who did not eat the fish, what do they eat? *Much of the food they ate centers around cassava, with the nightly meal being in the form of a stew. I don't know the names, but the food was a variety of domesticated raw and cooked plants parts, both vegetables and fruit, like banana and coconut from market, and foraged plant parts from leaves to berries. I don't remember if there were nuts, seeds, lentils, mushrooms, etc., my mind was distracted elsewhere.* **what is their general daily intake of food?** *They, and I, did not eat much in terms of quantity. Most of the vegetables were from forest gardens, so perhaps that made them somehow more filling, and required less time to gather and digest relative to foraging wild vegetables.* **what items?** *Wish I knew the fruit and vegetable names, but most of the people only knew their native language which I do not know.* **how do they obtain these things (grow or gather)?** *Combination of slash-and-burn cultivation and gathering mainly wild* *fruits. When I was there it was harvest season for cassava, most of which went into making a bread for market to trade for other mainly grown vegetables.*

c. are any of these 'vegans' entirely self-sufficient in terms of food?
Individually 'self-sufficient'? Food gathering seems to mainly be collective, I presume slash & burn has been well in effect and a vegan diet with grown foods combined with gathered wild foods is long established. **Or are there outside inputs coming in?** *Trading with other Pemón tribes at Friday markets. This case obviously cannot be used as a case of veganism subsisting on only foraged wild food, but combined with grown food, as done by indigenous people virtually worldwide for hundreds of years or more. I don't hide my personal belief that one could subsist wildly without meat. And humans adapting toward vegan primitivism is how Earth can thrive best.*

d. what is the normal day-to-day activity level and subsistence regime of the Pemón? *Imagine remote nature, no electric, no plumbing, no cars, and you can deduce just about almost all you need to know about the day-to-day life in this place of plenty. Humid mid days tamper activity, but overall comfortable temperatures make for plenty of time for both 'work' and fun. Every day before dusk all adults come together to play soccer, married people vs single. Point being, their workload is low enough and energy level high enough that they have plenty left to run & play.*

A work division between sexes emerged in teen years. Forest harvesting is tough work, and both men and women work together, with machetes and hauling too. More women than men forage. Women cook & do housework. Men seem to have more free time. Men were often off somewhere during the day, I assumed hunting, but if so their expeditions into the forest didn't seem productive. The dark night I stumbled upon the man spear fishing was the only meat for the community during my two week stay, and it only fed a couple men.

e. what role do the vegan members play in that regime? what is there contribution to the whole? *All people of all ages had a fairly high activity level, from my domesticated perspective, with no noted difference between people based on diet. A post-colonizer contact adaptation with the larger world of money exchange is mining diamonds. The Cherikayan chief considers the village fortunate to have a diamond mine within their 'property'. One morning just before sunrise he left with one of my visiting vegan friends and a few vegan Chirikayan children to fast hike to the mine. They arrived in time to eat the lunch they brought with them. They played in the mud, helped mine for diamonds, then trekked back by dusk. They all seemed to keep up the same.*

f. how much time did she spend with this group? *Two weeks.* **has she analyzed any of this at an extended temporal scale?** *No.* **can she cite any other examples in the anthropological literature of any non-agricultural (and thus civilized) indigenous people who are 100% vegan, whether as an entire group or who have 'vegan' members such as she asserts with the Pemón?** *The meat bias in historical documentation is so thick, I deem almost all of it unreliable. The mission of finding the dietary truth would need to start from scratch. It's too labor intensive for one person.*

g. If there are any verifiable citations for this then how many are there? *I haven't stumbled upon any.* **What is their geographical and ecological scope?** *The geographic scope was a swath of forest edge, savannah and tepuis compromising ~ <50 acres. The ecological scope emerged organically through my domesticated, modern mind through observing and interacting, i.e. likely scant in proportion to any scientist with a planned mission, or senses of a primitive mind. Sorry if it seems I'm avoid the scientific questions, hey I was just hanging out & contemplate the experience now only through memories.* **What are their specific colonial/industrial/agricultural contexts?** *Well of course there's the Spaniards, but I think the mountains prevented too much intrusion. The main one of relevance here, and the one you may find most informative from your perspective, is past 'encounter' with Seventh Day Adventist missionary. The church is still standing, and they still use it for service weekly. I attended a service. There were no bibles. They spoke their indigenous language, which I could not understand. To me it felt not that different than many typical mainstream quiet Christian churches, but I am generally repulsed by religion, so I'm not a good judge.*

I did not ask the diet of Pemón or Chirikayan pre-missionary contact, or if contact with the Adventists changed their dietary practices or mindset. If no individuals abstained from meat pre-contact, their current diet still shows how humans can and do adapt.

Many native people worldwide have actively fed life in their ecosystems, and show restraint in acts like hunting to maintain a thriving biota. One of the things that makes humans so special is our ability to adapt. We're super-adapters. No doubt time is now for some super-adapting. That doesn't mean to throw out the past, just continue doing what we've always done – adapt. If Earth is more viable with a future vegan primitive, then so be it.

AnPrim On Fire, JZ response with my reply

In response to my essay "AnPrim On Fire" John Zerzan stated refutations in his April 2, 2019 Anarchy Radio show, relevant to the EcoPatriarchy. Here are my responses in italics to his points in bold (paraphrased from my notes).

-Controlled fire was around 2 million years ago, very least several hundred thousand years ago.

Colonization tends to start innocently, linger for a long while, then erupt to top dominator position. For example, kudzu came to the states from Japan in 1876 for an exposition in Philadelphia, then in 1883 for an exposition in New Orleans. Home owners wanted it to provide shade, farmers wanted it to feed cows, and the government wanted it to control erosion. By 1946, kudzu had been planted by humans on 3,000,000 acres. It started spreading into cities and overtaking wild habitats. By 1997 the government listed kudzu as a noxious weed. Despite large scale efforts to eradicate it, today it has encroached into 7,400,000 acres. Since humans began colonizing, this story of unintended consequences is told again and again, with different characters and settings.

Comparing kudzu to controlling fire, kudzu in its co-adapted indigenous habitat in Japan is akin to earliest humans' first forays with fire, foraging in wakes of wildfires and moving food out of and into wildfire hotspots (earliest cooking).

This was a wildfire-nourishing-human relationship manifesting as erratic opportunity.

The first step to humans harnessing fire, akin to kudzu being brought from its home into far away expositions, is early humans maintaining fire over a period of time, transporting it, forming base camps around it.

The final step to humans harnessing fire, akin to kudzu's entwining with civilized human culture, is human's ability to make fire by hand. With this invention human's relationship with fire shifted from opportunistic to habitual and dependent, perhaps the first 'progress trap'. Archaeological evidence puts this at 700,000 to 120,000 years ago, though a long time passed before widespread use.

Anarcho-primitivism is not selecting a time to replicate, but understanding and finding wild paths forward.

-Fire was not just for cooking, but warmth and light to ward off predators.

*Temperature is one setter of habitat range boundaries. Like all bodies the human body living primitively thrives within a certain temperature spectrum. Areas falling outside that spectrum have a natural force to keep the species population in check. Ignoring and encroaching past temperature spectrum limits through innovations that increasingly disintegrate habitats as a whole is an act and ethos of colonization.

-In terms of domestication, when you use fire you don't change the nature of fire. He goes with domestication, with a definition of: changing the nature of something, namely animals or plants, about 10,000 years ago.

*What does it mean to 'change the nature'? Controlled fire sparked humans' protracted invasion of all bioregions leaving extinctions in their paths long before agriculture. This forever impacted, altered and degraded interconnections between life. This altered plant and animal cultures and biologies everywhere. All plants and animals 'change the nature' of one another as they form and reform, shift and reshift. That is the way of wild, so I don't understand the significance of 'change the nature'; but I do see intensifying control under colonization, with agriculture being a major intensification.

Regarding the mainstream's link between civilization and domestication (agriculture), defining 'domestication, 'civilization' and 'colonization' offers some clarity.

Domestication- the process of hereditary reorganization of wild animals and plants into domestic and cultivated forms according to the interests of people. In its strictest sense, it refers to the initial stage of human mastery of wild animals and plants.

Civilization- the stage of human social and cultural development and organization that is considered most advanced.

Colonization- the action of appropriating a place or domain for one's own use.

Since humans came down from the trees, they have had stage after stage of inventions that at the time would be considered increasingly organized 'advancements' that reorganized animals and plants. Some were slow and some fast, the latest was the organized 'advancement' of agriculture.

-If you want to argue that fire set in motion an ethos of control, domesticating vector, you have to show some evidence for that. Because nothing changed until actual domestication of plants and animals when everything changed, hierarchy & patriarchy. If you don't see a change in band society, egalitarian anti-hierarchal, that's common knowledge,

*After incursions dissolved into settlement, humans reigniting their innate yearning for embeddedness with nature. Even today humans long for wilderness connection at their core. Assuming fire played a role in humans' expansion out of Africa, here's evidence that early humans had behavior of control, predation and colonization, whether driven by or resulting in an ethos of control, predation and colonization:

Felisa A. Smith, Rosemary E. Elliott Smith, S. Kathleen Lyons, Jonathan L. Payne. Body size downgrading of mammals over the late Quaternary. Science, 2018; DOI: 10.1126/science.aao5987

"Elephant-dwarfing wooly mammoths, elephant-sized ground sloths and various saber-toothed cats highlighted the array of massive mammals roaming Earth between 2.6 million and 12,000 years ago. Prior research suggested that such large mammals began disappearing faster than their smaller counterparts — a phenomenon known as size-biased extinction...

With the help of emerging data from older fossil and rock records, the new study estimated that this size-biased extinction started at least 125,000 years ago in Africa...

...as humans migrated out of Africa, other size-biased extinctions began occurring in regions and on timelines that coincide with known human migration patterns, the researchers found. Over time, the average body size of mammals on those other continents approached and then fell well below Africa's. Mammals that survived during the span were generally far smaller than those that went extinct.

The magnitude and scale of the recent size-biased extinction surpassed any other recorded during the last 66 million years, according to the study, which was led by the University of New Mexico's Felisa Smith.

"It wasn't until human impacts started becoming a factor that large body sizes made mammals more vulnerable to extinction," said the University of Nebraska-Lincoln's Kate Lyons, who authored the study with Smith and colleagues from Stanford University and the University of California, San Diego. "The anthropological record indicates that Homo sapiens are identified as a species around 200,000 years ago, so this occurred not very long after the birth of us as a species...the research team found little support for the idea that climate change drove size-biased extinctions during the last 66 million years. Large and small mammals seemed equally vulnerable to temperature shifts throughout that span, the authors reported"

Lyons went on to say that restructuring from large to small mammals has "profound implications" for the world's ecosystems. Large mammals tend to be herbivores, devouring large quantities of vegetation and effectively transporting the associated nutrients around an ecosystem. When they disappear, the small mammals are poor substitutes for important ecological functions.

Further, controlled fire could be the birth of compulsory labor and taxation. When humans began coming together to share the fire, their relationships formed new intimacies and power dynamics. As today, there would have been a social pressure to gather a constant supply of firewood as the price to pay for benefiting from it.

With humanity's patriarchy comes speciesism, a new power over animals in humans' shift from prey to predatory. Fire was used to run large carnivores away from their kills, slowing starving them into extinction. Fire was used to clear out caves inhabited by other animals for shelter from the elements. Fire was used to engineer weapons to ambush larger herbivores. Fire was used to corral and entrap large mammals to kill and cook them.

Fire was the most important technology in expanding into new terrains and developing early human societies. Whoever wielded fire had more power. Once the terrains were dominated, early humans began managing the biomes, which benefited certain other life as well, often creating a new thriving diversity. Evidence of more complex management such as still practiced by some native people is found 100,000 – 200,000 years ago.

Before fire, the human diet was mostly plant based. After fire, which brought on organized hunting and meat, the human body slowly began adapting with changes in teeth, gut, etc. But at the human biological core, humans remain herbivores, and thrive best with that dietway.

-If you are a raw food vegan you might want to arrange the story of human species to fit that, the impulse of that then you don't like fire or cooking or hunting.

*The man-the-hunter story has been arranged to fit the violent lifeway of civilization. It's challenging for people today to conceive of a way without fire, cooking or hunting, just as people deny that our species is a colonizing one. Without fire, we would not have been able to colonize. Without a colonizing ethos, we would not have used fire to breech the wild limits of our primal human habitat. Just imagine, without fire humans may still be mostly in Africa, and a diversity of megafauna may still be in every land. And for certain, the life on Earth would not be in a death spiral. Fire mastery hoisted human ferocity, and with that wrought a fiery new lifeway onto all.

March 7, 2020

I email JZ a link to the study *"Empathy and Compassion toward Other Species Decrease with Evolutionary Divergence Time."* He responds:

Frankly, this paper sounds like a joke. Feelings, empathy, emotions? How about DOMESTICATION, the key shift that changes everything.

I reply: *It may be a question of which came first, chicken or egg, but doesn't it seem that changes in behavior, like domestication, and would correlate with changes in feelings? Perhaps even, if the feelings didn't change, domestication could not have happened?*

Do you disagree that compassion is a strong driver neglected by modern rationality? Can't imagine humans, and other animals too, being able to exist without compassion, even if only mother and baby.

211

Ria's Response to JZ & Bellamy Condemning Vegan Primitivism

Ria's response to Oak Journal's podcast "Rejecting the World Society Paradigm" with Bellamy, John Zerzan and Steve Kirk condemning vegan primitivism.

https://soundcloud.com/oakjournal/rejecting-the-world-society-paradigm

-<u>Veganism is hating power in oneself, hyper-pacifism, and that doesn't happen in the natural world</u> – Does compassion happen in the natural world? Does mutualism? Does symbiosis? Do those beings hate themselves for it? Is compassion not an act of power, or only killing and eating the bodies of others?

-<u>Not enough land for vegan primitivism</u> – How do you know how much land would be needed for wild foraging? How many seasons can an acorn harvest last? And wapato? And mongongo nut? And tubers of tiger-nuts? And ground nuts? Who still holds this knowledge to make the calculation? If collapse happened overnight, would there be enough land for everyone to hunt? Why are you imposing the excuse of overpopulation on vegans only?

-<u>Modern liberal values extending rights to animals</u> – Modern values and rights would not long for smashing civilization. It must be challenging to distinguish consumerist veganism from primitivist veganism, we're a rare breed.

-Utilitarianism to lower amount of suffering – Do anprims want to lower suffering in the world? I thought Anarchy Radio routinely reported on all the suffering. Why? Do animals not try to have less suffering in themselves and those around them?

-Rationally managed society – Once again, confusing consumerist veganism with primitivist veganism.

"Veganism is essential to wildness. Not only is exploiting and killing animals a humanape-constructed activity and form of authority, but it socially evolved into the leading political regime worldwide. Very often humans want to pinpoint about such questions as origins, saying that "it has always been so even prior to civilization", and extreme rationalization has destroyed the last bits of remorse that could be left - nonetheless, if there is any initial "project" for humans, here we are, and we fail." ~Nicolas Dupont

-The study mentioned was 'low meat', not 'no meat' - Being that alternatives to modern mainstream narratives tend to be silenced, scorned and sternly denied before considered, even when alternative 'proof' is discovered, is it recognized for what it is, or explained away with acceptable culturally mediated ideology, as in the points made in this podcast?

Challenges to inaccurate, propagated narratives do manifest, but face uphill battles in gaining mainstream acceptance. The study: DNA analysis shows that forest gathering Neanderthals found in a cave in Spain drew their food and medicine from plants, mushrooms, pine nuts, and moss.

Weyrich, Laura S., et al. "Neanderthal Behaviour, Diet, and Disease Inferred from Ancient DNA in Dental Calculus." *Nature, International Journal of Science* , vol. 544, 2017, pp. 357–61.
https://www.nature.com/articles/nature21674

At Spy cave, Belgium, Neanderthal diet was heavily meat based and included woolly rhinoceros and wild sheep (mouflon), characteristic of a steppe environment. In contrast, no meat was detected in the diet of Neanderthals from El Sidrón cave, Spain, and dietary components of mushrooms, pine nuts, and moss reflected forest gathering.

So here's DNA evidence that some pre-civ humans subsisted wholly on plants, mushrooms and moss challenging civilization's romanticized man-the-hunter image and pro-meat bias. Why is your first response to try to disprove it?

-Cannot survive vegan outside technology / Leviathan – It's been done, and you refuse to acknowledge it. Seasoned wild tender Finisia Medrano has told me it's very doable to subsist vegan on the sacred hoops, even in the scarce landscapes she tends. The only solid evidence of earliest bipedal human diet was of plants. What is the earliest solid evidence of meat eating? The man-the-hunter myth is popularized, overgeneralized, hyped up. Modern minds project modern indoctrination into early human narratives.   Scientific narratives are processed and molded through cultural values. For example, when modern meat eating paleoanthropologists find any evidence of hunting, they routinely deem all individuals comprising an entire group over vast areas and times as 'hunters'. Mainstream-embraced evolutionary narratives, that most anprims were indoctrinated into, tend to be value-laden and biased.

-Anthropocentricism to maintain world view - Is conjuring up a pre-civ ideal, egalitarianism with hunting, to recreate in the present and future an act of mindset morality? How is Paul Shepard not human-centric? And if you're against people with predatory sexuality, I don't know how you'd idealize him.

"The human hunter in the field is not merely a predator, because of hundreds of centuries of experience in treating the woman-prey with love, which he turns back into the hunt proper. The ecstatic consummation of this love is the killing itself. Formal consummation is eating… The prey must be eaten for ethical not nutritional value, in a kind of celebration."

-Veganism imposes universal moral rights – Vegan primitivists do? Or man-the-hunter ideologues like Paul Shepard, encouraging all boys & men to hunt? I am vegan because my entire animal being tells me to not kill or eat animals, without being indoctrinated into it, like human hunting. As a child I instinctively fought to be vegan in a world of killers. It seems unlikely a child born into a world of vegans would fight to kill animals. Would I like for humans to end the killing nonhuman animals? As much as I'd like for humans to end the killing of human animals. My animal being repels from humans killing.

Shepard comes off as a psychopath in saying he saw no difference between eating a vegetable and an animal, yet, he saw hunting as deeply spiritual: *"Hunting is a holy occupation, framed in rules and courtesy, informed by the beauty of the physical being and the numinous presence of the spiritual life of animals."* For Shepard, *"eating animals is a way to worship them." "(T)o be kindred… means… a sense of many connections and transformations – us into them, them into us, and them into each other from the beginning of time."* Shepard encouraged every man to hunt to recover *"…the ontogenetic movement;*

...the value of the hunt is in a single leap forward into the heart-structure of the world, the "game" played to rules that reveal ourselves. What is important is to have hunted. It is like having babies."

Marti Kheel wrote how sects of Deep Ecology *"employ ethical discourse as a means of shielding the hunter from the actual experience of the animal he kills... The focus of the hunter is on his own interior mental state. As long as his mental attitude is said to conform to a particular ethical code, his violent behavior is thought to be legitimized. The emphasis on the instinctual (sexual) nature of hunting functions to further remove the hunters' conduct from ethical reproach, since hunting is seen as a natural and elementary drive. The ethical discourse thus functions as a "decoy," focusing attention not on the state of the animal who is about to be killed, but rather on the hunter. What the holy hunters see as a "reciprocal" activity is, in reality, a unidirectional morality in which the hunter formulates and follows his own moral directives... the animal is reduced to an object, a symbol against which the hunter seeks to establish his masculine selfhood and moral worth."*

Andree Collard and Joyce Contrucci in Rape of the Wild: Man's Violence against Animals and the Earth, wrote that *"the efforts of modern man to rationalize the contradictions and delusions surrounding the hunt and the hunter extend to the romanticized images he fashions of primitive man as the archetypal hunter with the hunt as the sine qua non of his existence."*

Even if you embrace the spiritualism of hunting, how can a rewilder whose ideal is based on early cultures with spiritual hunting honed through generations, communicate with the spirit of the hunted animal? This may be why many hunt in rote form: I am wild by hunting and eating animals. How is the intimate connection between animal persons formed, when they don't experience other animals as persons? Their rewilding is artificial. They are a babe thinking themselves into a virile doer of civilization's 'rewilding'. Observing a lifetime would not bring them a step closer to their goal with their mindset. They cannot accept that ancient knowledge of ecological embeddedness has vanished, and reconstructing wild knowledge takes generations. In today's hurting wildscape, wildness requires immense healing first, lifetimes of giving back. When your friend is hurting, you don't use her, you offer aid. Wild is hurting, and if your animal being is open to sensing the pain and you don't give aid, instead exploit wild even more, your relationship is based in the disconnected aloofness of disregarded pain. Despite their justifications, they flail in attempts at ecological embeddedness by hunting animals, without perceiving their harm to the habitat.

And besides, how many people use man-the-hunter to justify buying pieces of tortured carcasses in stores & drive-through windows?

-No examples of indigenous subsistence – There are, but Leviathan doesn't want to know them. Man-the-hunter bias dominating archaeology and many other modern institutions makes searches contrasting propagandized narratives a challenge.

Christopher Ryan, author of Civilized to Death: The Price of Progress: *"The popularity and persistence of scientific narratives often have more to do with how well they support dominant mythologies than with their scientific veracity."*

James C. Scott: *"...if you were hunter-gatherers or nomads, however numerous, spreading your biodegradable trash thinly across the landscape, you were likely to vanish entirely from the archaeological record,"* Not only do hunter-gatherers leave little evidence, plant foragers leave even less, likely resulting in greatly overexaggerated claims of inherent human hunting.

Archaeobotanist Sarah Mason: *"For the most part the Pleistocene, and even the earliest post-glacial, is a blank when it comes to evidence of humans eating plants. No wonder the old men's stories, of chaps who hunt great mammals and eat their meat, still dominate our unthinking visions of hunter-gathering in that period."*

Andrée Collard and Joyce Contrucci, authors of Rape of the Wild: *"...denying validity or even recognition to alternative interpretations, access to alternative values and beliefs capable of freeing a society from its own self-destruction is closed."*

Archaeologist Lyn Wadley: *"Many archaeologists are not interested in botanical remains."*

Anthropologist Penny Spikins on Raymond Dart's 'killer ape' theory: *"A tendency to see what we think ought to be there was perhaps never best illustrated..."*

-Would have to migrate to equatorial climate – What are the natural human habitat limits? Is it not anthropocentric to think you have a right to live wherever you want? Why don't you have to abide by wild's invisible walls regulated by food opportunities and temperatures? Why not live under the sea if you want to. In space if you want to? That returning to wild habitat is not a part of anprim reveals a human supremacy that nixes return to wildness altogether.

-Dubious health value – Wow. Still clinging to that?

According to the sciences of evolution, anatomy, and physiology humans are herbivores, designed to thrive from a plant-based diet. As put by professor of physical anthropology Katharine Milton,

There is general agreement that the ancestral line (Hominoidea) giving rise to humans was strongly herbivorous… In hominoids, features such as nutrient requirements and digestive physiology appear to be genetically conservative and probably were little affected by the hunter-gatherer phase of human existence.

Milton, Katharine. "Hunter-Gatherer Diets—a Different Perspective." *The American Journal of Clinical Nutrition,* vol. 71, no. 3, 2000, pp. 665–667, doi:10.1093/ajcn/71.3.665.

Tharrey, Marion, et al. "Patterns of Plant and Animal Protein Intake Are Strongly Associated with Cardiovascular Mortality: the Adventist Health Study-2 Cohort." *International Journal of Epidemiology*, vol. 47, no. 5, Feb. 2018, pp. 1603–1612, doi:10.1093/ije/dyy030.

Miles, Fayth L, et al. "Plasma, Urine, and Adipose Tissue Biomarkers of Dietary Intake Differ Between Vegetarian and Non-Vegetarian Diet Groups in the Adventist Health Study-2." *The Journal of Nutrition*, vol. 149, no. 4, 2019, pp. 667–675, doi:10.1093/jn/nxy292.

Abete, Itziar, et al. "Association between Total, Processed, Red and White Meat Consumption and All-Cause, CVD and IHD Mortality: a Meta-Analysis of Cohort Studies." *British Journal of Nutrition*, vol. 112, no. 5, 2014, pp. 762–775, doi:10.1017/s000711451400124x.

Bernstein, Adam M., et al. "Major Dietary Protein Sources and Risk of Coronary Heart Disease in Women." *Circulation*, vol. 122, no. 9, 2010, pp. 876–883, doi:10.1161/circulationaha.109.915165.

Kim, Hyunju, et al. "Plant-Based Diets Are Associated With a Lower Risk of Incident Cardiovascular Disease, Cardiovascular Disease Mortality, and All-Cause Mortality in a General Population of Middle-Aged Adults." *Journal of the American Heart Association*, vol. 8, no. 16, 2019, doi:10.1161/jaha.119.012865.

Kelemen, L. E. "Associations of Dietary Protein with Disease and Mortality in a Prospective Study of Postmenopausal Women." *American Journal of Epidemiology*, vol. 161, no. 3, Jan. 2005, pp. 239–249, doi:10.1093/aje/kwi038.

Song, Mingyang, et al. "Association of Animal and Plant Protein Intake With All-Cause and Cause-Specific Mortality." *JAMA Internal Medicine*, vol. 176, no. 10, Jan. 2016, p. 1453, doi:10.1001/jamainternmed.2016.4182.

Stark, Philip B., et al. "Open-Source Food: Nutrition, Toxicology, and Availability of Wild Edible Greens in the East Bay." *Plos One*, vol. 14, no. 1, 2019, doi:10.1371/journal.pone.0202450.

Common garden weeds are more nutritious than kale, Berkeley researchers find.

https://returntonow.net/2018/09/29/weeds-more-nutritious-than-store-bought-produce/

Rebuttal of Paul Shepard's "The Vegetarians" in his essay "Post-Historic Primitivism" in *The Wilderness Condition: Essays on Environment and Civilization*

https://archive.org/stream/Post-historicPrimitivism/Post-historicPrimitivism_djvu.txt

Returning to Reality a response to Paul Shepard's "The Vegetarians"

By M.B.

Laying out a scathing illogical introduction, Shepard wastes no time in announcing his unsubstantiated generally held biases towards people who abstain from consuming animals and their secretions. The very first vague attack on vegan diets as being a "quantity over quality" ideology is a vile underlying theme of his essay which he relies on to build credibility with the reader.

Because of the unsupported assumptions Shepard has made about the inadequacy of a vegan diet in general ("quantity over quality") and especially in terms of "protein" and "long chain fats" these myths are best dispelled immediately. The notion that plants are an inadequate source of protein is ironically absolutely inimical to the truth. Plants being the most important primary producers on the planet not only create the energy that drives most life on Earth, but also the eight essential amino acids which primary consumers (herbivores) and all subsequent consumers obtain from them directly or indirectly and chemically rearrange to synthesize other amino acids(1,2). The concept of protein combining of plant foods is nutritional lore that is ripe for the tomb. All plant foods contain all essential amino acids albeit in varying quantities, with many having amino acid ratios considered to be "complete" sources of protein, such as soy and amaranth (3). It has been proven that diets that are adequately calorie dense are almost always adequately rich in protein (2). Interestingly, once believed to be caused by protein deficiency, recent evidence suggests that kwashiorkor is a "micronutrient deficiency" rather than a "macronutrient deficiency." (4). Additionally, more recent research has suggested that animal protein is carcinogenic (5), and that human omnivores have higher levels of C-reactive protein which in essence is wasted protein (6,7). Your idea of "protein hunger" is another stark untrue statement that has not been proven in humans and the fact that primates eat insects and that chimpanzees for instance sometimes cannibalize each other doesn't prove that a completely vegan diet is inadequate for humans, nor does this indicate that our evolutionary heritage has not been predominately herbivorous. Also there is evidence that feeding captive gorillas meat rich diets induces heart disease as it does for our own species(8).

Concerning fats, again the truth is oiled to fortify the bias of Mr. Shepard. Long chain fatty acids indispensable for life come in two general forms known as Arachidonic acid (from linoleic acid), the omega 6 and Eicosapentanoic (EPA) and Docohexasenoic (DHA, both of which come from alpha-linoleic acid) acids which are omega 3's(9). They are easily synthesized by the body from the essential short chain fatty acids which in the omega 6 form is linoleic acid (LA) and the omega 3 compound is alphalinoleic acid (ALA). A cursory review of the scientific literature illuminates the capacity of the human body to synthesize all the long chain fatty acids necessary to thrive as the brain and rest of the body needs very little and stores excess as well (10). Animal flesh contains minimal omega 3s, even that of grass fed or wild animals (11). Fish contains a considerable amount of DHA and EPA but these are obtained from consuming the algae that initially produces it (12). However the oceans fisheries are near annihilated by overfishing, and their tissues concentrate methylmercury, PCBs, dioxins and other lipophilic toxins (13,14). Despite the confusion raised by people who speculate fish cannot, they do in fact feel pain (15). As such the best option may be algae derived supplements that are available for those concerned about their body's ability to convert ALA to DHA, though for most people this is probably superfluous (10). Thus, it is not necessary and it is environmentally taxing to consume animals strictly to obtain long chain fatty acids.

To further confound the reader, the B12 issue is thrown in coupled with misinformation. Cobalamin or Vitamin B12 as it is commonly known, presents another can of worms to sort through but the tactic doesn't stand up to scientific scrutiny and careful review of the evidence. Studies like the Framingham Offspring Study which have demonstrated that up to 38 per cent of omnivores reviewed had marginal B12 status, as well as the fact that B12 does not come from meat nor plants but is synthesized by prokaryotic bacteria exclusively, materializes more questions than answers (16,17). Furthermore those with impaired digestion such as the elderly and those with gastrointestinal issues are at heightened risk of B12 deficiency(18,19). The evidence we have instructs us that it is prudent for the majority of people to consider supplementing B12 as the animals reared for slaughter in particular those in CAFO operations receive. In short, Shepard's lack of nutritional research and his reliance on the assumption that the reader will take his bias and lies at face value result in his argument rapidly disintegrating.

The American Academy of Dietetics has stated that a properly planned vegan diet is adequate for all stages of life, including pregnancy and infancy (20). Furthermore, there are many vegan athletes as well as professional vegan weightlifters who hold or have held world records, Carl Lewis being one of them. Clearly, animal foods are not "more critical for sound nutrition than plant foods." A near vegan diet is the only diet proven to not only prevent but also reverse the number one cause of death on Earth, heart disease (21,22). The final idea Shepard espouses is one which has been reiterated so frequently that it has become a cliché: the idea of the rugged noble savage who is the splitting image of health. This is an exhausting appeal to nature as if hunter gatherers were the standard of longevity and vigor. The fixation on this nonexistent anomalous nutritional mystery is irresponsible as writing like this can have considerable influence that will not only effect the environment and the lives of animals, but people's health. The fact is that hunter gatherers are not a standard of nutrition or wellbeing. The idea that the Masai and the Inuit had some immunity to atherosclerosis and the diseases of affluence has been totally refuted (23-26). As I have stated, knowledge of how to treat the cause of heart disease was already known by 1990 (20) as such you have no excuse in publishing the conjecture of a doctor who hasn't definitively proven his hypothesis. The same diet proven to reverse heart disease has also been shown by both Dr. Kempner and Swank to reverse diabetes and multiple sclerosis, respectively, long before Ornish's trial (27,28).

The egregious assertions that there is "no phylogenic felicity" and also a "reinventing of biology" for the vegan argument to stand is akin to the Politburo fat and malicious decrying the rachitic proletariat, such is the blind faith in a putrid and incredulous system. Comparative anatomy of humans and our closest herbivorous relatives anatomically, as well as with respect to dentition and physiology indicates our shared dietary heritage. The length of our digestive tract is not the only significant comparison as is done in the essay of interest, but a myriad of others such as dentition and the jaw, Stomach pH, Cholesterol metabolism, behavior, sense of taste, and other metabolic distinctions such as our inability to synthesize vitamin C as well as to detoxify retinol or preformed vitamin A, as carnivores ably do both (29,30).

The viewpoints presented concerning ethical and primarily environmental and existential aspects are similarly of a logically deficient stance. The notion that people who exclusively consume vegetables and plants/fungi are murderous and blood hungry is as ludicrous as the perverse propaganda used to attack enemies of the Nazi party. The audacity to enthusiastically describe the culture of animal murder (hunting) and then lead off his affront to vegans with such a hollow inflammatory statement demonstrates that the spiritual affinity for lifeforms described is a guise which is dropped readily when vegans are under attack. Zucchini, soybeans, and all plant and fungal life on Earth for that matter are sentient but lack nervous systems and science has not proven that they feel pain and they do not scream for their lives as animals being slaughtered. The sardonic attitude and previously stated spiritual insinuations are obviously incompatible. Animals that tangibly fight and run for their lives, vocalize in terror if they can and display systemic outward agony are certainly not equitable to the harvesting of soybeans and zuchhini. Obviously, this point is a red herring which is something Shephard accuses feminists of employing, which is besides the point- even if this were true, more plants perish to feed animals than if humans just ate the plants directly.

Not only are the majority of vegetables and plant foods consumed by the general population, but those who choose to eat plant foods alone are not only sparing the livelihood of farmed animals but also millions of small rodents and insects which die in the harvesting of crops raised for the feed of farmed animals, who require far more nutrition than human beings. Thus, the damage of "harvesting casualties" is far more pronounced when considering the crops destined for animal consumption.

The amount of feed per animal varies depending upon the definition (31) (For actual beef that 90 per cent of "First World" omnivores consume the ratio is about twenty pounds of feed/grain to one pound of red meat), but no matter the copious caveats and hair splitting, all energy in our world for our intents and purposes is derived from the Sun. Plants are the most direct source of this energy, and every time this energy is transferred to another trophic level such as herbivores and so on, energy is lost via the metabolism, growth, and death of these organisms (32). This is elementary science.

Logical fallacies are a hallmark of this essay, as after fishing emotional sympathy from the foolish with a red herring, Shepard next employs an appeal to obscurity. This delusional notion that the dietary pattern which requires the least amount of land to feed the most people having the most deleterious effect upon "The Fourth [and] Fifth World" is frustratingly unfounded. It's rather clear what happens to quality of life for those in these neatly compartmentalized "worlds" when in fact all "worlds" are tied together and so are our collective problems.

The insincere contrite nod at true vegetarians (vegans) and the idea that a vegan diet is only suitable for people who are malnourished, an ersatz substitute for the "traditional" diet which causes heart disease, diabetes, and colon cancer in the "First World."This is hardly the case. As proven above, plant food is wasted in excessive quantities to feed animals while impoverished humans starve, especially in the Third World (33). Not only are "calories" wasted on these animals, but as I have elucidated, "protein" as well. Furthermore, these animals are oftentimes supplemented with B12 which I have discussed.

So how is life for those poor people who had to "gulp" soya in lieu of eating animal corpse, the "preferred" cuisine? Well, there's no way to ascertain that, but it should be readily apparent that if that land was being used to rear farmed animals it wouldn't be for this destitute "Third World" refugee described but rather for the affluent meat consumer. Not to mention the fact that this diet is not a "better than nothing" approach which I have demonstrated.

But let me continue to shovel out the lies that have muddied the pure waters of truth. The same reasoning that I have used above applies to the "Fourth [and] Fifth Worlds" and to reply to the query posited about their wellbeing I simply ask one to look at the world, even as it was in the 1990's when "The Vegetarians" was written. Increased demand upon burgeoning middle classes in "Second World" countries has resulted in more acreage being devoted to raising animals and it often is like a raging cancer at the fringes of pristine habitat such as the Amazon rainforest, the home of many indigenous peoples and where untold numbers of species are extinguished, some perhaps never discovered from habitat destruction but also globally from the effect of climate change which animal agriculture plays a huge role in. This is what happens to the "fourth" and "Fifth World" when the world follows the egregiously dangerous advice noted in the essay of focus- the most diverse and unique life forms are destroyed directly, climate change from animal agriculture influences species extinction worldwide, and because of rainforest encroachment, tribal peoples such as the Guarani and Yanomamo are in jeopardy of losing their culture and livelihood (34,35). The Food and Agriculture Organization of the United Nations estimates that animal agriculture produces more greenhouse gases than all those emitted by worldwide transportation (36), both leading drivers of climate change and it's corresponding environmental havoc.

So in essence, Shepard is engaging himself in a tour de force of hypocrisy as everything he is claiming vegans are guilty of are failings of those who continue to demand the flesh and secretions of animals. The only ecologically shortsighted ideology here is the one that is currently exercised on a massive scale on our fragile interconnected world, Shepard's aloofness to facts and logic devastate any possibility his argument might convince anyone who does any veracious research. He errantly champions the dietary pattern which causes the most comprehensive ubiquitous malaise and decimation in the world. Not only in terms of environmental degradation and climate change, but also habitat destruction, ocean dead zones, abuse of antibiotics and the resulting consequences, widespread preventable chronic illnesses, and even increased incidence of violence in communities with abattoirs and increased cancer in communities near certain animal agribusiness operations (37,38). Thus, aligning the vegan diet with a "quantitative mindedness" as I have explained is totally inaccurate. The low fat, oil free, whole food vegan diet is the most complete diet as it does not detract from health the way that animal flesh does. It intrinsically ameliorates our world by virtue of being of a holistic mindset that acknowledges that everything is related in the vast web of life, and by endeavoring to be conscientious of this, to evolve mindfully, and let truth reign instead of wallow in darkness and ignorance, as Shepard's essay advocates.

Sources

Fowden L. (1980) Amino Acids: Production by Plants and the Requirements of Man. In: Blaxter K. (eds) *Food Chains and Human Nutrition*. Springer, Dordrecht. https://link.springer.com/chapter/10.1007/978-94-011-7336-0_6

McDougal J (2002),Plant Foods Have a Complete Amino Acid Composition, *Circulation*, https://doi.org/10.1161/01.CIR.0000018905.97677.
https://www.ahajournals.org/doi/10.1161/01.CIR.0000018905.97677.1F

https://www.huffpost.com/entry/vegetarian-protein-complete-meat_n_5a90357ae4b01e9e56bb3224

Heikens GT, Manary M. 75 years of Kwashiorkor in Africa. Malawi *Med J.* 2009;21(3):96–98. https://www.ncbi.nlm.nih.gov/pmc/articles/PMC3717488/

Campbell TC. Cancer Prevention and Treatment by Wholistic Nutrition. *J Nat Sci.* 2017 Oct;3(10):e448. PubMed PMID: 29057328; PubMed Central PMCID: PMC5646698.

Smidowicz A, Regula J. Effect of nutritional status and dietary patterns on human serum C-reactive protein and interleukin-6 concentrations. *Adv Nutr.* 2015 Nov 13;6(6):738-47. doi: 10.3945/an.115.009415. PubMed PMID: 26567198; PubMed Central PMCID: PMC4642421.

Sutliffe JT, Wilson LD, de Heer HD, Foster RL, Carnot MJ., C-reactive protein response to a vegan lifestyle intervention, *Complement Ther Med.* 2015 Feb;23(1):32-7. doi: 10.1016/j.ctim.2014.11.001. Epub 2014 Dec 3.

Cheryl Lyn Dybas, Ilya Raskin, Out of Africa: A Tale of Gorillas, Heart Disease… and a Swamp Plant, *BioScience*, Volume 57, Issue 5, May 2007, Pages 392–397, https://doi.org/10.1641/B570503

Linus Pauling Institute, Oregon State University, https://lpi.oregonstate.edu/mic/other-nutrients/essential-fatty-acids

Domenichiello AF, Kitson AP, Bazinet RP, Is docosahexaenoic acid synthesis from α-linolenic acid sufficient to supply the adult brain?, *Prog Lipid Res.* 2015 Jul;59:54-66. doi: 10.1016/j.plipres.2015.04.002. Epub 2015 Apr 25

Berkeley Health, Berekely University of California, https://www.berkeleywellness.com/healthy-eating/food/nutrition/article/grass-fed-beef-omega-3s

Doughman SD, Krupanidhi S, Sanjeevi CB. Omega-3 fatty acids for nutrition and medicine: considering microalgae oil as a vegetarian source of EPA and DHA, *Curr Diabetes Rev.* 2007 Aug;3(3):198-203.

Food and Agricultural Organization of the United Nations, The State of the World's Fisheries and Aquaculture, http://www.fao.org/3/i2727e/i2727e00.htm

Streit B. Bioaccumulation of Contaminants in Fish, *EXS.* 1998;86:353-87.

Sneddon LU, Pain perception in fish: indicators and endpoints, *ILAR J.* 2009;50(4):338-42.

Tucker KL, Rich S, Rosenberg I, Jacques P, Dallal G, Wilson PW, Selhub J, Plasma vitamin B-12 concentrations relate to intake source in the Framingham Offspring study. *Am J Clin Nutr.* 2000 Feb;71(2):514-22.

Fang H, Kang J, Zhang D. Microbial production of vitamin B12: a review and future perspectives. *Microb Cell Fact.* 2017 Jan 30;16(1):15. doi: 10.1186/s12934-017-0631-y. PubMed PMID: 28137297; PubMed Central PMCID: PMC5282855.

Allen LH1., Causes of vitamin B12 and folate deficiency., *Food Nutr Bull.* 2008 Jun;29(2 Suppl):S20-34; discussion S35-7.

Madanchi M, Fagagnini S, Fournier N, Biedermann L, Zeitz J, Battegay E, Zimmerli L, Vavricka SR, Rogler G, Scharl M; Swiss IBD Cohort Study Group. *Inflamm Bowel Dis.* 2018 Jul 12;24(8):1768-1779. doi: 10.1093/ibd/izy054.

Melina V, Craig W, Levin S., Position of the Academy of Nutrition and Dietetics: Vegetarian Diets., *J Acad Nutr Diet.* 2016 Dec;116(12):1970-1980. doi: 10.1016/j.jand.2016.09.025.

Ornish D, Brown SE, Scherwitz LW, Billings JH, Armstrong WT, Ports TA, McLanahan SM, Kirkeeide RL, Brand RJ, Gould KL. Can lifestyle changes reverse coronary heart disease? The Lifestyle Heart Trial. *Lancet.* 1990 Jul 21;336(8708):129-33

Esselstyn CB Jr, Gendy G, Doyle J, Golubic M, Roizen MF. A way to reverse CAD? *J Fam Pract.* 2014 Jul;63(7):356-364b.

Mann GV, Spoerry A, Gary M, Jarashow D, Atherosclerosis in the Masai, *American Journal of Epidemiology,* Volume 95, Issue 1, January 1972, Pages 26-37, https://doi.org/10.1093/oxfordjournal.aje.a121365

Mbalilaki JA, Masesa Z, Strømme SB, Høstmark AT, Sundquist J, Wändell P, Rosengren A, Hellenius ML, Daily energy expenditure and cardiovascular risk in Masai, rural and urban Bantu Tanzanians. *Br J Sports Med.* 2010 Feb;44(2):121-6. doi: 10.1136/bjsm.2007.044966. Epub 2008 Jun 3.

Fodor JG, Helis E, Yazdekhasti N, Vohnout B, "Fishing" for the origins of the "Eskimos and heart disease" story: facts or wishful thinking? *Can J Cardiol.* 2014 Aug;30(8):864-8. doi: 10.1016/j.cjca.2014.04.007. Epub 2014 Apr 13.

Bjerregaard P1, Young TK, Hegele RA, Low incidence of cardiovascular disease among the Inuit–what is the evidence? *Atherosclerosis.* 2003 Feb;166(2):351-7

McDougall J, Walter Kempner MD Founder of the Rice Diet, https://www.drmcdougall.com/2013/12/31/walter-kempner-md-founder-of-the-rice-diet/

Metropulos, Megan MS RDN, Ware, Megan RDN, *Does the Swank Diet help with multiple sclerosis?,* https://www.medicalnewstoday.com/articles/318665.php

Mills, Milton MD, *The Comparative Anatomy of Eating,* retrieved from https://www.adaptt.org/documents/Mills%20The%20Comparative%20Anatomy %20of%20Eating1.pdf

Drouin G, Godin JR, Pagé B. The genetics of vitamin C loss in vertebrates. *Curr Genomics.* 2011 Aug;12(5):371-8. doi: 10.2174/138920211796429736. PubMed PMID: 22294879; PubMed Central PMCID: PMC3145266.

USDA National Institute of Food and Agriculture, New Technologies for Ag Extension Project, https://articles.extension.org/pages/35850/on-average-how-many-pounds-of-corn-make-one-pound-of-beef-assuming-an-all-grain-diet-from-background

Department of Education Open Textbook Pilot Project, Transfer of Energy Between Trophic Levels, https://bio.libretexts.org/Bookshelves/Introductory_and_General_Biology/Book %3A_General_Biology_(Boundless)/46%3A_Ecosystems/46.2%3A_Energy_Fl ow_through_Ecosystems/46.2C%3A_Transfer_of_Energy_between_Trophic_L evels

Oppenlander, Richard DDS, *Animal Agriculture, Hunger, and How to Feed a Growing Population: Part One of Two,* https://www.forksoverknives.com/animal-agriculture-hunger-and-how-to-feed-a-growing-global-population-part-one-of-two/#gs.xjs3wg

Survival International, https://www.survivalinternational.org/tribes/brazilian

Yale School of Forestry and Environmental Studies, *Global Forest Atlas, Cattle Ranching in the Amazon Region,* https://globalforestatlas.yale.edu/amazon/land-use/cattle-ranching

Food and Agriculture Organization of the United Nations, *Livestock's Long Shadow,* http://www.fao.org/3/a0701e/a0701e00.htm

Fitzgerald, A. J., Kalof, L., & Dietz, T. (2009). Slaughterhouses and Increased Crime Rates: An Empirical Analysis of the Spillover From "The Jungle" Into the Surrounding Community. *Organization & Environment,* 22(2), 158–184. https://doi.org/10.1177/1086026609338164

Avery, Sarah, N.C Residents *Living Near Large Hog Farms Have Elevated Disease,* Death Risk, https://corporate.dukehealth.org/news-listing/nc-residents-living-near-large-hog-farms-have-elevated-disease-death-risks

https://veganprimitivist.wordpress.com/2019/08/25/returning-to-reality-a-response-to-paul-shepards-the-vegetarians-by-michael-b/

Ria & Oak Journal & JZ

*Note: Words in bold italics were my emphasis.

Hey Ria,

John sent over your piece, I'll dig into it in the next few days. There's a bit more to that section in the print version FYI. I'll make sure you get a copy when it comes out. Of course anything you'd like in print as a response since you are mentioned we will include, up to 1k words in this issue and more in the following maybe? Your call, I can send you copy of the print interview in the next few weeks.

Cheers
Steve

On Wednesday, February 5, 2020

Yes, that'd be nice.

Also, it seems fair to run a retraction of some of the interview where the Neanderthal study is portrayed as 'low meat' not 'no meat'.

"...ancient DNA from five specimens of Neanderthal calcified dental plaque (calculus) and the characterization of regional differences in Neanderthal ecology. At Spy cave, Belgium, Neanderthal diet was heavily meat based and included woolly rhinoceros and wild sheep (mouflon), characteristic of a steppe environment. In contrast, no meat was detected in the diet of Neanderthals from El Sidrón cave, Spain, and dietary components of mushrooms, pine nuts, and moss reflected forest gathering."

Thanks.
Ria

"We are dreaming of a time when the land might give thanks for the people."
-Robin Wall Kimmerer

Hi Ria,

If you can submit something for this issue by end of month that is under 1500 words we will certainly run it -- more space in issue 2 as well.

There is an extensive note on that section in the print copy describing the two cohorts with one very high and one no meat of detection, *one could imagine a margin of error* in both cohorts -- though I'm not at all a technical expert as to the methodology used in that study the authors displayed a relatively high degree of confidence. There *seems to have been at least some backlash* last year to the study as well

https://www.sciencedaily.com/releases/2019/02/190219111704.htm

On Wednesday, February 5, 2020

Browsing through your link, *I don't see any reference to the El Sidrón cave Neanderthals*. Also, that the phrasing 'no detectable meat' was added is evidence of the man-the-hunter bias presenting all pre-history people as hunters, otherwise, why include such a phrase? It's also interesting to note that the link you attached includes evidence of cannibalism, which anprims choose not to cherry pick into including in their diet.

If you'd like me to rebut something in print, could you email it to me? Otherwise, would you like me to focus just on the podcast section in question? My book has grown to over 300 pages, and will publish by the end of this month, so I could also include that after my signature.

Have you asked Layla if she'd like opportunity to reply as well?

Thanks,
Ria

No, it isn't directly mentioned but it seems clear from some reporting that it is at least partly responsible for the wording. Not a claim on the validity, just sharing. I don't think single pieces of empirical evidence are that interesting, but certainly homo genus can be or has been cannibalistic at times. As to your point about including it in diet based on evidence...that seems a bit hyperbolic or maybe you're serious? A bit of a false analogy to compare the evidence for cannibalism as broad dietary component to the evidence for meat eating!

Look forward to your response. My plan was to reach out to you both for issue 2, we're about maxed out with page length (in fact over projected by 10 pages). But since it wasn't the focus of the interview, and I had actually planned on not discussing it, it wasn't a priority for issue 1 unfortunately.

I don't quite understand the comment on detectable...it is factual. It was not observed or experience but extrapolated via data. I'm certainly not seeing that as

evidence of bias. Also, that wasn't what the note for the print version ,
"detectable" is not included.

*The phrasing of the one study I sent you is arguably over the top, but I haven't
read the study so I couldn't say for sure.*

Certainly, I'll get you the full print interview by Monday, sooner if possible so
you can have time to review, the topic is isolated to one section of the interview.

Good luck with the book launch, we will review for issue 2.

Best
Steve

*As you know, with DNA technology now being used a more accurate picture
of early human diet is coming to light. Scientists are just beginning to figure it
out, so the fact that a plant-moss-mushroom no detectable meat diet was
evidenced in Neanderthals 48,000 years ago in France is a significant finding
that challenges the mainstream man-the-hunter narrative.*

*I've read through the study you linked, and can't find its connection to the El
Sidrón cave study, and cannot find anywhere online that anyone is connecting
the two studies. All articles I found so far that include both studies do not have
one study negating the other in any way. If you find any connections, please
share, as I strive for accuracy.*

If you don't have space, that's fine. But to be fair, there were false
claims/opinions stated in the podcast, and if you're not intending to retract, then
an opportunity for Layla and/or me to respond would be essential for Oak's
credibility. That's why I appreciate you reaching out. Actually, three people
were given podcast time on one side of an issue, so giving Layla an opportunity
to address the accusations in podcast form would be even more fair. But she
may be too offended to reply, I don't know.

Sorry I wasn't clear. I just meant that if I write a commentary I could sign it as
Ria, author of *EcoPatriarchy: The Origins & Nature of Hunting*

I don't intend to eat up huge amounts of space. That last time was a quirk that
ended up ballooning into a book. Apologies for putting you through all that
effort. You were very patient, and your critique helped me in my writing too. So
thanks.

Ria

Certainly it is significant finding.

Would you be interested in doing audio interview for issue 2, that way you'd get more of the exact same platform. If you felt like I wasn't the best person to do the other side then I'd be open to hearing suggestions.

And no worries on book, it was invigorating process and I've appreciated our discussions.

Best, Steve

I think Layla would be best, maybe ask her first? She's more of a stand-alone guest, as her talk is lengthy Q & A, haven't heard her do quick give & take.

If she doesn't, I might consider doing it with Flower Bomb. We complement one another well.

The issue was that you, the interviewer, were on the same side as JZ & Bellamy, so it was very one sided. And Bellamy's not well versed in anprim, but you two let him run with it as if you agreed. John finally stepped in to call out his stance against the moralizing point. If you interviewed Flower Bomb and me, you'd just have to stick to the role of interviewer and let us state opinions that you may find disagreeable and just let our opinions hang there. Probably wouldn't be much fun for you.

Hope you're enjoying all of this project. It must be a huge beast.

***

We see the interview and issue very differently, which is a thing that happens and I don't take it personally that you feel it was unfair. It wasn't really meant to be fair or unfair, it was an open-ended discussion with three people that was intended to be interesting to the milieu -- and so far success on that end.

I don't know Layla and have a rapport with you so that's my preference. I'd interview you both with the intention of being more of a mediator of your discussion but I won't guarantee that my opinion will be invisible (if such a thing is possible).

I"ll write Layla about a chance to reply in writing but given your interaction to the episode already you are the logical choice I think.

It's been going well, just chip away every day and try to put out something engaging.

Steve

On Oak email to John Zerzan:

Hi John -

fyi, the study I referenced that Bellamy and you said indicated "low meat" not "no meat" was indeed "no meat". It seems you haven't read the study (below) and were relying on Steve's analysis, which falls apart to the point where he concedes that the study is a significant finding that challenges the man-the-hunter narrative (see relevant excerpts of emails below) -

Here's the study and pdf to which you and Bellamy were responding:

Laura Weyrich and others "Neanderthal Behaviour, Diet, and Disease Inferred from Ancient DNA in Dental Calculus." Nature, International Journal of Science , 2017
https://www.nature.com/articles/nature21674

https://www.researchgate.net/publication/314306629_Neanderthal_behaviour_diet_and_disease_inferred_from_ancient_DNA_in_dental_calculus

*Note: Words in bold italics were my emphasis.

On Wednesday, February 5, 2020

...Also, *it seems fair to run a retraction of some of the interview where the Neanderthal study is portrayed as 'low meat' not 'no meat'.*

"...ancient DNA from five specimens of Neanderthal calcified dental plaque (calculus) and the characterization of regional differences in Neanderthal ecology. At Spy cave, Belgium, Neanderthal diet was heavily meat based and included woolly rhinoceros and wild sheep (mouflon), characteristic of a steppe environment. In contrast, **no meat** was detected in the diet of Neanderthals from El Sidrón cave, Spain, and dietary components of mushrooms, pine nuts, and moss reflected forest gathering."

Thanks.

Ria

Hi Ria,

There is an extensive note on that section in the print copy describing the two cohorts with one very high and one no meat of detection, *one could imagine a margin of error* in both cohorts -- though I'm not at all a technical expert as to the methodology used in that study the authors displayed a relatively high degree of confidence. There *seems to have been at least some backlash* last year to the study as well *{The link he provides does not refer to the study, and I cannot find any such backlash elsewhere.}*

https://www.sciencedaily.com/releases/2019/02/190219111704.htm

On Wednesday, February 5, 2020

Browsing through your link, *I don't see any reference to the El Sidrón cave Neanderthals*....

Thanks, Ria

No, it isn't directly mentioned but it seems clear from some reporting that it is at least partly responsible for the wording. Not a claim on the validity, just sharing...

The phrasing of the one study I sent you is arguably over the top, but I haven't read the study so I couldn't say for sure.

Best, Steve

As you know, with DNA technology now being used a more accurate picture of early human diet is coming to light. Scientists are just beginning to figure it out, so the fact that a plant-moss-mushroom no detectable meat diet was evidenced in Neanderthals 48,000 years ago in France is a significant finding that challenges the mainstream man-the-hunter narrative.

I've read through the study you linked, and can't find its connection to the El Sidrón cave study, and cannot find anywhere online that anyone is connecting the two studies. All articles I found so far that include both studies do not have one study negating the other in any way. If you find any connections, please share, as I strive for accuracy.

Ria

...Certainly it is significant finding.

Steve

Email to JZ:

John, the points that Bellamy and you made against Layla and my vegan anarcho-primitivism have been refuted (see link). I'm fine if you'd like to defend the rebutted points, but honestly, I project I'd win this debate, if you choose to have it.

https://veganprimitivist.wordpress.com/2020/02/03/response-to-bellamy-jz-steve-kirk-condemning-vegan-primitivism/

I think it's fair to at least retract this part of your & Bellamy's errors on Anarchy Radio and/or Oak, for your credibility.

Despite any disagreements on points, respectfully,

Ria

Ria Letter to JZ

Hey John,

Without going into detail, I want you to know that you've significantly soothed my life, likely how you have so many others. That said, *EcoPatriarchy: The Origins & Nature of Hunting* was inspired mainly by my contrasting ethos with you and other anprims. The underlying speculative narrative is fairly aligned with Layla's predation theory. Since so much inspiration comes from you, including conflict with you presented in the book, I'm sending you a draft proof as invitation to write an honest response to be included at the end - negative, positive or both. If so, let me know so you can have time before final submission. No pressure, I just thought it would be fair to offer you the opportunity if you choose.

If it'd be ok with you, I'd like to call in your show to briefly announce my book (unless you'd like the honors). If you feel you'd need to state your opinion on it, I'd like an opportunity to state mine. Maybe we could collaborate in briefly announcing it, being upfront about our disagreement? Or, just announce it with no opinion? I'm fine either way.

I don't know if you read through my response to your & Bellamy's critique of vegan primitivism. I found the points fairly easy to rebut. But I'll just point out that the claim that the 2017 Neanderthal study referenced evidenced of 'low meat' not 'no meat' was incorrect.

...ancient DNA from five specimens of Neanderthal calcified dental plaque (calculus) and the characterization of regional differences in Neanderthal ecology. At Spy cave, Belgium, Neanderthal diet was heavily meat based and included woolly rhinoceros and wild sheep (mouflon), characteristic of a steppe environment. In contrast, no meat was detected in the diet of Neanderthals from El Sidrón cave, Spain, and dietary components of mushrooms, pine nuts, and moss reflected forest gathering.

I find it interesting that the Neanderthal sample from Spy cave in Belgium was around 42,000 years old, and samples from the individuals from El Sidrón cave in Spain were around 50,000 years old. I believe the caves are about 1,000 miles apart. I don't include speculation on this in my book, but I find it intriguing that there might have been a shift from forest gathering plants, mushrooms & moss to a diet heavy in meat in 8,000 years. As you know, there's really too little evidence of anything going that far back to draw solid conclusions. Narratives are a game of speculation. Even with the little we do know, much of it is culturally biased.

Since I criticize Paul Shepard, I thought you may be interested in something said by Jim Mason, author of *An Unnatural Order: Roots of Our Destruction of Nature*, which he gave permission to quote in my book:

I have taken a lot of flak from feminist and animal rights people over my use of Paul Shepard's ideas. I know where he's coming from, same place I came from, the southern Missouri Ozarks where hunting and fishing are a way of life. I cringed a lot when I read his views on hunting. Nevertheless, I think his most important idea, and the one that I tried to elaborate on in my book, is the importance of animals in the evolution of the human mind, speech, thought, and worldview: The ideas expressed in his early book, Thinking Animals. I think it is very important to try to understand those ideas apart from his obsessions with hunting. To me it shows the importance of animals to the human mind and worldview, and then we can understand the devastation brought on by domestication and animal slavery.

EcoPatriarchy will be available on Amazon at-cost, so as not to feed the beast.

Hey, perhaps we can agree that at least I don't cop out in the end!

Wishing you & Alice well.

Ria

PS – The last time I sent you a book, I was just regaining my ability to read & write after the trauma of my brother's murder. This book is kinda like a litmus test of my brain healing. Crazy fucking world.

Ryan the Green Anarchist Against Civilization & Ria Chat On Fire

Hey Ria,

I have a question on article you wrote: ANPRIM ON FIRE: HUMAN SUPREMACY WITHIN ANARCHO-PRIMITIVIST NARRATIVE.

I really admire your position based on the few things I've read, and I'm already coming at this as an anti-civilizationist and a vegetarian, though the concept of vegan primitivism is new to me.

Thank you!

Wow, thanks for this - very interesting. I answered your questions in bold… {Ryan's replies are in italics.}

I have a couple of questions on this. I agree that fire, rather than agriculture, seems to have been the first human invention that set us on the course towards the invasive colonizing species we are today. However, is it possible that although our natural habitat and lifeway was equatorial and herbivorous, our shift to hunter-gatherers, though initially unnatural, led to adaptations that make it more natural now? **How are you defining 'natural'?** Not that eating meat is necessary, as the science you've pointed out ensures that it's not. But rather that we are adapted to living in habitats that were not originally natural for us, and therefore our wild presence would no longer be unnatural; that it's possible for us to be connected and intimate with the land in a northern climate even though winter dominates much of the year and our nakedness and herbivorous origins make it impossible to live there without tools, animal flesh, and animal skin/fur.

I see. I'd say we are generalist>specialists. What I mean by that is that we are highly adaptable with an ability to invade & colonize outside our 'natural' habitat. But once we 'settle' we engineer the landscape to suit us, co-specializing the new habitat - we become reliant upon it, and it becomes reliant upon us. The problem is that once we create the world into our niche, we lose our generalist ability to easily back out of our creation. We sacrifice our resilience - perhaps colonizing-settling is even a self-domesticating device. If you call that 'natural' or 'naturalized' is a moot point really. The main point is that we've designed ourselves into a trap at the expense of ourselves and thriving ecology.

This makes a lot of sense to me, and I'm really glad somebody else recognizes this. When I say natural, it's for lack of a better word. I don't believe it's unnatural for a species to adapt to conditions and environments in order to survive that they didn't evolve in initially. If that were the case, we wouldn't have the diversity of life spread across Earth that we see. Engineering the landscape to "create the world into our niche" is a form of domestication though, and I like how you point out that we've designed ourselves into a trap at the expense of ourselves and thriving ecology. The Anprim philosophy doesn't include this thought process, and at least to my knowledge doesn't recognize the inherent domestication behind our migrations from our original range, fire as a colonizing catalyst, domestication through pre-civilized environmental engineering, and that there's anything dominating about utilizing animals to buffer ourselves from the lack of adaptions to an environment, such as fur for warmth and skin for shelter, and meat and fat for sustenance in landbases lacking suitable plant nutrition. Thank you for articulating this.

An example I think would be how we evolved naked and herbivorous near the equator, where nakedness was natural for heat exchange, dark skin protected us from the sun's rays, and the landscape was diverse enough and warm enough year round to provide adequate nutrition without animal flesh. But as we adopted fire and meat and other cooked foods after our scavenging period, and the tools to procure them, we were able to move to habitats and climates that would otherwise be inhospitable. So by the time some of our species reached places like what is now northern Europe, they required shelters and clothes made of animal furs, and a diet heavily based on meat, and tools and inventions to procure meat, and fire to cook it and keep warm. Because they didn't evolve in that habitat, they had to take the adaptions to the environment from other animals who had them, like the fur, or the meat of those animals because there wasn't year round plant material in sufficient type, quantity, and diversity.

Exactly. Similar to when early humans started herding, using other animals as larders to feed upon as they expanded into areas without known or stable food opportunities.

Good point. Unrelated, but related, our first foray out of Africa seemed to have been limited to eastern Eurasian coasts into what is now southeast Asia. As herding wasn't invented yet, the oceans served as a larder for human expansion into new areas. Only later migrations colonized interior Eurasia with its unknowables.

Though we were thus initial invasive and dominating in this sense, as time went on, the landscape adapted to our presence as much as we adapted to its. Wherever we moved, massive die-offs followed, as animals that had not co-evolved with us were suddenly faced with our predation and domination. But after those die-offs, we seem to have found equilibrium in those landscapes, where we thrived and the landscape was undegraded by our presence for thousands of years until the advent of agriculture and the encroachment of civilization.

Wow, you could have helped write my book. That's pretty much what I say in one section- you make the point so clearly.

In the case of northern Europeans, their dark skin moved to what we now consider white skin due to adaptations to ensure adequate sunlight absorption for vitamin d production. But we never evolved fur for warmth, a layer of thermos-regulating fat, or claws and teeth for carnivory. We didn't evolve those because we buffered our evolution from them through the use of tools and inventions. There's no selective pressure to evolve fur in a cold environment if you're kept warm by fire and fur. There's no selective pressure to evolve claws to hunt if you invent spears and knives and traps. But the things we can't buffer against, such as sunlight absorption, or gut length and internal physiology, seem have to adapt to this new environment.

Yes. I'd add the theory that 'selection pressures' stem initially from chance mutations, whether helpful or not is mere coincidence. But I've often wondered about what's behind the locations on our body that we retain hair, and the difference in hair locations between sexes. I have this guess that as humans first made clothes, they were wrapped around the limbs and torso, perhaps like a shawls and sleeves, leaving the armpits and genital area more exposed, hence hair there. And maybe hats came later, hence head hair. And that perhaps women tended to stay closer to the fire cooking and taking care of children while men were out in the elements more, hence facial hair. And children were kept warm with blankets, clothes and fire, hence delayed hair. I wonder what your honest opinion is on this?

This is interesting. I have thought of this as well, though not as thoroughly as you it seems. I've never thought of the genital area and armpits retaining hair because of exposure due to possible shawl-style clothing. That's actually a brilliant hypothesis. I assumed the pubic hair, from the mons in the front all the way to the back, is to keep the reproductive area warm. But why would it need extra warmth more than the rest of the body, especially areas with vital organs, unless it was exposed more than other areas? The scrotum especially, as it hangs outside the body to ensure it doesn't get as warm as the rest of the body, and only shrinks back when it actually needs it. Pubic hair could protect from dust and debris too, like eyelashes and brows, but that seems more relevant to females than males, but neither sex as far as I know differs much in pubic hair quantity. As for armpits, I have no idea. Yours is the most plausible explanation I've heard. Though I read once that vital arteries are really close to the skin there, and hair can help retain beat there. But then why not the neck and other areas too.

I would agree that head hair is for heat regulation, as much of our heat escapes there. Though the aquatic ape theory suggests body hair was lost due to an aquatic period in our history, rather than for heat exchange and sweat glands, but that head hair was retained for children to grasp and be carried along by us when swimming, similar to how the children of other apes now hold on to their mother's fur when she walks. It also suggests that human babies are born with so much fat for buoyancy, while other primates have to build fat after birth. Though that theory is far from proven at this point.

Regular body hair I assume is vestigial; there was no selective pressure to be completely bald after enough of it disappeared to suit the selective pressure for sufficient heat regulation in equatorial or near equatorial climates. But I suspect the sex differences in amounts of body hair and the facial hair in males and lack of facial hair in females, has more to do with sexual selection than actual function. The same goes for breast size, the curviness generally found in women, the disparity in muscles, the unnecessarily large penis size for male humans, and most other sexual dimorphic characteristics unrelated to reproduction.

Now if those of us of European heritage, with white skin, were to be truly wild again, we'd either have to live in the north where our white skin is most suitable, but which would require continued use of animals for fur and food, and the tool of fire for cooking it and for warmth, or we'd have to live in an equatorial habitat like we evolved to, but then our white skin would be a liability, and even hinder our ability to survive.

Exactly. Just as we adapted into our trap, we'll have to find a way to adapt out of our trap. And adaptation transitions can be... tense.

I'm really glad you said this. Most Anprims and the Jensen-ites don't acknowledge this.

The idea usually expressed is that if civ fell tomorrow, obviously our numbers would plummet, but those who survive will rewild, but that our range will not diminish. This is because it can't, without 'tense' re-adaptation. Rather than acknowledge that and accept that it will be necessary, it is ignored, and assumed all landscapes can remain our range. And I can see where this stems from supremacy.

Our invasiveness caused partial adaptations to new unnatural environments, while our tools and inventions buffered us from full adaptation. So do we really belong anywhere now? **Exactly! Where is the wild human habitat? We've so engineered the entire world, altering even our own original habitat out of existence.** In your opinion, does fire, though originally a tool that led to invasiveness and conquest, have a place in wildness now because we evolved into our current species using it? **Are we living 'wild' now? Fire led to this. The answer seems clear.** Is it really human supremacy to choose to live in northern climates even post-civ given that, although originally unnatural human terrain, we evolved to those places after moving to them, and the land-bases there adapted to our presence? **Did the land-bases have choice to co-adapt?**

Or did we make all the decisions on who lives and who dies and how all the survivors get to live? What remain are humans' slaves.

And what is your opinion on how people of white skin could truly be wild again, and accept human ranges rather than world presence, given that our partial adaption to the north in skin melatonin but non-adaptation in the form of fur and fat, kind of renders us unnatural in every environment, even the original human habitats we evolved from? **It's going to be a transition with future details unknown. But what choice do we have? Continue our path of ecocide?** And if partial but incomplete adaptation can occur through movement of place, making us unnatural tenants of any landscape without the use of some tools and inventions that ultimately mediate us from wildness, couldn't it be that our foray into meat eating, though originally unnatural, has led to the same situation, where now after hundreds of thousands of years of being a part of the human diet, some amount of animal products for some cultures at least can be beneficial, if not slightly necessary, in a wild situation without civ and agriculture and processed food, as we've partially adapted to them without the full adaptations of claws and fangs and short intestinal tracts and full immunity to atherosclerosis? **Beneficial for whom? Part of the problem that got us where we are today is that we stepped out of embeddedness with ecology community, we honed an ethos of supremacy over all. That too needs to change. If the world went anti-civ overnight, we're so overpopulated that there'd have to be a period of downsizing. Just imagine if most humans agreed to just stop breeding. It really wouldn't take long to rewild the planet. I see no reason why humans need to eat animals to live wild. Raw vegan was the original human diet, and to this day, raw vegan remains the healthiest diet, even though our biology has taken on an ability to handle meat.**

How do we deal with the legacy of our planetary colonization when its inception was so long ago that we have made partial adaptations to this unnatural state, and the land in many cases has adapted to us as well, to the point where what was once unnatural is no longer definitively so? **I give a quick suggestion to that in my book. Basically, one idea is to slow the colonizing human changes, and aim to restore ecologies to their last state of thriving. That would mean replicating controlled burns, reintroducing natural predators, etc. In time we'd have to phase ourselves out of the entirety of the world and re-locate ourselves into wild human habitat.** Even the burning of forests for field and forest edges, while a form of domination over land and plants and animals conducted by hunter-gatherers, over time has led to adaptations on the part of the land and animals and fire regimes, so much so that once they were stopped and allowed to rewild, thanks to indigenous displacement by Europeans but before being plowed over, the landscape suffered. **For more extensively degraded areas, replicate wildscape communities through reintroductions and expanding nearby natural areas. In time, bioregions will again live on their own terms.** Of course a new equilibrium would be found given enough unhindered time, but my point is that maybe our original unnaturalness in some aspects of our relationship to the land ceased to be unnatural once we and the land-base co-adapted to the new lifeway. And maybe now it is no longer correct to say that our natural human habitat is equatorial, or that our only natural wild diet should be 100% vegan." **It seems that after initial incursion & colonization, we settle into something that looks more embedded within ecosystem. However it's labeled is less important than realizing these colonization steps were early catalysts and need to be taken into account in rewilding. The only way our species is going to intentionally rewild is to drop our supremacist ethos. Otherwise, the collapse will be handled by humans quite disastrously, perhaps leading to extinction of our species.**

So correct me if I'm wrong, but what you're saying is that even though the indigenous wildness we've seen since fire and migration looks something like embeddedness, the co-adaptation of the land to us that gives that impression was not by 'choice,' and is therefore a slave to our presence. True wildness would mean accepting a limited human range we're adapted to that doesn't require domination and environmental engineering. And although it would be painful, it's necessary unless we're willing to maintain our supremacist ethos and continue to be an invasive colonizing species. And it'll be painful because we've designed ourselves into a trap, and we don't really belong anywhere anymore due to our new partial adaptations as well as the degradation of our original habitat.

On top of that, raw vegan is our original diet, the one that we evolved to, and that although fire and millions of years of incorporating meat in some amounts have led to adaptions that allow us to handle meat, it is not necessary, and is not beneficial to us or our landbases. That if the landbase doesn't support human life through wild plant nutrition, rather than close the gap with meat, that landbase should be abandoned for areas more suitable for wild humans and a wild vegan diet. And that our health, and the health of the land, and the shedding of power relations and supremacist ethos in general, depends on it.

And I know this might come across as dumb, but just so I have it straight, I assume too, that you're not against meat eating by other animals, or that you think predation is inherently dominating. But rather it is in the context of humans only because it's not our original diet, and requires tools and fire and expansion to acquire.

I also gather that you're not suggesting everyone who survives the collapse move to the equator and call it good overnight, that rewilding will have to come in steps and be a conscious act. To restore ecologies to an original state of thriving as much as possible rather than just abandon them to natural forces after millennia of interference, and that could include controlled burns, reintroduction of extirpated predators, and even meat eating, as you pointed out in another article, if the meat is from invasive destructive animals and is done in the service of rewilding, and with the ultimate goal of eliminating them and our consumption of meat. And ultimately to phase ourselves out and relocate to wild suitable human habitat.

And if so, do you think fire and meat consumption of even indigenous species has a place in rewilding? If the goal is to phase it out over generations and relocate? Like if civ fell tonight, are you on board with living off the land for the survivors, hunting and gathering since a vegan diet in non-equatorial climes is unlikely? But at least minimize meat consumption with the goal of weaning ourselves off as well as re-locate to more hospitable landbases over time?

NOTES

1 INTRODUCTION

1. Heller, Chaia. "For the Love of Nature: Ecology and the Cult of the Romantic." *Ecofeminism: Women, Animals, Nature*, Temple University Press, 1993, pp. 219–242, p. 227.
  Chaia Heller is the author of 'The Ecology of Everyday Life: Rethinking the Desire for Nature.' In her essay here Heller explores the domination and romanticization of women and nature, the use of this devise to rationalize domination, and the reflection away from inciting action on this patriarchal crisis. While much of her thinking is a renunciation of eco-patriarchy, she cites from Bookchin, advocating for ecology and society.
2. Dupont, Nicolas. Personal communication, 22 Jan. 2020.
  Dupont is a late 1980's European animalist gnostic.
3. Martins, Ricardo. Personal communication, 19 Jan. 2020.
  Martins is an author and editor on indigenous topics, and founder of a small eco-anarchist collective.
4. Montana, Ria. "Us Before Cave Art." *Vegan Primitivist*, 16 Sept. 2017, https://veganprimitivist.wordpress.com/2017/09/16/us-before-cave-art/
  Schooling is a main mechanism of indoctrination into civilization. The essay "Us Before Cave Art" is a speculative exercise comparing two hypothetical children, one born in a civilized setting, one primitive, exploring the process that separates or strengthens the intrinsic self connecting with wildness. It finds that mechanisms of civilization only allow for its repetition. In ecology there is no need for contrived, forced learning, as all animals, including humans, instinctively self learn what they need to survive and thrive. To maintain civilization, methodology schemes are essential to supplant organic human lifeways with civilized mindsets instilled with civilizing concepts and narratives that disconnect humans from growing wild attachments through free living.
5. Flower Bomb. Personal communication, 10 Nov 2019.
  Flower Bomb is a nihilist, individualist anarchist who has written personal texts on queer nihilism, anti-civ veganism, straight edge/radical sobriety, and social war.
6. Toynbee, Arnold Joseph. *Mankind and Mother Earth. A Narrative History of the World*. Oxford University Press, Incorporated, 1984.
  Toynbee was a history scholar, researcher, philosopher and prolific author of numerous books, well-read in many languages. He was renowned for his 12-volume A Study of History (1934–1961). He served many posts, including his 1919 appointment to professor of Byzantine and modern Greek studies at the University of London. Historians developed a disdain for his telling of myths, allegories, and religion over factual data. His critics argued that his conclusions are more of a Christian moralist rather than a historian.
  In his examination of the rise and fall of civilizations, he concluded civilizations arose in response to some set of challenges of extreme difficulty, when "creative minorities" devised solutions that reoriented their entire society. Challenges and

responses were physical, as when the Sumerians exploited the swamps of southern Iraq by organizing the Neolithic inhabitants in capable of carrying out large-scale irrigation projects... When a civilization responded to challenges, it grew. Civilizations disintegrate when their leaders stopped responding creatively, and the civilizations then sank in nationalism, militarism, and the tyranny of a despotic minority... Toynbee believed that societies always die from suicide or murder rather than from natural causes, and nearly always from suicide. He sees the growth and decline of civilizations as a spiritual process.

7. Perlman, Fredy. "Against His-story, Against Leviathan" *The Anarchist Library*, 1983.

https://theanarchistlibrary.org/library/fredy-perlman-against-his-story-against-leviathan

Against His-story, Against Leviathan, Fredy Perlman's most known book, critiques civilization at its origins focusing on not the man vs nature dichotomy, but the spiritual and ethos shift that manifested man's destruction of nature. The story borrows from others' stories to tell of Mesopotamian zeks transformed by a type of rust on the biosphere, a rust called civilization, unwittingly birthing anarcho-primitivist thought, an inspiration for anti-civilization and rewilding perspectives such as that of John Zerzan's. Perlman never embraced the story's implied ideological stance of anarcho-primitivism, yet believed wildness to be hiding in plain sight as here and now.

8. Ibid.

9. Huxley, Aldous. *Ape and Essence*. Heron Books, 1968.

Ape and Essence is a sardonic commentary on society, philosophy, science, nationalism, fear, industrialism, the myth of progress, and humans' ecological destruction. It is a triumph of the animal we carry within over the rational, serving as a warning on the progression of technology. It's interesting to note that Huxley was a vegetarian from 1945 until his death.

10. Ryan, Christopher. *Civilized to Death: The Price of Progress*. Avid Reader Press, 2019, p. 87.

This book is a perfect example of building a solid anti-civ case, but retreating from its natural conclusion in the end, that of a return to uncivilived. In this case Ryan eloquently illuminates the disaster of civilization, but holds on to human supremacy over all, on the final page concluding, "A movement to redesign the human zoo to reflect the origins and nature of Homo sapiens would represent a second, more brilliant Enlightenment, built to resonate with a more distant past." p. 252

11. Dennis, Stephen G. *Homo Dominus: a Theory of Human Evolution*. IUniverse, 2009, p. 3.

Book description: Homo dominus redefines what it means to be human. Starting with the component pieces of human uniqueness-cognition, self-awareness, language, technology, aggression, altruism, culture, the arts, and spirituality-it rebuilds the human species using a new conceptual blueprint. Sure to spark debate, Homo dominus offers a new vision of who we are and how we got here. Author Stephen Dennis draws from neuroscience, paleontology, psychology, and sociobiology to show that the impetus of human evolution is our propensity to control events and their consequences. This means simply that our root operating system is built on actions taken to bring perceptions into line with expectations. A pivotal genetic shift driven by ecological instability in the late Miocene era triggered this evolutionary divergence and propelled us out of apedom. From our hardscrabble origins on the forest margins to our current position of global dominance, Homo dominus recasts traditional human evolutionary theory in terms of basic control theory. It is a powerful organizing principle that puts our past in a new context and projects our future in a new light.

12. AbdelRahim, Layla. *Wild Children-Domesticated Dreams: Civilization and the Birth of Education.* Fernwood Publishing, 2013, p. 40.

Comparative anthropologist Dr. Layla AbdelRahim is an anarcho-primitivist writer and speaker who examines civilization premises and predatory pathologies, proposing a return to the human primate's mutualistic lifeway and frugivore dietway.

"In contrast to wilderness, where presence and empathy are critical for vitality, civilization functions on alienation and absence. This entails physical and emotional absence, but also includes a metaphysical dimension, since technological development is literally linked to death. Namely, the rise of hunting, i.e. killing of others for food…

The creation of distance between the one who inflicts pain and the victim makes it possible for frugivores to switch to serial killing on a regular basis. In this respect, language provides the grammar for ritualized murder. The purpose of language is to generate regularity…In this sense, language differs from communication – which is the foundation of life – in the same way that technology differs from tools. Tools and communication are irregular and respond to the needs of the moment. They do not require a system to ensure standardization and both have an important place in wilderness. Language and technologies, in contrast, are systems that allow a ritualistic behaviour regardless, or even in spite of, need" ("Children's Literature, Domestication, and Social Foundation: Narratives of Civilization and Wilderness", 2015, pp 15-16).

More on her work can be found at http://layla.miltsov.org/

13. Kropotkin, Petr. "Mutual Aid as a Factor in Evolution", 1902 in *The Cry for Justice: An Anthology of the Literature of Social Protest*, Upton Sinclair, The John C. Winston Co, 1915.

"As soon as we study animals — not in laboratories and museums only, but in the forest and prairie, in the steppe and in the mountains — we at once perceive that though there is an immense amount of warfare and extermination going on amidst various species, and especially amidst various classes of animals, there is, at the same time, as much, or perhaps even more, of mutual support, mutual aid, and mutual defence amidst animals belonging to the same species or, at least, to the same society. Sociability is as much a law of nature as mutual struggle. Of course it would be extremely difficult to estimate, however roughly, the relative numerical importance of both these series of facts. But if we resort

to an indirect test, and ask Nature: "Who are the fittest: those who are continually at war with each other, or those who support one another?" we at once see that those animals which acquire habits of mutual aid are undoubtedly the fittest. They have more chances to survive, and they attain, in their respective classes, the highest development and bodily organization."

14. Moore, John. *Anarchy & Ecstasy: Visions of Halcyon Days.* Aporia Press, 1989, pp. 32-3.

Moore interpreted Perlman's zeks as individual inspirations to live free in wildness. He too saw the term 'anarcho-primitivist' as limiting.

"John Moore is a wildly under-valued voice in the realm of anarcho-primitivism most obviously, but also in a vision of anarchy as a flexible, current, non-ideological way of approaching life and thought."

15. Young, Jon, and Dan Gardoqui. *What the Robin Knows: How Birds Reveal the Secrets of the Natural World.* Mariner Books, 2013.

"Jon Young is a nature connection mentor, naturalist, wildlife tracker, peacemaker, author, workshop leader, consultant, sought after public speaker and storyteller. He founded of Wilderness Awareness School. Under the tutelage of Tom Brown Jr., Jon developed a deep connection to the natural world. His learning journey was not easy - most of the lessons were hard-earned through days, weeks, and months of study."

16. Robertson, Jim. *Exposing the Big Game: Living Targets of a Dying Sport.* Earth Books, 2012, p. 39.

Book description: Exposing the Big Game challenges the archaic, yet officially endorsed, viewpoint that the primary value of wildlife in America is to provide cheap entertainment for anyone with a gun and an unwholesome urge to kill. Portraits and portrayals of tolerant bears, loquacious prairie dogs, temperamental wolves, high-spirited ravens and benevolent bison will leave readers with a deeper appreciation of our fellow beings as sovereign individuals, each with their own unique personalities. Above all, this book is a condemnation of violence against animals, both historic and ongoing. It explores the true, sinister motives behind hunting and trapping, dispelling the myths that sportsmen use to justify their brutal acts. Exposing the Big Game takes on hunting and defends the animals with equal passion, while urging us to expand our circle of compassion and reexamine our stance on killing for sport.

17. Suzman, James. *Affluence without Abundance: What We Can Learn from the World's Most Successful Civilisation.* Bloomsbury, 2019, p. 169.

Anthropologist James Suzman has done field work with the Bushmen of Botswana's eastern Kalahari for more than 25 years.

18. Huxley, 1968, p. 68.

19. Merchant, Carolyn. *The Death of Nature: Women, Ecology and the Scientific Revolution.* HarperSan Francisco, 1980.

In Merchant's ecofeminist thesis the shift from enlightenment to the scientific revolution corresponded with a Western ethos shift to a machine-like state that intensified hierarchies rooted in domination over Earth. This shift not only hyper-manipulated and exploited, but killed nature.

20. Bekoff, Marc, and Jessica Pierce. *The Animals Agenda: Freedom, Compassion, and Coexistence in the Human Age*. Beacon Press, 2018.

21. Tokarczuk, Olga, translated by Antonia Lloyd-Jones. *Drive Your Plow over the Bones of the Dead*. Fitzcarraldo Editions, 2019, p. 202.

Olga Tokarczuk is a Polish writer of poetry and literature, an animal rights activist, feminist, public intellectual, and psychologist. She has been described in Poland as one of the most critically acclaimed and commercially successful writers, and as unpatriotic, anti-Christian and a promoter of eco-terrorism.

Drive Your Plow over the Bones is a murder mystery thriller of hunters turning up dead via wild justice.

22. Ibid, p. 155.

23. Sussman, Robert. "The Myth of Man the Hunter/Man the Killer and the Evolution of Human Morality." *The Evolution of Human Behavior: Primate Models*, State Univ of New York Press, 1985, pp. 121–129, p. 128. https://www.unl.edu/rhames/courses/current/readings/sussman.pdf

Anthropologist Sussman analyzise the social constructs of man-the-hunter. Abstract: Since the discovery of the first man-ape, many have assumed that the earliest humans were hunters and that this was associated with a "killer instinct." The myth of "man the hunter" was repeated in the 1960s in anthropology texts and popular literature. In the 1970s it was adopted by sociobiologists to explain human nature. "Man the hunter" is used to explain not only human biology but also human morality.

24. Zerzan, John. *Why Hope? The Stand Against Civilization*. Feral House, 2015, p. 130.

Zerzan lays the foundation for anarcho-primitivism as an anthropological exploration of the origin of division of labor, specialization, domesticating plants and animals, symbolic culture, etc.

"There were choices thousands of generations earlier than these developments, based on an intelligence equal to ours. Paul Tacon is on good grounds to surmise that very early humans (e.g. Homo erectus) probably "questioned their position in the universe." They were far more robust than we are, and recent scholarship has significantly raised estimates of their longevity. Research has also confirmed very early cooking with fire: the appearance of small molars at 1.9 million years ago is evidence of cooked food, compared with the large molars of other primates who spend much more time chewing. And it may not be amiss to bring in Montaigne's sixteenth-century essay, 'Of the Custom of Wearing Clothes', where he observes that people remain who wear none, "situated under much the same sky as ours [France's]. Montaigne found it unhealthy, our practice of being so mediated against the elements, when we "are naturally equipped with sufficient covering…"

JZ is an anarcho-primitivist ecophilosopher, author, speaker, and host of Anarchy Radio. He criticizes agricultural civilization as inherently oppressive, and advocates drawing upon the ways of life of hunter-gatherers as an inspiration for rewilding.

25. Ryan, 2019, p. 87.

26. Scott, James C. *Against the Grain: A Deep History of the Earliest States.* Yale University Press, 2018, p. 13.

Scott is a political scientist and comparative anthropologist focusing on agrarian and non-state societies, subaltern politics, and anarchism. His primary research has centered on peasants of Southeast Asia and their strategies of resistance to various forms of domination.

27. Mason, Sarah L. R., et al. "Preliminary Investigation of the Plant Macro-Remains from Dolní Věstonice II, and Its Implications for the Role of Plant Foods in Palaeolithic and Mesolithic Europe." *Antiquity*, vol. 68, no. 258, 1994, pp. 48–57. Quote from abstract.
doi:10.1017/s0003598x00046184.

28. Collard Andrée, and Joyce Contrucci. *Rape of the Wild: Mans Violence against Animals and the Earth.* Indiana University Press, 1989, p. 41.

Ecofeminists Collard and Contrucci address not just the patriarchal oppression of both women and animals, but also man's destruction of the earth as a whole. While they postulate romantic ideals of early human matriarchal societies living in harmony with Earth, their detailed analysis of later times focuses on animals' individual experiences under human control. They end with their image of the future as a techno-ecocide, patriarchy-prompted human and other species mass extinction.

29. Martins, 2020.

30. Humboldt, Alexander von. *Personal Narrative of a Journey to the Equinoctial Regions of the New Continent during the years 1799–1804.* Translated by Jason Wilson, Penguin, 2006.

Humboldt was touted as the first scientist to 'relate colonialism to the devastation of the environment.' He also said, "Cruelty to animals is one of the most significant vices of a low and ignoble people. Wherever one notices them, they constitute a sure sign of ignorance and brutality which cannot be painted over even by all the evidence of wealth and luxury."

The Ecologist: A Journal for the Post-Industrial Age highlighted writing of Andrea Wulf on Humboltd:"Considered the most famous man of his time after Napoleon he talked and lectured incessantly holding entire rooms captive for hours...

First and foremost he adored scientific field work, particularly botany and geology although his masterstroke was to see "this great chain of causes and effects" that connect diverse natural phenomena and to conceive of the concept of the web of life.

His first major expedition began in 1799 when he managed to buy a place on a Spanish ship heading to its Latin American colonies. He stuffed his allocated space under his hammock with the world's most cutting-edge scientific instruments including a barometer, cyanometer and sextant.

He would be gone for five years fearlessly pushing himself and his loyal companions to extremes to learn what he could of uncharted natural systems. Wulf describes Humboldt and his team climbing Mount Chimborazo:

"At 18,000 feet they saw a last scrap of lichen clinging to a boulder. After that all signs of organic life disappeared, because at that height there were no

plants or insects... No one had ever climbed this high before... As he stood on top of the world, looking down upon the mountain ranges folded beneath him, Humboldt began to see the world differently. He saw the Earth as one great living organism where everything was connected, conceiving a bold new vision of nature that still influences the way that we understand the natural world."
https://theecologist.org/2016/mar/03/invention-nature-adventures-alexander-humboldt-lost-hero-science

31. Dupont, 2020.
32. Montana, Ria. "Anarcho-Primachismo: Primitivism Or Patriarchy?" *Vegan Primitivist*, 19 June 2019.
veganprimitivist.wordpress.com/2019/06/01/anarcho-primachismo-primitivism-or-patriarchy/
33. Cartmill, Matt. *A View to a Death in the Morning: Hunting and Nature through History.* Harvard University Press, 1996, p. 30.
*   Biological anthropologist Cartmill offers an expansive cultural history of evolving practices and views of hunting and humans' relationship with nature.*
34. Ibid, p. 30.
35. Adorno, Theodor. "Wozu noch Philosophie? [Why still philosophy?]," 1963, *Critical Models,* 1998, p. 7.
*   Theodor Adorno was a critical philosopher focused on human suffering—especially in modern society. Oppression is created through politics, economics, culture, and materialism, but is maintained most through consciousness. Therefore the focus of action must come from consciousness.*
36. Barnes, Simon. *Rewild Yourself: Making Nature More Visible in Our Lives.* Pegasus Books, 2019.
*   Back cover: For those readers who want to get closer to the nature all around them and bring it back into focus within their lives, this book is the ideal companion.*
We're not just losing the wild world. We're forgetting it. We're no longer noticing it. We've lost the habit of looking and seeing and listening and hearing.
But we can make hidden things visible, and this book features numerous spellbinding ways to bring the magic of nature much closer to home.
Mammals you never knew existed will enter your world. Birds hidden in treetops will shed their cloak of anonymity. With a single movement of your hand you can make reptiles appear before you. Butterflies you never saw before will bring joy to every sunny day. Creatures of the darkness will enter your consciousness. And as you take on new techniques and a little new equipment, you will discover new creatures and, with them, new areas of yourself that had gone dormant. Once put to use, they wake up and start working again. You become wilder in your mind and in your heart. Once you know the tricks, the wild world begins to appear before you.
37. Corby, Rachel. *ReWild Yourself: Becoming Nature.* Amanita Forrest Press, 2015.
*   Back cover: Over the last millennia or so, as humanity has become more civilised, humankind has found itself increasingly removed from its own innate*

wildness. At the same time society has found itself beset with ever greater incidences of mental illness, stress, depression and antisocial behaviour. In Rewild Yourself: Becoming Nature Rachel Corby addresses the longing search for meaning, what she calls the dark cries of the soul, that have emerged alongside the human-nature disconnect. Rachel writes with a passion and a deep love for the wild. In developing ones senses and natural instincts she invites you to join her in finding ways to redress the balance. She encourages you to find the wild place inside and overcome a little of your own domestication, to rebuild connections and communications with nature allowing for a free-flow between the wildness of the world and your wild heart. Considering many aspects of our modern lives, this book offers a path which leads to a personal and cultural transformation; a future where there is space for the wild to grow.

38. Baker, Nick. *Rewild: The Art of Returning to Nature.* White Lion Pub, 2020.

As our busy, technology-driven lives become more sedentary we have become less connected to our natural surroundings. In these challenging times, it is by rediscovering our links to the world around us that we can rekindle the natural, human connection we have to the wild.

Nick Baker introduces rewilding as a concept that needs to be established at a personal level. Taking the reader back to their natural sensitivities, we rediscover the instinctive potential of our senses. From learning to observe the creatures and beasts within hands' reach and seeing and hearing the birds and trees of our forests, Baker's expert advice offers the practical tools to experience the wilderness on your own doorstep, as well as in the wider, wilder world.

ReWild mixes memoir with practical advice, to delight, inform and inspire us all to discover the art of returning to nature.

39. Gooley, Tristan. *The Lost Art of Reading Natures Signs: Use Outdoor Clues to Find Your Way, Predict the Weather, Locate Water, Track Animals--and Other Forgotten Skills.* The Experiment, 2015.

Back cover: When writer and navigator Tristan Gooley journeys outside, he sees a natural world filled with clues. The roots of a tree indicate the sun's direction; the Big Dipper tells the time; a passing butterfly hints at the weather; a sand dune reveals prevailing wind; the scent of cinnamon suggests altitude; a budding flower points south. To help you understand nature as he does, Gooley shares more than 850 tips for forecasting, tracking, and more, gathered from decades spent walking the landscape around his home and around the world. Whether you're walking in the country or city, along a coastline, or by night, this is the ultimate resource on what the land, sun, moon, stars, plants, animals, and clouds can reveal—if you only know how to look!

40. Liedloff, Jean. *The Continuum Concept.* Penguin, 2009, pp. 92-3.

During a fluke diamond-hunting expedition to Venezuela, Jean came into contact with the Yequana. She became fascinated with them and decided to live with them. Based on these experiences, she wrote The Continuum Concept to describe her new understanding of how modern humans have lost much of our natural well-being, and to show practical ways to regain, particularly for children, an attached style of child-rearing. She was a founding member of The Ecologist magazine.

41. Bickle, Penny, and Linda Fibiger. "Ageing, Childhood and Social Identity in the Early Neolithic of Central Europe." *European Journal of Archaeology*, vol. 17, no. 2, 2014, pp. 208–228, doi:10.1179/1461957114y.0000000052.

42. Jones, Pattrice. *Aftershock: Confronting Trauma in a Violent World: a Guide for Activists and Their Allies.* Lantern Books, 2007, pp. 172-3.

"Pattrice is an ecofeminist writer, educator, and activist. She is the co-founder of VINE Sanctuary in Springfield, Vermont, an LGBTQ-run farmed animal sanctuary. "pattrice jones sets the stage to begin healing the trauma associated with not just resisting oppression and injustice, but having to experience it. She offers real steps toward recognizing and correcting the problems facing humans, our planet and our animal relations. This book is a light in the dark for those of us who have dared to challenge the status quo." —Jeffrey "Free" Luers, Imprisoned Eco-Activist"

43. Mandeville, Bernard. *The Carnivorous Custom and Human Vanity: The Fable of the Bees; or, Private Vices*, Publick Benefits, vol. 1, Oxford, 1705, pp. 172-181. http://www.animal-rights-library.com/texts-c/mandeville01.htm

44. Heller, 1993, p. 219.

45. Ibid, p. 220.

46. Ibid, p. 235, 239.

47. Livingston, John A. *Rogue Primate: An Exploration of Human Domestication.* Rinehart Publishers, 1994, p. 176.

Livingston reviewed origins of and sinking dependence on human's increasingly calamitous Great Leap Forward of inventiveness, language, abstract thinking, controlled fire and hunting. The clever human apes inadvertently decimated and domesticated other species, including themselves. As with Daniel Quinn and Adorno, he positions the root of the problem in mindsets malleable to change, including the notion of human superiority.

2 ORIGINS OF RATIONALIZING

1. Livingstone, David. *Missionary Travels and Researches in South Africa.* National Trust for Scotland, 2013, pp. 562-3.

"Includes Sketchings of Sixteen Years' Residence in the Interior of Africa, and a Journey from the Cape of Good Hope to Loanda on the West Coast, Thence Across the Continent, Down the River Zambesi, to the Eastern Ocean. London: John Murray, 1857."

2. Damro, Kenneth. *A Northwoodsman's Guide to Everyday Compassion.* Wingspan Press, 2006, p. 51.

Bird enthusiast and outdoorsman Kenneth Damro reveals animal (human and non) realities of modern hunting culture, sharing the logical and emotional reasons he turned from avid hunter to vegan. Ken was interviewed in the documentary "On The Wild Side", on his perspective for the anti-hunting movement.

3. Shepard, Paul. *The Tender Carnivore and the Sacred Game.* Scribners, 1973, p. 173.

Environmentalist and professor of nature philosophy and human ecology Paul Shepard was an influential and profoundly original thinker in evolutionary theory and developmental psychology. He critiqued civilization juxtaposed primitivism, advocated a return to mystical prehistoric hunting, and spurred Deep Ecology. His books were candy reinforcement to anarcho-primitivism, including The Tender Carnivore and the Sacred Game, Thinking Animals, Coming Home to the Pleistocene, and Nature and Madness His main theme is that the essence of human nature evolved during the Pleistocene, and domestication caused today's ecological and social deterioration. Perhaps the only philosopher to have focused fully and directly on how human development relies on the natural environment and how culture facilitates or disrupts this process, he explores how and theorized that humans are evolutionarily dependent on sustained contact with nature for emotional and psychological growth and maturity.

4. Collard and Contrucci, 1989, p. 52.

5. Ardrey, Robert, and Berdine Ardrey. *African Genesis: a Personal Investigation into the Animal Origins and Nature of Man.* Story Design Limited, 2014.

In the end science screenwriter and anthropologist Ardrey concluded that what he and Dart had written in the late 1950s had been warped by a 'weapon fixation'. "These were Cold War years dominated by our fears concerning the ultimate weapon. Like Dart, I was preoccupied by the implications of the hypothesis in terms of our ancient dependence on the weapon." pp. 13-14.

6. Hart, Donna, and Robert W. Sussman. *Man the Hunted: Primates, Predators, and Human Evolution.* Westview Press, 2005, pp. 23-29.

"Man the Hunted" is an anthropology classic in redressing Dart's Man-the-Hunter mythology, laying out evidence of early humans being prey of various other animals longer than humans have hunted.
Dart's famous 1924 "Taung baby" discovery which Dart evidenced as proof of 'man the killer ape' is found instead to have been the prey of a large proto-eagle, with typical "can opener" marks of eagle talons on Taung's skull. "The evidence to support a Man the Hunter hypothesis has been, and continues to be, very weak. Raymond Dart based his "killer-ape" hunting theory on the holes and dents in some fossil australopithecine skulls that he conjectured were the murderous actions of fellow hominids. But we now know these holes and dents were undoubtedly caused by the fangs of predators and the processes of fossilization." p. 220.

7. Spikins, Penny. *How Compassion Made Us Human: the Evolutionary Origins of Tenderness, Trust and Morality.* Pen & Sword Archaeology, 2015, pp. 24-28.

Archaeologist Penny Spikins makes the case that the feeling and ethos of care is central to what made Homo 'human'. Her review of paleo-artifacts interprets and re-interprets how social emotions and organization evolved with and for compassion.

Spikins sums up the cultural bias behind Dart's erroneous 'killer ape' theory as "A tendency to see what we think ought to be there was perhaps never best illustrated..." p. 24.

8. Kover, T.R. "Of Killer Apes and Tender Carnivores." *Studies in Religion/Sciences Religieuses,* vol. 46, no. 4, 2017, pp. 536–567, doi:10.1177/0008429817735302.

Shepard's view is that "far from producing a "killer ape," the evolutionary transition of early hominids into a predatory niche resulted in a "tender carnivore" with an increased capacity for empathy with other humans and animals."

9. Braudy, Leo. *From Chivalry to Terrorism: War and the Changing Nature of Masculinity.* Vintage Books, 2005.

Cultural historian Braudy lays out an expansive study of war covering the last 2,500 years centering on the shifting facades of 'masculinity'. He explores how this shift is tied to a culture's defense, colonizing adventures, and pathological leaders, detailing the effect on society.

10. Collard and Contrucci,1989.

11. Ehrenreich, Barbara. *Blood Rites: Origins and History of the Passions of War.* Grand Central Publishing, 2020.

In this researched exposition on the origins of war, social critic Ehrenreich posits that earliest humans were a prey species. When shifting from prey to predator small bands re-enacted the trauma of being prey in sacrificial blood rites. By onset of agricultural, humans had hunted into extinction vast numbers of large species. Men shifted from hunters to warriors, initially capturing others for blood rites and slavery. War evolved as a central theme of modern human lifeway.

12. Flower Bomb. "Vegan Means Attack: Fomenting A Wildfire Against Speciesism and Moral Anthropocentrism" *The Anarchist Library.* https://theanarchistlibrary.org/library/Flower-bomb-vegan-means-attack

13. Turnbull, Colin M. *The Mountain People.* Simon & Schuster, 2007.

Colin was an anthropologist and ethnographer who became well known with his idealized, portrayal of the Mbuti Pygmies in The Forest People. Ten years later, he wrote an antithetical book, The Mountain People, about Uganda's starving Ik tribe. He advocated that the Ik, for their own good, should be relocated in small groups of less than ten, in distances so far from each other that their culture would collapse and be destroyed, although later he acknowledged his own inability to see their humanity. Turnbull was highly controversial, with a passion for involvement with his subjects rather than practicing conventional scientific objectivity. His work led to debate on the value of ethnography as a scientific discipline.

14. Shepard, Paul. *The Others: How Animals Made Us Human.* Island Press, 1997, p. 9.

15. Conrad Justice Kiczenski. Personal communication, 24 Aug. 2019.

Kiczenski wild tends and wild seed propagates continuing earlier human lifeways.

16. Melamed, Yoel, et al. "The Plant Component of an Acheulian Diet at Gesher Benot Ya'Aqov, Israel." *Proceedings of the National Academy of Sciences*, vol. 113, no. 51, May 2016, pp. 14674–14679, doi:10.1073/pnas.1607872113.

17. Barras, Colin. "Ancient Leftovers Show the Real Paleo Diet Was a Veggie Feast." *New Scientist*, 5 Dec. 2016. https://www.newscientist.com/article/2115127-ancient-leftovers-show-the-real-paleo-diet-was-a-veggie-feast/

18. Wadley, Lyn, et al. "Cooked Starchy Rhizomes in Africa 170 Thousand Years Ago." *Science*, vol. 367, no. 6473, Feb. 2020, pp. 87–91, doi:10.1126/science.aaz5926.

19. "Earliest Roasted Root Vegetables Found in 170,000-Year-Old Cave Dirt." *New Scientist*, 2 Jan 2020. https://www.newscientist.com/article/2228880-earliest-roasted-root-vegetables-found-in-170000-year-old-cave-dirt/#ixzz69z24y5FA

20. Spikins, Penny, et al. "From Homininity to Humanity: Compassion from the Earliest Archaics to Modern Humans." *Time and Mind*, vol. 3, no. 3, 2010, pp. 303–325, doi:10.2752/175169610x12754030955977.

21. Spinkins, 2015.

22. Robinson, Kirk. "A Philosophical Critique of the North American Model of Wildlife Conservation." *Rewilding*, 26 Jan. 2020.
Kirk Robinson is a professor of philosophy, founder and executive director of the Western Wildlife Conservancy, interviewed on Rewilding Podcast, https://rewilding.org/episode-37-kirk-robinson-on-state-wildlife-governance-and-the-north-american-model-of-wildlife-conservation/

23. Tokarczuk, 2019, p. 22.

24. "The Real Reason Humans Have Those Sharp Front Teeth." *Science Insider,* YouTube, 27 Apr. 2019. https://www.youtube.com/watch?v=Fu3AGteE210

25. Robinson, Joshua R., et al. "Late Pliocene Environmental Change during the Transition from Australopithecus to Homo." *Nature Ecology & Evolution*, vol. 1, no. 6, 2017, doi:10.1038/s41559-017-0159.
Archaeologist Robinson's study finds environmental conditions at the origins of Homo were similar to earlier ancestors, "indicating that the emergence of Homo from Australopithecus did not involve a dietary shift" Analysis of an early Homo jawbone from Ledi-Geraru in the lower Awash Valley of Ethiopia dated 2.8 million years ago indicates a diet similar to Australopithecus afarensis Lucy 3.2 million years ago.

26. Faurby, Søren, et al. "Brain Expansion in Early Hominins Predicts Carnivore Extinctions in East Africa." *Ecology Letters*, 2020, doi:10.1111/ele.13451.
Astract: ...We test this using the East African carnivore fossil record. We analyse the diversity of carnivores over the last four million years and investigate whether any decline is related to an increase in hominin cognitive capacity, vegetation changes or climatic changes. We find that extinction rates in large carnivores correlate with increased hominin brain size and with vegetation changes, but not with precipitation or temperature changes. While temporal analyses cannot distinguish between the effects of vegetation changes and hominins, we show through spatial analyses of contemporary carnivores in

Africa that only hominin causation is plausible. Our results suggest that substantial anthropogenic influence on biodiversity started millions of years earlier than currently assumed.

27. Briggs, Helen. "Human Impact on Nature 'Dates Back Millions of Years'." *BBC News*, 20 Jan. 2020. www.bbc.com/news/science-environment-51068816?fbclid=IwAR0CNooBYC-NWM-Jv0tdhW9Tm3LixsqqvqkpAOBOWdiTpZa4nEPtQDxanhE

28. Hardy, Karen, et al. "The Importance of Dietary Carbohydrate in Human Evolution." *The Quarterly Review of Biology,* vol. 90, no. 3, 2015, pp. 251–268, doi:10.1086/682587.

29. Thompson, Jessica C., et al. "Origins of the Human Predatory Pattern: The Transition to Large-Animal Exploitation by Early Hominins." *Current Anthropology*, vol. 60, no. 1, Feb. 2019, pp. 1–23, doi:10.1086/701477.

Jessica C. Thompson (anthropologist), Susana Carvalho (cognitive and evolutionary anthropologist), Curtis W. Marean (professor of human evolution and social change), and Zeresenay Alemseged (professor of organismal biology and anatomy):

"We argue that concepts of meat-eating and tool use are too loosely defined: outside-bone nutrients (e.g., meat) and inside-bone nutrients (e.g., marrow and brains) have different macronutrient characteristics (protein vs. fat), mechanical requirements for access (cutting vs. percussion), search, handling and competitive costs, encounter rates, and net returns. Thus, they would have demanded distinct technological and behavioral solutions. We propose that the regular exploitation of large-animal resources—the "human predatory pattern"—began with an emphasis on percussion-based scavenging of inside-bone nutrients, independent of the emergence of flaked stone tool use."

30. Briggs, 2020.

31. Moore, 1989, pp. 53-4, 58, 62.

32. Spikins, 2015, pp. 66-7.

33. Spikins, Penny. "Goodwill Hunting? Debates over the 'Meaning' of Lower Palaeolithic Handaxe Form Revisited." *World Archaeology*, vol. 44, no. 3, 2012, pp. 378–392, doi:10.1080/00438243.2012.725889.

34. Long, TJ. Personal communication, 28 Nov 2019.

TJ Long is a raw fruitarian.

35. Ibid.

36. Whiten, Andrew, and David Erdal. "The Human Socio-Cognitive Niche and Its Evolutionary Origins." *Philosophical Transactions of the Royal Society B: Biological Sciences*, vol. 367, no. 1599, May 2012, pp. 2119–2129, doi:10.1098/rstb.2012.0114. https://royalsocietypublishing.org/doi/full/10.1098/rstb.2012.0114

37. Spikins, 2015, pp. 182-3.

38. Ibid, p. 175.

39. Power, Camilla. "Gender Egalitarianism vs Patriarchy Theory." *Freedom News*, 28 Jan. 2019. https://freedomnews.org.uk/gender-egalitarianism-vs-patriarchy-theory/

Evolutionary anthropologist Camilla Power has published many articles on evolutionary origins of ritual, gender and the use of cosmetics in African initiation. Her current interest is origins of religion, Neanderthal symbolic revolution, grandmothers and cooperative breeding, kinship and Hadza women's ritual. She may be considered a radical anthropologist.

40. Spikins, 2015, p. 146.

41. Aubert, Maxime, et al. "Earliest Hunting Scene in Prehistoric Art." *Nature,* Dec 2019, doi.org/10.1038/s41586-0198-1806-y.

42. de Waal, Frans. *The Bonobo and the Atheist.* W.W. Norton & Company, 2014.

As a Professor in a Department of Psychology, primatologist de Waal's observations of empathy and care make the case for evolutionary biological origins of human fairness that emphasizes human connection with other animals through natural instincts for cooperation and empathy.

43. Tweet, #SIBERIAISBURNING, 2019.

44. Honan, Kim, et al. "'Screaming Animals in Pain': Beekeepers Traumatised as They Check on Hives after Fires." *ABC News*, 20 Nov. 2019. https://www.abc.net.au/news/2019-11-20/beekeepers-traumatised-by-screaming-animals-after-bushfires/11721756?pfmredir=sm&fbclid=IwAR1OO0VoOYBCluL2OkdAqD7_XHH3jo3TBYLVfeRfO_dxgnkXYsWY4zKHBvo

45. Wiber, Melanie. *Erect Men/ Undulating Women: the Visual Imagery of Gender, Race and Progress in Reconstructive Illustrations of Human Evolution.* W. Laurier U.P., Canada, 1999.

Based on intensive study of human origin illustrations, responses from students and colleagues, and research into reconstructive illustration and feminist criticism of Western art, Wiber traces the subtle ways paleoanthropological conventions have influenced and shifted in the creation of illustrations. Wiber reveals that embedded meanings in these illustrations go beyond gender to include two other ubiquitous themes--racial superiority and upward cultural progress. Underlying all these themes, she finds a basic conservatism in the paleoanthropological approach to evolutionary theory.

46. Luke, Brian. "Taming Ourselves or Going Feral?: Toward a Nonpatriarchal Metaethic of Animal Liberation." *Animals & Women: Feminist Explorations*, Duke University Press, 1995, pp. 290-319, doi.org/10.1215/9780822381952-013.

"So long as we remain committed to animal liberation, yet also see the direct sympathetic responsiveness of individual humans to animal suffering as undependable, we will be drawn toward authoritarian structures that promise this taming, through the domination of emotion by reason, selfishness by patriarchal ethics, and people by political authorities and their philosophical advisors." *Luke contends that humans override their innate interspecies empathy on three fronts: denying personal responsibility, denying the harm done, and objectification of animals.*

47. Collard and Contrucci, 1989, p. 33.

48. Spikins, 2015, p. 37.

49. Gero, Joan M., and Margaret W. Conkey, *Engendering Archaeology: Women and Prehistory*. Blackwell, 2002.
Gero was an archaeologist and pioneer of feminist archaeology. She focused on early human gender and power issues in studies with contemporary indigenous peoples of the Andean regions of Argentina and Peru.
50. Jensen, Derrick, "'If We Wish to Stop the Atrocities, We Need Merely to Step Away from the Isolation. There Is a Whole World Waiting for Us, Ready to Welcome Us Home." https://www.derrickjensen.org/endgame/too-much-to-lose/
Derrick Jensen is a Deep Ecology environmental activist, writer, and leader of Deep Green Resistance (DGR), a leftist environmentalist project co-founded with Lierre Keith. Keith, an ardent trans-exclusionary radical feminist (TERF) famous for excluding trans women and specious nutrition science throughout her book, The Vegetarian Myth.
51. Spikins, 2015, p. 164.

3 HUNTING AS TRANSITORY

1. Taylor, Timothy. *The Artificial Ape: How Technology Changed the Course of Human Evolution*. Palgrave Macmillan, 2010, pp. 18-9.
Archaeologist and anthropologist Timothy Taylor explains how an early human artefact explains human evolution and led to "survival of the weakest" https://www.newscientist.com/article/mg20727741-700-artificial-ape-man-how-technology-created-humans/#ixzz64zdkmUb8
2. Damro, 2006, pp. 11-52, p. 16.
3. Williams, Joy. "The Killing Game: Why the American Hunter Is Bloodthirsty, Piggish, and Grossly Incompetent." *Esquire*, 1 Oct. 1990. https://classic.esquire.com/article/1990/10/1/the-killing-game
4. Mason, Jim. *An Unnatural Order: Why We Are Destroying the Planet and Each Other,* The Continuum Publishing Company, 1998, p. 116.
In the chapter "Animals: The Most Moving Things in the World." pp. 91–117 psychiatrist Stephen Katcher and others find that humans have fundamental feelings and empathy for animals possibly stemming from human instinct for nurturing and social bonding. p. 95. Mason posits this human instinct is impaired due to conditioning in utilitarian culture. p. 100. Mason disagrees with Shepard's interpretation of adults hiding animal killing and war from children as giving an idealized view of nature. Mason says "We have long been ill at ease with human-animal killing, and we have hidden, disguised, ritualized, rationalized, and ideologized it – pardon the expression – to death throughout the ages." p. 105. Mason sees hiding killing from children then exposing it to them later as an "implanting process" and as possible "child abuse – emotional, psychic, and possibly cultural abuse." p. 106. Primal Guilt and Ritual Atonement are covered pp 109-11.
5. Benítez-López, Ana, et al. "Intact but Empty Forests? Patterns of Hunting-Induced Mammal Defaunation in the Tropics."
PLOS Biology, vol. 17, no. 5, 2019, doi:10.1371/journal.pbio.3000247.

"The pervasive effects of overhunting on tropical mammal populations may have profound ramifications for ecosystem functioning and the livelihoods of wild-meat-dependent communities, and underscore that forest coverage alone is not necessarily indicative of ecosystem intactness."

6. IUCN Red List. "Unsustainable Fishing and Hunting for Bushmeat Driving Iconic Species to Extinction – IUCN Red List." *IUCN Red List*, 18 July 2019. https://www.iucn.org/news/species/201907/unsustainable-fishing-and-hunting-bushmeat-driving-iconic-species-extinction-iucn-red-list

"Overfishing has pushed two families of rays to the brink of extinction, while hunting for bushmeat and habitat loss have led to the decline of seven primate species, according to the latest update of The IUCN Red List of Threatened Species. "

7. Hance, Jeremy. "How Laos Lost Its Tigers." *Mongabay Environmental News*, 7 Nov. 2019. https://news.mongabay.com/2019/10/how-laos-lost-its-tigers/?fbclid=IwAR3IBGtv91-h03jrOgPu4EcdvT8nzN8ehi7JWkXUiawFtVoj94ueWH43N5g

The last tiger in Lao PDR likely died in terrible anguish. Its foot caught in a snare, the animal probably died of dehydration. Or maybe, in a desperate bid to free itself from a snare crafted from a simple and cheap motorbike cable, it tore off a leg and died from the blood loss. Perhaps the Indochinese tiger (Panthera tigris corbetti), a distinct subspecies, was able to free itself from the snare, only to have the wound fester and kill it in the end. Or, and this isn't impossible either, the last tiger of Lao PDR (or Laos) was simply shot to death by poachers who then butchered its body and sold its parts in the illegal trafficking trade to feed a seemingly insatiable demand for tiger bits and bones for sham medicine or status symbols.

However it died, it probably wasn't peaceful.

A new paper in Global Conservation and Ecology finds that the last tigers of Laos vanished shortly after 2013 from Nam Et-Phou Louey National Protected Area. And the scientists believe it was most likely a surge in snaring that did them in, despite large-scale investments in the park, relative to the region. With the loss of tigers in Laos's largest protected area, the tiger is most likely extinct in Laos, as it probably is in both Cambodia and Vietnam.

...And the tiger isn't the only victim: the researchers also believe Indochinese leopards (Panthera pardus delacouri) are extinct in Laos now, wiped out from Nam Et-Phou Louey and other protected areas by the same snaring crisis.

This tragedy is simply another sign of industrial-scale "empty forest" syndrome across Southeast Asia, as poachers with guns and snares continue to wipe out animal populations, targeting anything the size of a mouse or sparrow and larger.

...Tigers are massive, easily distinguished from other animals, tend to use well-trodden paths, and cover huge areas of territory, making photographing them far easier than many other more cryptic species on camera.

The only other place in Laos tigers were thought to maybe persist was Nakai-Nam Thuem National Biodiversity Conservation Area.

"Recent camera trapping in Nakai-Nam Thuen suggests that tiger, leopard, clouded leopard, and golden cats have now been extirpated from this protected area," said a conservationist who spoke on the condition of anonymity.

So, tigers are very likely gone from Laos, just as they have recently been wiped out from Cambodia and Vietnam. Given all the attention and money for tigers, how did this happen?

Again.

What the #!*&*$ happened?

Jessica Hartel, the director of the Kibale Snare Removal Program in Uganda, told me in 2015 that snares are "the landmines of the forest."

"Like landmines, snares do not discriminate, are virtually undetectable, and can cause irreversible permanent physical damage within a split second," she said.

"Like landmines, snares are unforgiving death traps that cause pain, suffering, and mutilation. Like landmines, snares are detonated automatically by way of pressure from the animals stepping into or through it."

And big cats like tigers and leopards are "particularly vulnerable to snaring," says Jan Kamler, co-author of the recent study also with WildCRU — even if snares are mostly set for bushmeat animals, such as deer and wild pigs.

"[Tigers and leopards] occur at relatively low densities to begin with (compared to prey species), and they have the widest ranging movements of all species," Kamler wrote to me. "Consequently, even if snaring is stopped within a protected area, as long as snaring occurs along the boundary, then tiger and leopard populations may ultimately become extirpated."

With only a handful of tigers left to begin with, it only takes a few encounters with snares to kill off an entire population. Ditto for leopards."

8. McKibbin, Phillip. "But What about Boil up? How Māori Are Embracing Veganism." *The Spinoff*, 16 Nov. 2018.
https://thespinoff.co.nz/atea/16-11-2018/but-what-about-boil-up-how-maori-are-embracing-veganism/

9. Robinson, Margaret. ELK, Earthling Liberation Kollective -. "Margaret Robinson - Indigenous Veganism: Feminist Natives Eat Tofu – Human Rights Are Animal Rights." *YouTube,* 10 June 2014.
ww.youtube.com/watch?v=ahD6uz1mYJA

Margaret Robinson is a Mi'kmaq feminist Dalhousie University professor and activist noted for her research on sexuality, specifically bisexuality, sexual and gender minority people's experiences of mental health and Indigenous health. Earthling Liberation Kollective – ELK: "ELK is intended to exist as a grassroots, community collective composed of people following these 3 agreements: 1. We envision the radical goal of total liberation for all species. This means we promote anti-oppressive community empowerment and species-inclusive social justice for humans & non-humans alike. 2. We manifest this radical goal through transformative justice. This means we are creating and supporting solutions that both address underlying cycles of violence and which offer potential to collectively transform our communities away from dependencies of violence against all humans, animals, and our Earth. 3. We reject single-issue, superficial, inaccessible, tokenizing and otherwise non-

intersectional responses to the oppression of humans, animals and our Earth. This means we do not support or make space for any & all efforts that ignore, dismiss or simply fail to account for the complexities of power and privilege."
https://humanrightsareanimalrights.com/about-elk/

10. Robinson, Margaret and Michael Sizer. "Dr. Margaret Robinson at the AR Academy." *YouTube,* 22 Feb. 2014.
www.youtube.com/watch?v=8t2mK92H63E

11. Robinson, 2014.

12. Laws, Rita. "Choctaw Nation – a (Mainly) Vegetarian Tribe." *The Lotus Post*, 13 Jan. 2019.
https://www.thelotuspost.com/choctaw-nation-a-mainly-vegetarian-tribe/

Rita Laws is Choctaw and Cherokee. She lives and writes in Oklahoma. Her Choctaw name, Hina Hanta, means Bright Path of Peace, which is what she considers vegetariansim to be.

13. Montana, Rio. Personal observation, 2019.

During a 2008 stay with the Pemón people of southeast Venezuela in the Gran Sabana, between jungle edge and tepui flat-topped mountains, this essay's author notes that children did not eat meat and on rare occasion adults ate meat, moreso men. When the chief learned this author was vegan, he told her "You are closer to the gods." It was later learned that, while most missionaries of the region were Catholic, the missionary that stayed with these people was a Seventh Day Adventist who preached the sacredness of meatless life. Since the missionaries left many years ago, local spiritualism blended with colonizer religious mythologies. Still, the same dietary practice existed amongst neighboring Pemón people whose missionaries were meat eating Catholics.

14. Fisher, Linda. "On the 'Right to Hunt' by a Native American Vegan." *Scavenger,* www.thescavenger.net/social-justice-sp-24912/animals/768-on-the-right-to-hunt-by-a-native-american-vegan.html

Linda Fisher is an "animal communicator, vegan activist and artist Linda G. Fisher, of Ojibway and Cherokee heritage and a tribal member of the Ojibway Nation.

Linda sees through the eyes of an animal and feels interconnectedness with all life saying,"I have had a passion for animals, the natural world, and art, since I was old enough to hold a crayon. It was during those very early years that my psychic abilities and deeper understanding of animals became apparent. Upon reaching adulthood, my Ojibwa/Cherokee mother fondly called me Gizhaadamokwe (Guardian Spirit Woman). What I understood about the feelings of animals prompted me to become a voice to protect them."

As an animal communicator, Linda "sees" the primal essence of an animal and conveys that information to the animal caretakers in an effort to help them better understand their animal companions' deeper needs and feelings. Linda integrates her psychic skills as an accredited animal behavior specialist and consultant to help her clients and their caretakers.

A woman of many talents, Linda is also a professional artist with paintings found in local galleries and private homes worldwide. She has co-authored

several published books about animals and shares her home with an adopted dog and six rescued parrots."
https://www.idausa.org/native-american-reflections-vegan-spirituality/
15. Atjecoutay, Kerry Redwood. Personal communication. 24 Aug. 2019. https://kredatjecoutay.wordpress.com/2017/04/04/kerry-m-redwood-atjecoutay/
Atjecoutay is an abstract mixed media artist for Earth-Animal Liberation from human greed. He is Great Plains Ojibway/Cree from Ka-wezauce (cowessess - Saskatchewan Canada) of the Ojibwa Nation, a descendant of the Anishinabek.
16. Schlesier, Karl. *The Wolves of Heaven: Cheyenne Shamanism, Ceremonies, and Prehistoric Origins.* University of Oklahoma Press, 2013, p 12.
Action and cognitive anthropologist Schlesier had vast field experience with the Cheyenne. He theorized based on the archeological remains that Cheyenne lived on the plains from 500 B.C emerging as a distinct people with their creation of the Massaum, a ceremony of earth-giving. According to Schlesier, the Massaum was an elaborate ceremony of world revitalization, ritual theater, and performances of magic. Peter Nabokov, writing in the Journal of Religion stated that "Schlesier is trying to conjure up a nonstatic American Indian world in which peoples and ideas circulate, constellate, and periodically achieve new plateaus of religious-social integration."
17. Cameron, Anne. *Daughters of Copper Woman.* Press Gang Publishers, 1981, p. 97.
In this re-telling of Northwest Coast Native myths, Cameron weaves together the lives of legendary and imaginary characters, creating a work of fiction with an intensity of style matched by the power of its subject.
18. Solazzo, Caroline, et al. "Proteomics and Coast Salish Blankets: a Tale of Shaggy Dogs?" *Antiquity,* vol. 85, no. 330, 2011, pp. 1418–1432, doi:10.1017/s0003598x00062141.
https://www.academia.edu/1179226/Proteomics_and_Coast_Salish_blankets_a_tale_of_shaggy_dogs
19. Lewis, Jerome. "Ekila: Blood, Bodies, and Egalitarian Societies*." Journal of the Royal Anthropological Institute,* vol. 14, no. 2, 2008, pp. 297–315, doi:10.1111/j.1467-9655.2008.00502.x.
Jerome Lewis is a field work social anthropologist with Central Africa hunter-gatherer societies, focused on Yaka forest hunter-gatherers.
20. Native America Calling. "Monday, July 16, 2018 – Plant-Based Natives; What It Takes to Go Vegan » Native America Calling." *Native America Calling,* 18 July 2018. https://www.nativeamericacalling.com/monday-july-16-2018-plant-based-natives/
Native America Calling is a live call-in podcast with thought-provoking national conversation about issues specific to Native communities.
21. C. Personal communication, 1 Dec 2019.
22. Emily Victoria. Personal communication, 20, Dec 2019.
Emily Victoria is Toltec tribal member, organizer at Bay Area Chapter of Animal Save Movement, and contributor to Vegan News.

23. Gaard, Greta. "Ecofeminism and Native American Cultures: Pushing the Limits of Cultural Imperialism?" *Ecofeminism: Woman, Animals, Nature*, Temple University Press, 1993, pp. 295–314, p. 296.

Greta Gaard is an ecofeminist writer, activist, and women's studies scholar, focusing on ecofeminism, queer theory, queer ecology, vegetarianism, and animal liberation.

24. Mason, Sarah L. R., et al. "Preliminary Investigation of the Plant Macro-Remains from Dolní Věstonice II, and Its Implications for the Role of Plant Foods in Palaeolithic and Mesolithic Europe." *Antiquity*, vol. 68, no. 258, 1994, pp. 48–57.

25. Hockett, Bryan. "The Consequences of Middle Paleolithic Diets on Pregnant Neanderthal Women." *Quaternary International*, vol. 264, 2012, pp. 78–82, doi:10.1016/j.quaint.2011.07.002.

26. Henry, Amanda G., et. al. "The Diet of Australopithecus Sediba." *Nature: International Journal of Science*, vol. 487, 2 June 2012, pp. 90–93, doi: 10.1038/nature11185.

This study finds a feeding ecology, from extraction of dental calculus of an early hominin and dental microwear texture of Australopithecus. sediba in palaeoenvironmental evidence. The two individuals examined consumed an almost exclusive C_3 diet that probably included harder foods, and both dicotyledons (for example, tree leaves, fruits, wood and bark) and monocotyledons (for example, grasses and sedges). Like earlier Ardipithecus ramidus (approximately 4.4 myr ago) and modern savanna chimpanzees, A. sediba consumed C_3 foods in preference to widely available C_4 resources.

27. Woodburn, James, and Richard B. Lee "An Introduction to Hazda Ecology," *Man the Hunter*. Routledge, 2017, pp 49-55.

Man the Hunter was a 1966 symposium organized by Richard Lee and Irven DeVore, held at the Center for Continuing Education, University of Chicago. The symposium resulted in a book of the same title and attempted to bring together for the first time a comprehensive look at ethnographic research on hunter-gatherers. Mostly American cultural anthropologists contributed, and several of the most influential figures in then contemporary anthropology attended. In addition to Lee and DeVore, the symposium was attended by Marshall Sahlins, Aram Yengoyan, George Peter Murdock, Colin Turnbull, Lewis Binford, and Julian Steward. The main point of the conference was that given that hunting was humanity's original source of livelihood, any theory of society and the nature of Man would require a deep knowledge of how hunters live.

28. Marlowe, Frank W. *The Hadza: Hunter-Gatherers of Tanzania*. University of California Press, 2010.

Anthropologist Frank Marlowe pioneered the field of human sociobiology, focusing on human evolution, the behavior of hunter-gatherers, comparisons among human societies such as parenting, mating, sexual selection, the evolution of human life history, cooperation and economic behavior. His field research occurred in harsh conditions for the foraging Hadza hunter-gatherers, among whom he was with between 1993 and 2014.

29. Milton, Katharine. "Hunter-Gatherer Diets—a Different Perspective." *The American Journal of Clinical Nutrition,* vol. 71, no. 3, 2000, pp. 665–667, doi:10.1093/ajcn/71.3.665.
https://academic.oup.com/ajcn/article/71/3/665/4729104

Katharine Milton is an anthropologist focused on the dietary ecology of primates, including human ancestors and modern humans. She has worked extensively on the dietary ecology of a number of indigenous groups in the Brazilian Amazon to document their uses of forest food and medicine.

30. O'Dea, Kerin, et. al. "Traditional Diet and Food Preferences of Australian Aboriginal Hunter-Gatherers." *Philosophical Transactions of the Royal Society of London. Series B: Biological Sciences,* vol. 334, no. 1270, 1991, pp. 233–241, doi:10.1098/rstb.1991.0112.

Kerin O'Dea is a professor of Nutrition and Population Health at the University of South Australia. She studies the relationship between diet and chronic diseases She investigates the therapeutic and health impacts of traditional diets and lifestyles upon population health, and is well-known for her research into how a reversion to a traditional hunter-gatherer lifestyle had a beneficial impact upon diabetes and associated conditions in Australian Aborigines.

31. Psihoyos, Louie, director. *The Game Changers.* 2018.
https://gamechangersmovie.com/the-film/

"After eight years in the making the highly anticipated movie produced by James Cameron and featuring Arnold Schwarzenegger finally debuted at the prestigious Sundance film festival…

The Game Changers tells the story of James Wilks — elite special forces trainer and winner of The Ultimate Fighter — as he travels the world on a quest for the truth behind the world's most dangerous myth: that meat is necessary for protein, strength and optimal health. Meeting elite athletes, special ops soldiers, visionary scientists, cultural icons, and everyday heroes, what James discovers permanently changes his relationship with food and his definition of true strength.

In the film, super athletes…testify that a plant-based diet propelled them to their athletic successes. The documentary clearly shows how people are far healthier when they adopt a plant-based diet and eliminate meat from their diet.

Also amongst the cast are leading research scientists and medical doctors who convey solid evidence of the benefits of a plant-based diet both for the environment and for people's overall health leading to a better quality of life.

… The myths 'meat is masculine', as well as the 'meat helps athletic performance' is debunked by top scientists clearly demonstrating that, in fact, the exact opposite is true."
https://www.riseofthevegan.com/blog/the-biggest-film-of-2018-the-game-changers-documentary

32. Clifton, Merritt, et al. "Killing the Female: The Psychology of the Hunt." *Animals 24-7,* 2 Jan. 2019. https://www.animals24-7.org/2018/12/29/killing-the-female-the-psychology-of-the-hunt/

"Committing journalism since 1968, mostly on animal-related news beats, and an active charter member of the Society of Environmental Journalists since 1990, ANIMALS 24-7 editor Merritt Clifton in 2010 received the 15th annual ProMED-mail Award for Excellence in Outbreak Reporting on the Internet for contributions to understanding the animal behavioral and cultural aspects of emerging zoonotic disease." https://www.animals24-7.org/

33. Milton, 2000.

34. Macho, Gabriele A. "Baboon Feeding Ecology Informs the Dietary Niche of Paranthropus Boisei." *PLoS ONE*, vol. 9, no. 1, Aug. 2014, doi:10.1371/journal.pone.0084942.

Gabriele Macho is a biological anthropologist at the University of Oxford.

35. Milton, 2000.

36. Shelley, Percy Bysshe. "A Vindication of Natural Diet." *Animal Rights Library*, 1813. http://www.animal-rights-library.com/texts-c/shelley01.htm

37. Long, TJ. Personal communication, 28 Nov 2019.

38. Kimmerer, Robin Wall. *Braiding Sweetgrass: Indigenous Wisdom, Scientific Knowledge and the Teachings of Plants.* Milkweed Editions, 2015.

Robin Wall Kimmerer is a Potawatomi botanist, professor and director of the Center for Native Peoples and the Environment, and co-founder of the Traditional Ecological Knowledge section of the Ecological Society of America. Her focus is on the role of integrating native ecological knowledge in ecological restoration and the ecology of mosses. She has taught on in botany, ecology, ethnobotany, indigenous environmental issues and the application of traditional ecological knowledge to conservation. She is engaged in programs which introduce the benefits of traditional ecological knowledge to the scientific community, in a way that respects and protects indigenous knowledge and creating new models for integration of indigenous philosophy and scientific tools on behalf of land and human relationship with the land.
She has written numerous scientific papers on the ecology of mosses, restoration ecology, contributions of traditional ecological knowledge to understanding of the natural world, and the book "Gathering Moss" incorporating traditional indigenous knowledge and scientific perspectives.

39. Benzie, Iris, et al. "Effects of a Long-Term Vegetarian Diet on Biomarkers of Antioxidant Status and Cardiovascular Disease Risk." *Nutrition,* vol. 20, no. 10, 2004, pp. 863–866, doi:10.1016/j.nut.2004.06.006.

Conclusions: Long-term vegetarians have a better antioxidant status and coronary heart disease risk profile than do apparently healthy omnivore, in addition to a better overall health status.

40. Thompson, Randall C., et al. "Atherosclerosis Across 4000 Years of Human History: The Horus Study of Four Ancient Populations." *Journal of Vascular Surgery,* vol. 58, no. 2, 2013, p. 549, doi:10.1016/j.jvs.2013.06.006.

Interpretation: Atherosclerosis was common in four preindustrial populations including preagricultural hunter-gatherers. Although commonly assumed to be a modern disease, the presence of atherosclerosis in premodern human beings raises the possibility of a more basic predisposition to the disease.

41. Tharrey, Marion, et al. "Patterns of Plant and Animal Protein Intake Are Strongly Associated with Cardiovascular Mortality: the Adventist Health Study-2 Cohort." *International Journal of Epidemiology*, vol. 47, no. 5, Feb. 2018, pp. 1603–1612, doi:10.1093/ije/dyy030.

Healthy diets can be advocated based on protein sources, preferring low contributions of protein from meat and higher intakes of plant protein from nuts and seeds

42. Miles, Fayth L, et al. "Plasma, Urine, and Adipose Tissue Biomarkers of Dietary Intake Differ Between Vegetarian and Non-Vegetarian Diet Groups in the Adventist Health Study-2." *The Journal of Nutrition*, vol. 149, no. 4, 2019, pp. 667–675, doi:10.1093/jn/nxy292.

43. Abete, Itziar, et al. "Association between Total, Processed, Red and White Meat Consumption and All-Cause, CVD and IHD Mortality: a Meta-Analysis of Cohort Studies." *British Journal of Nutrition*, vol. 112, no. 5, 2014, pp. 762–775, doi:10.1017/s000711451400124x.

44. Bernstein, Adam M., et al. "Major Dietary Protein Sources and Risk of Coronary Heart Disease in Women." *Circulation*, vol. 122, no. 9, 2010, pp. 876–883, doi:10.1161/circulationaha.109.915165.

45. Kim, Hyunju, et al. "Plant-Based Diets Are Associated With a Lower Risk of Incident Cardiovascular Disease, Cardiovascular Disease Mortality, and All-Cause Mortality in a General Population of Middle-Aged Adults." *Journal of the American Heart Association*, vol. 8, no. 16, 2019, doi:10.1161/jaha.119.012865.

46. Kelemen, L. E. "Associations of Dietary Protein with Disease and Mortality in a Prospective Study of Postmenopausal Women." *American Journal of Epidemiology*, vol. 161, no. 3, Jan. 2005, pp. 239–249, doi:10.1093/aje/kwi038.

47. Song, Mingyang, et al. "Association of Animal and Plant Protein Intake With All-Cause and Cause-Specific Mortality." *JAMA Internal Medicine*, vol. 176, no. 10, Jan. 2016, p. 1453, doi:10.1001/jamainternmed.2016.4182.

48. B., M. "Returning to Reality: A Response to Paul Shepard's 'The Vegetarians', by Michael B." *Vegan Primitivist,* 25 Aug. 2019. https://veganprimitivist.wordpress.com/2019/08/25/returning-to-reality-a-response-to-paul-shepards-the-vegetarians-by-michael-b/

49. Stark, Philip B., et al. "Open-Source Food: Nutrition, Toxicology, and Availability of Wild Edible Greens in the East Bay." *Plos One*, vol. 14, no. 1, 2019, doi:10.1371/journal.pone.0202450.

"Common garden weeds are more nutritious than kale, Berkeley researchers find.

Researchers from the University of California Berkeley have identified 52 edible weeds growing in abundance in the poorest neighborhoods of San Francisco, surrounded by busy roads and industrial zones.

At least six of them are more nutritious than kale, according to a new study.

The three low-income neighborhoods the researchers studied have been classified as "urban food deserts" — meaning they are more than a mile from the nearest shop that sells fresh produce.

Of the 52 species of wild-growing "weeds" they found, they tested six for nutrition content:
Chickweed
Dandelion
Dock
Mallow
Nasturtium
Oxalis
All six were more nutritious, by most accounts, than kale – arguably the most nutritious domesticated leafy greens.

The weeds boasted more dietary fiber, protein, vitamin A, calcium, iron, vitamin K, and provided more energy.

The only nutrient kale scored higher in was vitamin C, but the researchers suspect other weeds they found, such wild mustard and wild radish, might rival it in that category.

Many of the edible weeds they found have been used in folk medicine, including plantain, cat's ear, fennel, sow thistle, wild lettuce, and wild onions.

The really exciting part about the study, is that these weeds were foraged in the middle of a drought.

"Foraged leafy greens are consumed around the globe, including in urban areas, and may play a larger role when food is scarce or expensive," writes Philip Stark, statistics professor and founder of the Berkeley Open Source Food Project.

"Even during this low-production period, almost every address in all three study areas had several servings of several different species, suggesting that wild edible greens are a reliable source of nutrition all year round," writes Stark.

Soil at some survey sites had elevated concentrations of lead and cadmium, but tissue tests suggest the weeds don't take up much of these or other heavy metals.

After being rinsed, they tested at less than the dosages considered safe by the EPA, the researchers said.

Pesticides, glyphosate, and PCBs were undetectable.

How can people identify which wild greens are edible?

"Familiarity," says Stark. "Most people have no trouble telling the difference between, say iceberg lettuce and romaine lettuce."

He recommends people educate themselves and gradually start adding new weeds into their diets.

The report notes there are only 1.7 cups of farmed vegetables available per person per day in the United States, less than the recommended serving of two to three cups.

The researchers suggest wild food could fill in the gap and improve nutrition security.

"Wild foods might also contribute to a healthy ecosystem by building soil organic matter, retaining water and nutrients in the soil, and reducing erosion," Stark wrote."

https://returntonow.net/2018/09/29/weeds-more-nutritious-than-store-bought-produce/

50. Weyrich, Laura S., et al. "Neanderthal Behaviour, Diet, and Disease Inferred from Ancient DNA in Dental Calculus." *Nature, International Journal of Science*, vol. 544, 2017, pp. 357–61.

https://www.nature.com/articles/nature21674

At Spy cave, Belgium, Neanderthal diet was heavily meat based and included woolly rhinoceros and wild sheep (mouflon), characteristic of a steppe environment. In contrast, no meat was detected in the diet of Neanderthals from El Sidrón cave, Spain, and dietary components of mushrooms, pine nuts, and moss reflected forest gathering.

51. Mason, 1998.

"Male chauvinism... has long been at work in the field of anthropology. Male anthropologists have tended to play up male contributions to humanity and to ignore those of the female... Until recently, for example, male-dominated anthropology had not bothered to study and catalog the large numbers of grinding stones that women used. The study of (presumed) male tools, on the other hand, went to obsessive proportions. Nearly everything with a sharp edge got identified as an early great hunter's spearhead. Then thousands of these "spearheads" were classified into types and subtypes upon subtypes. From this perspective, it looked as if men were sophisticated tool-makers and –users, while women were all thumbs. Lately, better analysis has revealed that many of these "spearheads" were actually digging, stripping, and chopping tools-probably made and used by women.

When they study contemporary tribal people, male anthropologists again tended to follow male interests. Reviews of their studies show that male anthropologists spent more time talking and being with men than with women. When they studied relations between men and women, male scientists tended to inject their own notions of power, hierarchy, and intersexual dynamics. After such biased spadework by male scientists, male popularizers... carried the man-as-hunter myth another step or two. Their speculations and interpretations came largely from the realm of the subjective-a place where biases can run unnoticed and unchecked." p. 73

52. Mowat, Farley. *Never Cry Wolf.* Langara College, 2019.

Never Cry Wolf is an account of the Mowat's experience observing wolves in subarctic Canada, first published in 1963, adapted into a film in 1983. It has been credited for dramatically changing the public image of the wolf to a more positive one. In the book, Mowat describes his experiences in a first-person narrative that sheds light on his research into the nature of the Arctic wolf. In 1948–1949, the Dominion Wildlife Service assigns the author to investigate the cause of declining caribou populations and determine whether wolves are to blame for the shortage. Upon finding his quarry near Nueltin Lake, Mowat discovers that rather than being wanton killers of caribou, the wolves subsist quite heavily on small mammals such as rodents and hares, "even choosing them over caribou when available." He concludes: "We have doomed the wolf not for what it is but for what we deliberately and mistakenly perceive it to be: the mythologized epitome of a savage, ruthless killer—which is, in reality, not more than the reflected image of ourselves. We have made it the scapewolf for our own sins." Mowat writes to expose the onslaught of wolfers and government exterminators who are out to erase the wolves from the Arctic.

Mowat's book says that:

•*The main reason for declining population of caribou is human hunters from civilization.*

•*Wolves that hunt a large herd animal would rather attack weaker, injured, or older animals, which helps rid the herd of members that slow its migration.*

•*Arctic wolves usually prey on Arctic ox, caribou, smaller mammals, and rodents—but since they rely on stamina instead of speed, it would be logical for the wolves to choose smaller prey instead of large animals like caribou, which are faster and stronger, and therefore a more formidable target. One of these animals may include mice.*

•*A lone Arctic wolf has a better chance of killing small prey by running alongside it and attacking its neck. The wolf would be at a disadvantage if it attacked large prey from behind, because the animal's powerful hind legs could injure the wolf. However, a group of wolves may successfully attack large prey from a number of positions.*

•*Since Arctic wolves often travel in a group, their best strategy is not to kill surplus prey, since the whole group can sate themselves on one or two large animals. There are, however, exceptions to this.*

•*There are many local Eskimos, the majority of whom are traders.*

•*The Eskimos can interpret wolves' howls. They can tell things such as whether a herd or a human is passing through the wolves' territory, the direction of travel, and more.*

53. Walia, Arjun. "Anthropologists & Scientists Explain How Ancient Humans Were Predominantly Vegan" *Collective Evolution,* 1 Nov. 2019. https://www.collective-evolution.com/2019/11/01/anthropologists-scientists-explain-how-ancient-humans-were-predominately-vegan/

Many of Walia's highlighted citations are included in this book.

4 HUNTING'S CIVILIZED WRATH

1. Washburn, 1968, pp. 293–303.

2. Robinson, 2020.

3. Milton, Katharine. "Diet and Primate Evolution." *Scientific American: Becoming Human, Evolution and the Rise of Intelligence,* 19 Sept. 2006, p. 30. file:///C:/Users/Robert/AppData/Local/Microsoft/Windows/INetCache/IE/FPGR DKVO/becoming_human from Scientific American.pdf

Many characteristics of modern primates, including our own species, derive from an early ancestor's practice of taking most of its food from the tropical canopy.

4. Schreve, Danielle, et al. "Shoot First, Ask Questions Later: Interpretative Narratives of Neanderthal Hunting." *Quaternary Science Reviews*, vol. 140, 2016, pp. 1–20, doi:10.1016/j.quascirev.2016.03.004.

"This paper examines the hunting strategies employed by Neanderthals at a series of kill or near-kill sites from the Middle Palaeolithic of Europe (Mauran, La Borde, Taubach, Zwoleń and Salzgitter Lebenstedt). Using palaeolandscape reconstructions and animal ethology as our context, we adopt a multifaceted approach that views hunting as a chaîne opératoire involving the decisions and actions of both the hunter and the hunted, which together help reconstruct a forensic picture of past events as they unfolded. Our conclusions indicate that Neanderthals did not necessarily pre-select individuals from a herd, who they then isolated, pursued and killed, but rather ambushed whole groups, which they slaughtered indiscriminately. There is strong evidence, however, that Neanderthals were highly selective in the carcasses they then chose to process. Our conclusions suggest that Neanderthals were excellent tacticians, casual executioners and discerning diners."

5. "Mexico Finds Human-Built Mammoth Traps 15,000 Years Old." *The New York Times*, 7 Nov. 2019.
https://www.nytimes.com/aponline/2019/11/06/world/americas/ap-lt-mexico-mammoth-trap.html

"Archaeologists have said they have made the largest discovery of mammoth remains, with a trove of 800 bones from at least 14 of the extinct giants found in central Mexico. At least five mammoth herds lived in the area of the find...They also found two human-built pits dug 15,000 years ago to trap mammoth, believed to have been the first find of mammoth traps set by humans...

The institute said hunters may have chased mammoths into the traps. Remains of two other species that disappeared in the Americas — a horse and a camel — were also found... Some of the remains bore signs that the animals had been hunted, leading experts to conclude that they had found "the world's first mammoth trap", the statement said."

6. Carlson, Kristen, and Leland Bement. "Organization of Bison Hunting at the Pleistocene/Holocene Transition on the Plains of North America." *Quaternary International*, vol. 297, 2013, pp. 93–99, doi:10.1016/j.quaint.2012.12.026.

Organization of bison hunting at the Pleistocene/Holocene transition in Plains of North America found development of large-scale bison hunting across the North American Great Plains. Prehistoric hunters were not merely opportunistic. An understanding of topography, environment, bison behavior, and migration patterns was necessary to perform complex, large scale bison kills. In turn, these kills required the existence of social complexity whereby multiple groups of hunters worked in unison toward a successful kill event. On the southern Plains of North America, evidence suggests large scale bison hunting arose as mammoths and other megafauna became extinct 11,000 radiocarbon years ago

7. Hogan, Linda. Personal communication, 15 Sep. 2019.

8. Darwin, Charles. *The Origin of Species by Means of Natural Selection: or the Preservation of Favoured Races in the Struggle for Life ; The Descent of Man and Selection in Relation to Sex*, Modern Library, 1872.

In the book Civilized to Death: The Price of Progress, Christopher Ryan relays a an inter-primate occurrence interpreted by Darwin as "Many a civilized man who never before risked his life for another, but full of courage and sympathy, has disregarded the instinct of self-preservation and plunged at once into a torrent to save a drowning man, though a stranger. In this case man is impelled by the same instinctive motive, which made the heroic little American monkey, formerly described, save his keeper by attacking the great and dreadful baboon." p. 79

9. Schlesier, 2013, p. 53.

10. Hager, Lori. "Sex and Gender in Paleoanthropology." *Women in Human Evolution*, Routledge, 1997, p. 4.

Hager examines the role of women paleontologists and archaeologists in a field traditionally dominated by men. Women researchers in this field have questioned many of the assumptions and developmental scenarios advanced by male scientists. As a result of such efforts, women have forged a more central role in models of human development and have radically altered the way in which human evolution is perceived.

11. Shepard, 1973, pp. 122-3.

12. Zerzan, John. "Patriarchy, Civilization, And The Origins Of Gender." *The Anarchist Library*, 2008.
http://theanarchistlibrary.org/library/john-zerzan-patriarchy-civilization-and-the-origins-of-gender.html

13. Kheel, Marti, et al. "License to Kill: An Ecofeminist Critique of Hunters' Discourse." *Animals & Women: Feminist Theoretical Explorations,* Duke University Press, 1995, pp. 85-111.

Author of "Nature Ethics: An Ecofeminist Perspective" Marti Kheel, co–founded Feminists for Animal Rights (FAR) in 1982, hoping to link feminism and animal advocacy through exploring ways women and other–than–human animals are viewed under patriarchy. Her well-known 1985 article "The Liberation of Nature: A Circular Affair" published in Environmental Ethics was perhaps the first published feminist critique of environmental ethics. Kheel's primary aim was to develop a holistic philosophy bridging the seemingly unrelated ethos of feminism, animal liberation and nature ethics, all under ecofeminism. By exposing root causes of social problems, ecofeminism widens human empathy for all living beings.

14. Zihlman, Adrienne, "The Paleolithic Glass Ceiling: Women in Human Evolution." *Women in Human Evolution,* edited by Lori D. Hager, Routledge, 1997, pp. 94–96.

Adrienne Zihlman is a prominent feminist combining fields of paleoanthropology, biological anthropology and primatology. In collaboration with Nancy Tanner she critiqued the "Man the Hunter" hypothesis (men's hunting drove evolution while women passively followed as recipients of their provisions.) Zihlman and Tanner's study revealed women were inventors, tool

271

makers and socially central to the thriving group, and those roles were more flexible than rigid division of labor.

15. Nibert, David A. *Animal Oppression & Human Violence: Domesecration, Capitalism, and Global Conflict.* Columbia University Press, 2013, p. 10.

Sociologist David Nibert expounds on the history linking human oppression of one another with human oppression over nonhuman animals from origins of speciesism in the shift from egalitarian foraging to hunting and eventual domesticated animals for food. The book interweaves oppressions exponentially empowered to those benefiting, who use their power to reinforce and perpetuate the ideology of civilization's progress and internalize powerlessness in the exploited. Utilitarian relationships are neither natural nor inevitable, but a socially constructed paradigm. Modern humans are indoctrinated through institutional and cultural economic hegemonies. The oppressed are silenced when oppression is normalized, becoming invisible. Nibert warns that a gentler economic system will not end the oppression that hierarchies need to be addressed by using opportunities within the capitalist system to overcome it.

16. Spielvogel, Jackson J. *Western Civilization to 1500.* Wadsworth, 2014, p. 4.

17. Nibert, 2013.

18. AbdelRahim, Layla, 2013, pp. 31-4.

19. Collard, 1989.

20. Luke, Brian. *Brutal: Manhood and the Exploitation of Animals.* University of Illinois Press, 2007.

Through an ecofeminist lens at the intersection of gender and power, philosopher Brian Luke explores the role of the social construction of masculinity in exploiting other animals. His deconstruction of hegemonic myths and misconceptions on human supremacy, predation and eroticization of men hunting, serves as a calling for activist animal liberation.

21. Luke, Brian. "Violent Love: Hunting, Heterosexuality, and the Erotics of Mens Predation." *Feminist Studies,* vol. 24, no. 3, 1998, p. 627, doi:10.2307/3178583. http://www.brown.uk.com/brownlibrary/luke.pdf

22. Turnbull, Colin M., "Mbuti Womanhood." *Woman the Gatherer,* edited by Frances Dahlberg, Yale University, 1981, p. 219.

"If anything dominates it is that prime quality of interdependence."
Anthropologist Colin Turnbull had a special interest in hunter-gatherer semi-nomadic tribes of Africa, from rain forests to mountains. His classic book "The Mountain People" is his study of the tribe Ik he lived with from 1964-1967 in their temporary high mountain villages as their lifeway transitioned. As nations harden their boundaries excluding Ik from their traditional hunting grounds, Turnbull details how they adapt their foodway. Men hunt what they can and eat it far away and women collect only for themselves. As starvation sets in unfed children and old people die. The tribe steals cattle from neighboring peoples. Thieving intensifies even within their tribe becoming the new norm as honesty is predated upon and deceit becomes an art for surviving.

23. Potts, Malcolm, and Martha Campbell. "The Origins and Future of Patriarchy: the Biological Background of Gender Politics." *Journal of Family Planning and Reproductive Health Care,* vol. 34, no. 3, 2008, pp. 171–174,

doi:10.1783/147118908784734792.
https://pdfs.semanticscholar.org/448b/3258e7b95b633d9f8b2ad4a44aa6c6fdf28
8.pdf

Through the lens of evolutionary biology, a look at varied levels of patriarchy from human origins on shows dimorphism leads some hunter-gatherer men to dominate women, though some are "slightly less paternalistic than others… in some hunter-gatherer societies the girl's family decides whom she will marry, or in more war-like tribes women are captured, raped and then assigned to a particular man. Sometimes men and women choose their sexual partners." Women killing their infants "are optimizing their reproductive potential over the long term, because if a romantic relationship fails, a woman will not receive the support she needs from the father of the child, while over the next few years of breastfeeding and childcare she will be excluded from exploring a new romantic relationship. The most cost-effective reproductive strategy is to kill the child and start again.

24. Shostak, Marjorie. *Nisa: the Life and Words of a !Kung Woman.* Routledge, 2015.

Untrained anthropologist Marjorie Shostak authored this anthropological life history of an !Kung San woman of the Kalahari Desert. When traveling in Botswana in 1969 Shostak spontaneously began recording life stories of women in the Dobe camp, including a lively and candid storyteller who offered insight into womanhood and human nature to whom Shostak gave the penname "!Nisa. When Nisa appeared in 1981, it quickly became the most widely read anthropological life history, translated into many languages, and a foundational text in feminist anthropology.

25. Chagnon, Napoleon A. *Noble Savages: My Life among Two Dangerous Tribes - the Yanomamö and the Anthropologists.* Simon & Schuster, 2014, pp. 82-3.

Chagnon spent 30 years living with and accumulating data on the Stone Age Yanomamö, bow and arrow war-making people before they were acculturated in vast isolated wild land along Brazil and Venezuela. Noble Savages tells of scathing truths of a people whose primitive lifeway is now irrevocably blended into modernity. For studying and concluding that men who killed one or more enemies on raids, had almost three times greater reproductive success (more wives, more offspring) than those who did not kill (tables pp. 275-6), Chagnon was professionally vilified. Linking Yanomomö motivation for war-making to virility challenged liberal cultural anthropology orthodoxy's blame for war on resource competition or colonial repression, as opposed to evolutionary science.

26. Ibid, p. 9.

27. Thomas, Elizabeth Marshall. *The Harmless People.* Vintage Books, 1989, pp. 51-2.

This idealized ethnography is an anecdotal, qualitative case portrayal of primal humans embedded in habitat. Thomas visited with and learned from Kalahari desert Bushman people in the 1950s. They strived for peacefulness and togetherness within harsh climate until they were acculturated by the 1980s.

28. Berndt, Catherine H., "Interpretations and "Facts" in Aboriginal Australia" *Woman the Gatherer,* edited by Frances Dahlberg, Yale University, 1981, p. 153.

Bi-cultural anthropologist Catherine Berndt was world renowned for her gender studies of Aboriginal women of Australia and Papua New Guinea highlands. She sought out gender independence within an overarching context of interdependence.

29. Lerner, Gerda. *The Creation of Patriarchy.* Oxford University Press, 1986, p. 30. https://radicalfeministbookclub.files.wordpress.com/2018/03/women-and-history_-v-1-gerda-lerner-the-creation-of-patriarchy-oxford-university-press-1987.pdf

Historian Gerda Lerner examines how women's ability to procreate led to the rise of male power, female subordination, and society's dominance hierarchies, becoming a patriarchy foundational to civilization. The advent of hunting and gathering spurred division of labor that compelled women to choose a foodway that melded with mothering. Early humans cooperated for survival in near egalitarianism, until agriculture. With the drive to control nature men took control of women's reproduction for economic reasons. Children became an asset as labor to till soil and shepherd herds. Women's bodies became an exchangeable commodity, private property belonging to men.

30. Derricourt, Robin M. *Unearthing Childhood: Young Lives in Prehistory.* Manchester University Press, 2018, p. 179.

In prehistory children comprised about half the human population, but have taken a back seat to 'man the hunter' in study. Archeologist Robin Derricourt digs up this ignored cohort by professionally reviewing research from multiple disciplines to assay what is known and unknown to date. Chapter 1 is an introductory examination of cave paintings, footprints, toys, and skeletal remains available to interpret the experience and meaning of childhood. Chapter 2 and 3 focuses on birth, motherhood, infancy and family dynamics. Chapters 4-8 survey diets, clothing, socialization, play and conflict. Chapters 9 and 10 are a comparative analysis of death, burial sites and child status. Chapter 11 outlines study suggestions to advance understanding of prehistory childhood.

31. Good, Kenneth, and David Chanoff. *Into the Heart: One Man's Pursuit of Love and Knowledge among the Yanomama.* Touchstone, 1991, p. 62.

"Anthropologist Kenneth Good went to the rain forests of the Amazon to study the Yanomami. He found more than one of the few remaining peoples untouched by modern civilization. During more than a decade of observation, Good found himself accepted, indeed virtually adopted, by the tribe and eventually fell in love with a young Yanomami woman. In the process, he made exciting new discoveries about the tribal people and about himself. Into the Heart is the fascinating story of his journey of discovery."

32. Mason, Jim. Personal communication, 5 Sep. 2019.

33. Collard and Contrucci,, 1989, p. 48.

34. Adams, Carol J. *The Pornagrphy of Meat.* Bloomsbury Academic; Little Simon Ed. Edition, 2004.

Prominent author at the intersection of feminism and animal rights Carol Adams says "Vegan-feminism is an intervention that critiques and is visionary, that looks at individuals and at social structures, that deconstructs but also offers solutions. Vegan-feminism is always a question of now. Knowing what I know, now what will I do? It comes with an insistence! "Pay attention!" Pay attention, now. The process of objectification/fragmentation/consumption can be interrupted by the process of attention/nowness/compassion."
https://caroljadams.com/why-vegan-feminist

35. Kheel, Marti. *Nature Ethics: an Ecofeminist Perspective.* Rowman & Littlefield, 2008, pp. 49, 73.

"Frequently, rites of initiation into manhood include violence toward nature and separation from the sphere of women... and the seizure of her power... One of the most commonly found cross-cultural rites of initiation into manhood involves the young boy's killing of an animal. p. 49. Also see p. 73.

36. Gilmore, David D. *Manhood in the Making: Cultural Concepts of Masculinity.* Yale University Press, 1991, back cover.

"Anthropologist professor and author on the cross-cultural connection between hunting and rites of passage into manhood. The aim and outcome of the initiation is "to detach the boy from natural affection and natural role, to teach him that a man does not act on feelings but rather on meeting an external societal standard of manliness that is focused on exhibiting self-control and control over others."

37. Daly, Martin and Margo Wilson, "Evolutionary Psychology of Male Violence." *Male Violence,* edited by John Archer, Routledge, 1994, p. 275.

"Men lay claim to particular women as songbirds lay claim to territories, as lions lay claim to a kill, or as people of both sexes lay claim to valuables," wrote evolutionary psychologist Margo Wilson.
https://www.theglobeandmail.com/news/national/margo-wilsons-research-shed-light-on-evolutionary-psychology/article1203620/

38. Hite, Shere. *The Hite Report on the Family: Growing up under Patriarchy.* Grove Press, 1994, pp. 239-40.

"In 1976, a young grad student from Missouri dropped a bombshell into the bedrooms of the world, and blew apart our preconceptions about women's sexuality. The Hite Report on Female Sexuality challenged the sexual status quo and defied male dominance. It became a worldwide publishing sensation, and turned its author into a hate figure among some men.
Feminist and sexologist Shere Hite... scandalized the whole country. In her report, she posited a radical and utterly far-out theory: that women didn't need men to give them an orgasm.
But rather than welcoming Hite's book, a serious academic study based on interviews with more than 3,000 women, the American male population saw it as an attack on their virility. Hite was cast as the witch queen of feminism, out to steal men's mojo and turn women into animistic she-devils...
http://www.hiteresearchfoundation.org/biography-pg46

39. Kheel, Marti, "License to Kill: An Ecofeminist Critique of Hunters' Discourse." *Animals & Women: Feminist Theoretical Explorations*, edited by Carol J. Adams and Josephine Donovan, Duke University Press, 1995, p. 109.

In her essay here Kheel analyzes and critiques writings of Deep Ecologists' perspectives on hunting.

40. Shepard, Paul. "Searching Out Kindred Spirits." *Parabola, The Magazine of Myth and Religion,* 1991, p. 86.

The human hunter ideates on but stops short of empathizing with his prey: "Hunting is a holy occupation, framed in rules and courtesy, informed by the beauty of the physical being and the numinous presence of the spiritual life of animals"

41. Shepard, Paul. *Nature and Madness.* Alfred A. Knopf, *The Anarchist Library* 1967, p. 125.

Excerpt from Shepard's "Nature and Madness"
https://theanarchistlibrary.org/library/paul-shepard-nature-and-madness

42. Shepard, Paul,. "A Post-Historic Primitivism.*" The Wilderness Condition: Essays on Environment and Civilization,* edited by Max Oelschlaeger, Sierra Club Books, 1992, p. 81.

From Stuart Smithers' review of Shepard's essay: "Shepard reintroduces the basic themes of his earlier work, "The Tender Carnivore and the Sacred Game... But in the course of restating his thesis, Shepard adds new "research" that seems to trivialize the discussion as a whole and at the same time seems to turn his article into a sophomoric apology for hunters and meateaters, even going so far as to volunteer that "meat is always the 'relish' that makes the meal worthwhile." https://tricycle.org/magazine/wilderness-condition-essays-environment-and-civilization/

43. Shepard, 1991, p. 87.

44. Shepard, 1992, p. 86.

45. Gasset José Ortega y. *Meditations on Hunting.* Wilderness Adventures Press, 2007.

This book is scientifically unreliable and logically absurd. Ortega's view of the 'natural' relation between humans and wild animals is the exemplar of eco-patriarchy, anthropocentric bias in his ideal world dominated by blood-thirsty predators among which he includes humans. Like Shepard, Ortega claims humans have inherent 'natural' killing instincts that 'naturally' manifest in violence towards wild animals. He reasons that since the essence of wild life is escaping from predators, humans honor other animals even by killing them for 'fun' with no other legitimate need such as sustenance. In fact, wild animals are made for hunters to kill them, and if you don`t kill animals you are repressing your 'true' humanity, your masculine wanes. The damage this type of propaganda does in the age of the human caused 6th mass extinction event is heartbreaking.

46. Williams, 1990.

47. Collard and Contrucci, 1989, pp. 49-50.

48. Kheel, 1995, p. 110.

49. MacCaughey, Martha. *The Caveman Mystique: Pop-Darwinism and the Debates over Sex, Violence, and Science.* Routledge, 2008, p. 140.

Feminist sociologist Martha McCaughey's critique of how evolutionary psychology forms masculine identities and prescripts through science ideologies and mainstream culture, asserting potential for liberation from contrived masculinities.

50. Baba Yaga. "From Identity to Individualist: A Nihilist's Personal History in Leftism." *The Anarchist Library*, 2019. https://theanarchistlibrary.org/library/baba-yaba-from-identity-to-individualist-a-nihilist-s-personal-history-in-leftism?fbclid=IwAR20NtFWSxGca3ijDHAeWIMPwANiiecx80ysdBMHRKQ8IQFraVBRB48nFYU

51. Dunayer, Joan, "Sexist Words, Speciesist Roots." *Animals & Women: Feminist Theoretical Explorations,* edited by Carol J. Adams and Josephine Donovan, Duke University Press, 1995, p. 19. https://nomorelockeddoors.files.wordpress.com/2013/12/sexist-words-speciesist-roots.pdf

52. Wright, Ronald. *A Short History of Progress.* House of Anansi Press, 2019.

A Short History of Progress is concise & entertaining historical highlights of failed techno-societies since the arrival of Homo sapiens. Each step of 'progress' comes with its unexpected destructive consequences. But with all the progress' benefits it's too late to turn back, so 'mistakes' are left to fester, ignored, built upon toward inevitable immense failure. Civilization's increasingly complex infrastructure and hierarchical human social organization is destined for eventually collapse.

53. Schmookler, Andrew Bard. *The Parable of the Tribes.* University of California Press, 1984.

Wild humans enjoyed lives of wholeness and freedom with self-sustaining lifeways in nature. The locus of control was with nature, not any particular species. As civilizations gradually emerged human inventiveness brought on power over and exploitation of nature. Gradually humans turned wildlife's habitat into domesticated monocultures on 'private property'. As human monopoly on food production overpopulated the human species, inter-human clashes for territory escalated. Spoils went to the ruthlessly mighty. Social organization became increasingly hierarchal to keep order. The only way to keep control was through domination. The system humans inadvertently invented became mega-destructive and caught all humans in the conundrum with little realistic hope for escape.

54. Dunayer, 1995, p. 23.

55. Tokarczuk, 2019, p. 114.

56. Hultman, Martin, and Paul M. Pulé. *Ecological Masculinities: Theoretical Foundations and Practical Guidance.* Routledge, 2018.

This interdisciplinary text paves a path for 'ecological masculinities' toward Earthcare from Deep Ecology, Ecological Feminism, and Feminist Care models, toward an ecologically thriving planet for all life.

57. Ryan, 2019, pp. 121-2.

58. Alvarez, Natasha. *Liminal: a Novella.* Black and Green Press, 2014.
"A novella that grabs you by the heart and brings you down into that uncomfortable space between love, rewilding, and the suffocating despair of a civilization in decline. An activist dedicates herself to a deed to undo the means of power becomes a mother and lover in the meantime. Through joy and sorrow, the question is asked: what would you do? Powerful, moving, and compelling, this novella covers it all. Foreword by Kevin Tucker."
59. Flower Bomb. "What Savages We Must Be: Vegans Without Morality." *The Anarchist Library*, https://theanarchistlibrary.org/library/Flower-bomb-what-savages-we-must-be-vegans-without-morality
60. Ibid.
61. Vierich, Helga. "Addendum to Gardening in Eden." *Anthroecologycom*, 1 Dec. 2019, https://anthroecologycom.wordpress.com/2019/12/01/addendum-to-gardening-in-eden/
Anthropologist Vierich lived with Bushmen in the Kalahari for three years. She then became principal anthropological research scientist at a green revolution institute in West Africa. She currently teaches at the University of Kentucky and the University of Alberta.
62. Ibid.
63. Ibid.
64. Scott, James C. *The Art of Not Being Governed: an Anarchist History of Upland Southeast Asia.* Yale University Press, 2011.
65. Foreman, Dave, and Bill Haywood. *Ecodefense: a Field Guide to Monkeywrenching.* Abbzug Press, 2002.
Dave Foreman is an American environmentalist and co-founder of the radical environmental movement Earth First!
66. Foreman, Dave. *Confessions of an Eco-Warrior.* Crown, 1993.

5 REWILD ETHOS TO REWILD EARTH

1. Hogan, Linda. "Our Animal Selves." *Transcend Media Service,* 21 Mar. 2011, https://www.transcend.org/tms/2011/03/our-animal-selves/.
Linda K. Hogan is a poet, storyteller, academic, playwright, novelist, environmentalist and writer of short stories. She is currently the Chickasaw Nation's Writer in Residence.
2. Savoy, Ty. "Halifax Native Vegan Scholar Margaret Robinson on Cross Country Checkup 2019-01-28." *YouTube*, 28 Jan. 2019. https://www.youtube.com/watch?v=YESJ6daVg7U.
3. Messenger, Stephen. "Entire Village in` India Relocates so Nature Can Move In." *TreeHugger*, 11 Oct. 2018. https://www.treehugger.com/natural-sciences/entire-village-india-moves-out-so-nature-can-move.html.
4. Vogt, Benjamin. A *New Garden Ethic: Cultivating Defiant Compassion for an Uncertain Future.* New Society Publishers, 2017, p. 150.

"Our gardens are places of arrogance and alienation. We are a species very much alone in the world, trying to find an intimate, stabilizing connection we once had with other species. But somehow we are unable to give ourselves to the rather simple communication of empathy, compassion, and shared fate. In our gardens, we may show the greatest alienation, placing plants how and where we want and using species unrecognizable to wildlife. In our gardens, then, is arrogance- that we matter more, that our passions and loves, our losses and agonies, are separate and even superior to those of other species. While our gardens could ideally function as bridges between our world and the worlds of an infinite number of lives, too often they are walls of hubris and human-made disorder we impose upon a world already ordered to maximum benefit through millions of years of trial and error. What we wish to improve upon may be our own human-made alienation as creatures who struggle with an ethics that must encompass not just different races and creeds, but also animals, plants, and fungi. In a world of climate change and mass extinction, intimate gardens out our back door might be the best places to generate a landscape ethic that evolves into an activist-based global ethic of creation care for all life." pp. 96-7.

5. Jamieson, Dale, "Animal Liberation Is an Environmental Ethic." *Reflecting On Nature: Readings In Environmental Ethics and Philosophy*, Edited by Lori Gruen, Dale Jamieson and Christopher Schlottmann, Oxford University Press, 2013, pp. 174–5.
http://www.environmentandsociety.org/sites/default/files/key_docs/ev_7no.1_ja mieson_dale_0.pdf
Dale Jamieson is a scholar of environmental ethics and an analyst of climate change discourse
6. Bar-On, Yinon M., et al. "The Biomass Distribution on Earth." *Proceedings of the National Academy of Sciences*, vol. 115, no. 25, 2018, pp. 6506–6511, doi:10.1073/pnas.1711842115.
7. AbdelRahim, 2013, p. 116.
8. Hall, Lee. *On Their Own Terms: Animal Liberation for the 21st Century.* 2016.
Hall is a lawyer, writer, philosopher and a liberation activist for both other animals and the human spirit.
9. Wrenn, Corey. "Human Supremacy, Post-Speciesist Ideology, and the Case for Anti-Colonialist Veganism." *Animals in Human Society*, University Press of America/Hamilton Books, 2015, pp. 56 and 68.
Corey Lee Wrenn, PhD is an American sociologist specializing in animals and society, the animal rights movement, ecofeminism, and vegan studies.
http://www.coreyleewrenn.com/
10. Morris, Desmond. *The Naked Ape: A Zoologists Study of the Human.* McGraw-Hill Book Co., 1967, pp. 238-9.
The Naked Ape concluded that humans really were just apes, and much modern human behavior could be understood in terms of animal behavior and its evolution. Beneath the veneer of culture lurked an ancestral avatar.
11. Pointing, Charlotte. "Texas Hunter-Turned-Vegan Is Now Protecting 900 Acres for Wildlife." *Live Kindly,* 10 Apr. 2019,

https://www.livekindly.com/former-hunter-vegan-activist/?fbclid=IwAR3RuUrNWDAM1h678X_ZIzD32SjvCVJEHBc8f4quvDI bief93vXncotBRTU

12. Schmookler, 1984.

13. Moore, 1989, p. 57.

14. Zihlman, Adrienne, and Nancy Tanner. "Gathering and the Hominid." *Female Hierarchies,* Lionel Tiger, 2017, 163–188, doi:10.4324/9780203792018-7.

"This chapter presents a reconstruction of the way of life of Australopithecus, based on interpretations of new evidence and reinterpretation of the old. It explores the assumption that hunting arose early in human evolution and that meat was a primary food source. The chapter proposes that gathering of plant foods was the basic adaptation, and interprets social organization, parental investment, and mating patterns within this framework."

15. Hall, Lee. Personal communication, 27 July 2019.

16. Smith, Felisa A., et al. "The Accelerating Influence of Humans on Mammalian Macroecological Patterns over the Late Quaternary." *Quaternary Science Reviews,* vol. 211, 2019, pp. 1–16, doi:10.1016/j.quascirev.2019.02.031.

The transition of hominins to a largely meat-based diet ~1.8 million years ago led to the exploitation of other mammals for food and resources. As hominins, particularly archaic and modern humans, became increasingly abundant and dispersed across the globe…extinction of large-bodied mammals followed; the degree of selectivity was unprecedented… Today, most remaining large-bodied mammal species are confined to Africa, where they co-evolved with hominins… (A)nalysis demonstrates that anthropogenic impact on earth systems predates the terminal Pleistocene and has grown as populations increased and humans have become more widespread. Moreover, owing to the disproportionate influence on ecosystem structure and function of megafauna, past and present body size downgrading has reshaped Earth's biosphere. Thus, macroecological studies based only on modern species yield distorted results, which are not representative of the patterns present for most of mammal evolution. Our review supports the concept of benchmarking the 'Anthropocene' with the earliest activities of Homo sapiens.

17. Darimont, Chris T., et al. "The Unique Ecology of Human Predators." *Science,* vol. 349, no. 6250, 21 Aug. 2015, pp. 858–860, doi:10.1126/science.aac4249.

"Paradigms of sustainable exploitation focus on population dynamics of prey and yields to humanity but ignore the behavior of humans as predators. We compared patterns of predation by contemporary hunters and fishers with those of other predators that compete over shared prey (terrestrial mammals and marine fishes). Our global survey (2125 estimates of annual finite exploitation rate) revealed that humans kill adult prey, the reproductive capital of populations, at much higher median rates than other predators (up to 14 times higher), with particularly intense exploitation of terrestrial carnivores and fishes. Given this competitive dominance, impacts on predators, and other

unique predatory behavior, we suggest that humans function as an unsustainable "super predator," which—unless additionally constrained by managers—will continue to alter ecological and evolutionary processes globally."

18. Olsen, Jack. *Slaughter the Animals, Poison the Earth*. Manor Books, 1971.

Book description: It is the extermination of the coyote --a shrewd, wily, solitary scavenger-- that serves as the central theme of Jack Olsen's ragingly indignant, beautifully written and deeply moving book, perhaps the most gripping and important work of its kind since the publication of Rachel Carson's "Silent Spring".

Poisoned, hunted, a bounty placed on their heads, their pelts nailed to fenceposts, the coyotes symbolize the heartless and brutal way in which man has made the West his own as if nature had no place there.

Jack Olsen describes how, in the vast stretches of the American West, the wildlife is being systematically exterminated for the profit of the ranchers and stockmen... with the cooperation of government agencies. Hardest hit of all the animals are the great predators-- wildcats, wolves, eagles, bears, mountain lions, coyotes-- all now on the verge of extinction.

By decimating those species which seem to him inconvenient or wasteful or unprofitable, man has laid waste to his own heritage, sown the seeds of a poisoned earth, a dead land... and gone far along in the destruction of his own humanity.

19. Hall, 2016, p. 92.

20. Doe, Jane. *Anarchist Farm*. III Pub., 1996.

21. Scott, James C. *Two Cheers for Anarchism Six Easy Pieces on Autonomy, Dignity, and Meaningful Work and Play*. Princeton University Press, 2014, p. 64.

22. Yaga, 2019.

23. White, E. B. *Charlotte's Web*. Harper & Brothers, 1952.

24. Wilder, Laura Ingalls, and Renee Graef. *Deer in the Wood: My First Little House Books*. Harper Collins, 1995.

25. Hayduke. Personal communication, 8 Dec 2019.

26. Merwe, Marcel Van der. *Rewilding the Lost Wilderness: Green Heritage of the Forgotten Cape*. Marcel Van Der Merwe II, 2017. https://www.indiegogo.com/projects/rewilding-the-lost-wilderness-preserving-green-heritage-communities#/

"First came the Stone Age hunter-gatherers with power over the element of fire. On the heels of the San followed the Stone Age Khoikhoi pastoralists with their herds of sheep, goats and cattle. As the Khoikhoi spread across the entire face of the Cape, the Iron Age dawned with the arrival of the Bantu-speaking Nguni and later Tswana farmers. By 1488 European forays to these shores commenced as Portuguese seafarers set foot on South African soil. And after Dutch colonization in the year 1652 the Cape was never to be the same again.

However, the real Africa is a land of innovation, optimism and restoration. After much environmental and socio-political unrest, as various cultures surpassed their predecessors and came to define their own borders within this multi-

cultural blend, the Cape was left in a state of wildlife neutrality. Vast Karoo plains devoid of springbok, blesbok, black wildebeest and quagga; Fynbos laden mountains devoid of red hartebeest, eland and elephant; and water courses devoid of hippopotamus. But the modern African was not satisfied to have African bush devoid of African wildlife, and so we embark on the quest to 'rewild' this forgotten wilderness."

27. Olsen, 1971, pp. 267-8.
28. Sonnenblume, Kollibri terre. *The Failures of Farming and the Necessity of Wildtending: a Collection of Essays by Kollibri terre Sonnenblume.* Macska Moksha Press, 2018, p. 113.

Book description: The "Agricultural Revolution" is celebrated as one of the greatest achievements in the history of the human race, proof positive of "Progress" and of our own exalted status, only "a little lower than angels." Certainly, it was a huge change, on par with the taming of fire, the development of language and the splitting of the atom. However, a closer look shows that the adoption of farming led to declines in human health, caused sharp social inequities, started a war on the environment, and put us on a road that's headed towards extinction. In this collection of essays, the author —a former farmer— draws on both scholarship and personal experience to illuminate the emerging, contemporary understanding of agriculture as "wrong turn."

29. Perlman, 1983.
30. Pettorelli, Nathalie, et al. *Rewilding.* Cambridge University Press, 2019.

Back cover: Through a global and interdisciplinary lens, this book discusses, analyzes and summarizes the novel conservation approach of rewilding. The volume introduces key rewilding definitions and initiatives, highlighting their similarities and differences. It reviews matches and mismatches between the current state of ecological knowledge and the stated aims of rewilding projects, and discusses the role of human action in rewilding initiatives. Collating current scholarship, the book also considers the merits and dangers of rewilding approaches, as well as the economic and socio-political realities of using rewilding as a conservation tool. Its interdisciplinary nature will appeal to a broad range of readers, from primary ecologists and conservation biologists to land managers, policy makers and conservation practitioners in NGOs and government departments. Written for a scientifically literate readership of academics, researchers, students, and managers, the book also acts as a key resource for advanced undergraduate and graduate courses.

31. Foreman, Dave. *Rewilding North America A Vision For Conservation In The 21St Century.* Island Press, 2013.
32. Anderson, Kat. *Tending the Wild: Native American Knowledge and the Management of California's Natural Resources.* University of California Press, 2013.

Before Europeans arrived in 'California' there were 500 - 600 tribes living without domesticated plants or animals, without plowing or herding. "Tending the Wild" describes how the California Indians tended the land with a symbiotic intimacy. Nuts, grains, and seeds rich in oils, calories, and proteins were stored for long periods, enabling survival through harsher seasons and lean years. The amount of acorns foraged each year varied, but huge quantities were gathered as they were the main staple. A diverse variety of wild flowers and grasses provided a dependable supply of seeds and grains.

Indians tended the growth of plants by pruning, weeding, burning, watering, replanting bulbs, and sowing seeds. Soil disturbance was limited to digging bulbs, corms, and tubers, and planting. Disturbed soil was immediately reseeded. This lifeway sustained the ecosystem for a diversity of life without harm. And wild life tended toward content.

33. Medrano, Finisia. *Growing Up in Occupied America.* Lulu, 2013.

This true life story of 'tranny granny Finisia', long lived bundle carrier on traditional wild tended Sacred Hoops, carrying on lifeways of First Nations of the Great Basin. Her teachings offer a glimpse into an almost forgotten way of walking in with and nourishing the land. She is one of the last to live and hold the knowledge of dying ancient lifeways tending the wild.

34. Deur, Douglas *Pacific Northwest Foraging: 120 Wild and Flavorful Edibles from Alaska Blueberries to Wild Hazelnuts.* Timber Press, 2014, pp. 16, 18.

Foraging guidebook includes ethnobotanical information and emergent wild tending ethos through replanting indigenous species.

35. Kheel, 2008, p. 246.

36. Oppenlander, Richard A. *Comfortably Unaware: Global Depletion and Food Responsibility... What You Choose to Eat Is Killing Our Planet.* Langdon Street Press, 2011.

Richard Oppenlander is an activist, lecturer and author of two books on the impact food choice has on the environment, biodiversity, global warming, water scarcity, health, world hunger, and the cruelty inherent in all types of animal agriculture.

37. Torres, Bob. *Making a Killing: the Political Economy of Animal Rights.* AK Press, 2007, p. 133.

Torres was an assistant professor of sociology at St. Lawrence University in Canton, New York. He is the co-author, with his wife Jenna Torres, of Vegan Freak: Being Vegan in a Non-Vegan World, and the author of Making A Killing: The Political Economy of Animal Rights.

38. Bradley, Joan. *Bringing Back the Bush: the Bradley Method of Bush Regeneration.* New Holland, 2002.

The Bradley Method is a simple and adaptable approach to nature regeneration that is based on helping nature to help itself. This text outlines the basic principles underscoring the Bradley method, and provides the practical techniques required to put them into practice.

39. Perkins Gilman, Charlotte. *Herland,* The Forerunner, 1911.

Born in 1860, Perkins Gilman was a feminist, lecturer, writer, and publisher, a leading theorist of the women's movement in U.S.

40. Huxley, Aldous. *Island.* Heron Books, 1962.

Island is the final book by Aldous Huxley, published in 1962. It is the account of Will Farnaby, a cynical journalist who is shipwrecked on the fictional island of Pala. Island is Huxley's utopian counterpart to his most famous work, the 1932 dystopian novel Brave New World. The ideas that would become Island can be seen in a foreword he wrote in 1946 to a new edition of Brave New World: "If I were now to rewrite the book, I would offer the Savage a third alternative. Between the Utopian and primitive horns of his dilemma would lie the possibility of sanity... In this community economics would be decentralist and Henry-Georgian, politics Kropotkinesque and co-operative. Science and technology would be used as though, like the Sabbath, they had been made for man, not (as at present and still more so in the Brave New World) as though man were to be adapted and enslaved to them. Religion would be the conscious and intelligent pursuit of man's Final End, the unitive knowledge of immanent Tao or Logos, the transcendent Godhead or Brahman. And the prevailing philosophy of life would be a kind of Higher Utilitarianism, in which the Greatest Happiness principle would be secondary to the Final End principle – the first question to be asked and answered in every contingency of life being: "How will this thought or action contribute to, or interfere with, the achievement, by me and the greatest possible number of other individuals, of man's Final End?"

41. Powers, Richard. *The Overstory: a Novel.* W.W. Norton & Company, 2019.

Richard Powers is a novelist who explores the effects of modern science and technology. "A sweeping, impassioned work of activism and resistance that is also a stunning evocation of—and paean to—the natural world. From the roots to the crown and back to the seeds, Richard Powers's twelfth novel unfolds in concentric rings of interlocking fables that range from antebellum New York to the late twentieth-century Timber Wars of the Pacific Northwest and beyond. There is a world alongside ours—vast, slow, interconnected, resourceful, magnificently inventive, and almost invisible to us. This is the story of a handful of people who learn how to see that world and who are drawn up into its unfolding catastrophe."

42. Abbey, Edward. *Desert Solitaire.* University of Arizona Press, 2010.

Abbey's writings set primarily in the southwestern are an uncompromising environmentalist philosophy into action. http://www.abbeyweb.net/

43. Abbey, Edward. *The Monkey Wrench Gang.* Olive Editions, 2014.

The Monkey Wrench Gang recounts the exploits of a band of guerrilla environmentalists; both it and Desert Solitaire became handbooks of the environmental movement. The strain of cynicism that runs through much of Abbey's writing is leavened by a bracing prose style and mischievous wit. His advice was unorthodox: "This is what you shall do: Love the earth and sun and animals. Stand up for the stupid and crazy. Take your hat off to no man." And his opinions pithy: "Anarchism is not a romantic fable but the hardheaded realization, based on five thousand years of experience, that we cannot entrust the management of our lives to kings, priests, politicians, generals, and county commissioners." His appreciation for the natural and distrust of machines and the modern state resonated through the 1960s, '70s, and beyond. After his death, he was buried as he had requested: in a sleeping bag, without embalming fluid or casket. His body was surreptitiously interred in an unmarked desert grave somewhere in Arizona.

44. Tokarczuk, 2019.

45. James, Tania. *The Tusk That Did the Damage.* Vintage Books, 2016.

46. Webb, Mary. *Gone to Earth.* 2020. Originally published in 1917.

47. Costello, Emily, editor. "Before You Vote, Read Mary Webb's 1917 Novel on the Barbarism of Fox Hunting." *The Conversation*, 7 June 2017, from *Gone to Earth* chapters 1 and 28. https://theconversation.com/before-you-vote-read-mary-webbs-1917-novel-on-the-barbarism-of-fox-hunting-78620

48. Butler, Octavia E. *Dawn.* Aspect, 1989.

"In a world devastated by nuclear war with humanity on the edge of extinction, aliens finally make contact. They rescue those humans they can, keeping most survivors in suspended animation while the aliens begin the slow process of rehabilitating the planet. When Lilith Iyapo is "awakened", she finds that she has been chosen to revive her fellow humans in small groups by first preparing them to meet the utterly terrifying aliens, then training them to survive on the wilderness that the planet has become. But the aliens cannot help humanity without altering it forever.

Bonded to the aliens in ways no human has ever known, Lilith tries to fight them even as her own species comes to fear and loathe her. https://octaviabutler.org/

49. Harper, Breeze. "The Absence of Meat in Oankali Dietary Philosophy: An Eco-Feminist-Vegan Analysis of Octavia Butler's *Dawn*" *The Black Imagination: Science Fiction, Futurism and the Speculative*, Peter Lang, 2011, p. 112.

Breeze Harper is a critical race feminist, diversity strategist, and author of books and studies on veganism and racism. https://www.abreezeharper.com/

50. Williams, Cara. "Ecofeminism in the Speculative Fiction of Ursula K. LeGuin, Octavia Butler, and Margaret Atwood", 2018, pp. 42-3.

"The aim of this article is to explore the speculative fiction works of three prominent, female speculative fiction writers: Ursula K. Le Guin, Margaret Atwood, and Octavia Butler through an ecofeminist lens. Noting how Le Guin, Atwood, and Butler portray women and the environment in post-apocalyptic science fiction, this article looks at how these authors explore food acquisition and consumption in their various worlds. This article asks the question, how does our relationship with food (acquisition, agriculture, manufacturing, and consumption) reflect our relationship with our ecological environment and our understanding of women and the female role."

51. Coetzee, J. M. *Elizabeth Costello.* Brombergs, 2003.

"In this novel, Elizabeth Costello, a celebrated aging Australian writer, travels around the world and gives lectures on topics including the lives of animals and literary censorship. In her youth, Costello wrote The House on Eccles Street, a novel that re-tells James Joyce's Ulysses from the perspective of the protagonist's wife, Molly Bloom. Costello, becoming weary from old age, confronts her fame, which seems further and further removed from who she has become, and struggles with issues of belief, vegetarianism, sexuality, language and evil. Many of the lectures Costello gives are edited fragments that Coetzee had previously published. The lessons she delivers only tenuously speak to the

work for which she is being honored. Of note, Elizabeth Costello is the main character in Coetzee's academic novel, The Lives of Animals (1999).

52. Paula, Rodrigo Martini. "Rethinking Human and Nonhuman Animal Relations in J.M. Coetzees Elizabeth Costello." 2012.

"For the past four decades, scholarship on the relationship between human and nonhuman animals has been growing inside the academy and sprouting ontological and epistemological concerns about the status of the Humanities as an institution. Between 1997 and 2003, South-African author and Nobel Laureate J. M. Coetzee created Elizabeth Costello, an Australian writer that delivers lectures at certain universities and causes controversy when addressing the nature of animal rights movements. This work aims at analyzing the situations in which Coetzee uses Costello to speak about the cruelty to nonhuman animals. What I argue is that in entering the conversation through the use of a fictional character, Coetzee puts the discourse of both philosophy an science in perspective and forces the reader to rethink the politics involved in the ways disciplines speak of animals."

53. Coetzee, 2003, p. 70.

54. Randall, Don. "The Community of Sentient Beings: J. M. Coetzees Ecology in Disgrace and Elizabeth Costello." *ESC: English Studies in Canada*, vol. 33, no. 1-2, 2008, pp. 209–225, doi:10.1353/esc.0.0054.
https://journals.library.ualberta.ca/esc/index.php/ESC/article/view/25145/18650

55. Wright, Laura. "A Feminist-Vegetarian Defense of Elizabeth Costello: A Rant from an Ethical Academic on J.M. Coetzee's The Lives of Animals" *J. M. Coetzee and the Idea of the Public Intellectual*, Ohio Univ. Press, 2008.

Laura Wright explores the dichotomy between reason and emotion in the realm of animal rights in literature and feminist philosophy.

56. Stowe, Harriet Beecher. *Uncle Tom's Cabin.* Wordsworth Classics, 2002, p. 14.

57. Babbitt, Natalie. *Tuck Everlasting.* Square Fish, 2018.

58. Weyrich, 2017.

59. Nibert, 2013.

60. Plumwood, Val. *Environmental Culture: the Ecological Crisis of Reason.* Routledge, 2007.

Val Plumwood was a philosopher and ecofeminist known for her work on anthropocentrism. From the 1970s she played a central role in the development of radical ecosophy.

61. Voigt, 2017, pg. 151.

62. Weaner, Larry, and Thomas Christopher. *Garden Revolution: How Our Landscapes Can Be a Source of Environmental Change.* Timber Press, 2016.

An ecological approach to planting that bucks much of conventional gardening's counter-productive, time-consuming practices while restoring native ecology.

63. Montana, Ria. "Dog Versus Wildlife." *Vegan Primitivist,* 2 Dec. 2017.
https://veganprimitivist.wordpress.com/2017/12/02/dog-versus-wildlife/

64. Tokarczuk, 2019, pp. 47, 100-1.

65. Zakin, Susan. *Coyotes and Town Dogs: Earth First! and the Environmental Movement*. Markham Books, 2018.
   Historical Abbeyesque accounting of the first decades of Earth First!
66. Tokarczuk, 2019, pp. 15, 53.

6. RESURGENT SAVAGERY

1. Zerzan, John. *Running on Emptiness: The Pathology of Civilization*. Feral House, 2002, pg. 202.
   "Thinker and revolutionary John Zerzan has been widely credited with inspiring the new generation of antiglobalization activists. Collecting essays and interviews, Running on Emptiness reflects Zerzan's wide range of interests, from the political ("We All Live in Waco") to the personal ("So... How Did You Become an Anarchist?"). This book deftly mixes history, anthropology, science, cultural theory, and politics to offer a critique of society as well as a blueprint for change"
2. Tokarczuk, 2019, pp.195-6.
3. Collard and Contrucci,, 1989, p. 46.
4. Farnish, Keith. *Times up!: an Uncivilized Solution to a Global Crisis*. Green Books Ltd., 2009, p. 201.
   Book description: This is not an environmental book, even though it is concerned with the environment. It is not a book to save the world, even though the world is clearly in trouble. Ultimately, Time's Up! is a book about survival; about ensuring that every individual human has the means to save herself or himself from the global crisis that is unfolding. People know that the climate is changing, that species are being removed from the Earth at a rapidly increasing rate, that entire ecosystems are becoming shadows of their former richness; they know, but they do not understand. The global environmental crisis is closing in on humanity from all directions, yet the crisis barely registers on this culture's list of problems. As we stand, humanity is doomed to a collapse that will leave only a few nomads, and a toxic, barely survivable Earth in its wake. So why is nothing being done beyond changing light bulbs, recycling and buying organic food? It's certainly not for a lack of good reasons. Humans have no motivation stronger than survival, yet the culture that dominates "the culture we call Industrial Civilization" has created a set of priorities that value financial wealth, the possession of superfluous goods and short, cheap thrills, above that most basic need. In short, we are prepared to die in order to live a life that is killing us. Time's Up! is all about changing this. It describes what our actions are doing to the very things on Earth that we depend on for survival, at scales that we rarely contemplate. It arms us with the tools to free us from the culture that has blinded us for centuries, and which will allow us to live lives that will give the Earth, and ourselves, a future. Time's Up! proposes something radical, fundamental and frightening; something longterm, exhilarating and absolutely necessary; something totally uncivilized.

5. Wilkinson, Todd. "A Death Of Ethics: Is Hunting Destroying Itself? From Killing Baboon Families to Staging Predator-Killing Contests, Hunters Stand Accused of Violating the North American Model of Wildlife Conservation. Now They're Being Called out by Their Own." *Mountain Journal*, 12 Dec. 2018. https://mountainjournal.org/hunting-in-america-faces-an-ethical-reckoning?fbclid=IwAR2AxsoWzhRvEhkveJTw_RN6ReGzPYsEY62aruGxZQbC5rwd8Drr6wQ3d-w.

6. Huxley, 1968.

7. Schipani, Sam. "13 Unlucky Animals That Are Killed for Fun." *Sierra Club*, 16 July 2018. www.sierraclub.org/sierra/thirteen-unlucky-animals-wildlife-killing-contests?fbclid=IwAR1Zcx7OMoVV6EREsABkHoc5jUeG2VyypIUwa35Xzgrfxe9aOFhQypwhMDA

8.Adorno, Theodor W., and Anson G. Rabinbach. "Culture Industry Reconsidered." *New German Critique*, no. 6, 1975, p. 12, doi:10.2307/487650.

9. Rich, Adrienne, "Compulsory Heterosexuality and Lesbian Existence.*" Powers of Desire: The Politics of Sexuality,* edited by Martha E. Thompson, Monthly Review Press, 1983. http://www.posgrado.unam.mx/musica/lecturas/Maus/viernes/AdrienneRichCompulsoryHeterosexuality.pdf

This essay is a vital and clever critique of institutionalized lifeways that have traditionally controlled women— patriarchal motherhood, economic exploitation, the nuclear family, and compulsory heterosexuality.

10. Smuts, Barbara. "The Evolutionary Origins of Patriarchy." *Human Nature,* vol. 6, no. 1, 1995, pp. 1–32, doi:10.1007/bf02734133.

"This article encourages expansion of feminist analyses on an evolutionary basis of male motivations in controlling female sexuality. Evidence from other primates of male sexual coercion and female resistance to it indicates that the sexual conflicts underlying patriarchy predate the emergence of the human species. Humans, however, exhibit more extensive male dominance and male control of female sexuality than is shown by most other primates. Six hypotheses are proposed to explain how, over the course of human evolution, this unusual degree of gender inequality came about. The findings emphasizes behavioral flexibility, cross-cultural variability in the degree of patriarchy, and possibilities for future change."

11. Callenbach, Ernest. *Ecotopia: a Novel about Ecology, People and Politics in 1999.* Pluto Press, 1978.

"Twenty years have passed since Northern California, Oregon, and Washington seceded from the United States to create a new nation, Ecotopia. Rumors abound of barbaric war games, tree worship, revolutionary politics, sexual extravagance. Now, this mysterious country admits its first American visitor: investigative reporter Will Weston, whose dispatches alternate between shock and admiration. But Ecotopia gradually unravels everything Weston knows to be true about government and human nature itself, forcing him to choose between two competing views of civilization.

Since it was first published in 1975, Ecotopia has inspired readers throughout the world with its vision of an ecologically and socially sustainable future."

12. Stabile, Carol A. *Feminism and the Technological Fix*. Manchester University Press, 1994, p. 5.

Stabile explores various feminist assumptions and notions on technology and modernity, revealing their incongruences.

13. Kaczynski, Ted. "Ship of Fools." *Crime Scene*, 1999. http://www.sacredfools.org/crimescene/casefiles/s2/shipoffoolsstory.htm.

14. Gould, Stephen Jay. "On Replacing the Idea of Progress with an Operational Notion of Directionality." *Evolutionary Progress*, University of Chicago Press, 1988.

Gould was a paleontologist, evolutionary biologist, and historian of science. And one of the most influential and widely read authors of popular science. He taught at Harvard University and worked at the American Museum of Natural History in New York.

15. Harlan, Will. *Untamed: the Wildest Woman in America and the Fight for Cumberland Island*. Grove, 2015.

This inspiring biography of wild naturalist Carol Ruckdeschel is her battle to protect an island habitat she shares with other animals, in particular sea turtles.

16. Hegland, Jean. *Into the Forest*. Cornerstone Digital, 2016.

From Hegland's website: Set in the near-future, Into the Forest focuses on the relationship between two teenaged sisters as they struggle to survive the collapse of society.

In many ways, Nell and Eva have experienced a near-idyllic childhood, growing up miles from the nearest neighbor in the forests of northern California. Their father, an iconoclastic grade school principal, has decided to keep them out of school, and their mother has encouraged each of them to follow her own passions. As a result, Eva is determined to become a ballet dancer, while her younger sister, Nell, hopes to matriculate at Harvard.

Despite the fact that their happy world is rocked when their mother dies of cancer, they and their father are determined to carry on. Even as terrorism, a distant war, increasingly unpredictable weather, and an unstable economy, challenge the reliability of social order and infrastructure, their little family continues to hoard its resources and attempts to keep up its spirits as they wait for the lights to come back on, the phone to ring, and the lives they have been anticipating to return to them. But when their father is killed in an accident, and a dangerous stranger arrives at their door, the girls confront the fact that they must find some new way to grow into adulthood. http://jean-hegland.com/

17. Rozema, Patricia, director. *Into the Forest*. Elevation Pictures, 2016.

18. Lawrence, Andrew D., et al. "Construction of Fluorescent Analogs to Follow the Uptake and Distribution of Cobalamin (Vitamin B12) in Bacteria, Worms, and Plants." *Cell Chemical Biology*, vol. 25, no. 8, 2018, doi:10.1016/j.chembiol.2018.04.012.

"...seedlings of higher plants such as Lepidium sativum are also able to transport B12."

19. Shai, Iris, et al. "Protein Bioavailability of Wolffia Globosa Duckweed, a Novel Aquatic Plant, a Randomized Controlled Trial." *Clinical Nutrition*, vol. 38, no. 5, 2019, p. 2464, doi:10.1016/j.clnu.2019.08.007.

20. Mic the Vegan. "It's Official, There's a Plant Source of B12" *YouTube*, 27 Dec. 2019. https://www.youtube.com/watch?v=QHvRArWglRY

21. Nakos, M., et al. "Isolation and Analysis of Vitamin B12 from Plant Samples." *Food Chemistry*, vol. 216, 2017, pp. 301–308, doi:10.1016/j.foodchem.2016.08.037.

22. Hervey, Annette, et al. "Studies on Euglena and Vitamin B 12." *Bulletin of the Torrey Botanical Club*, vol. 77, no. 6, 1950, p. 423, doi:10.2307/2482180.

23. Craighead George, Jean. *Julie of the Wolves*. HarperCollins Publishers, 1972.

24. Ibid, p. 141.

25. Melamed, 2016.

26. Scott, 2018, pp. 39, 42.

27. Koch, Alexander, et al. "Earth System Impacts of the European Arrival and Great Dying in the Americas after 1492." *Quaternary Science Reviews*, vol. 207, 2019, pp. 13–36, doi:10.1016/j.quascirev.2018.12.004.

28. Long, TJ. Personal communication, 27, Nov 2019.

29. Mayton, Dave. Personal communication, 4 Feb 2020.

30. Ellul, Jacques. *The Technological Society*. Vintage Books, 1967.

Ellul explains the dystopian reality technology determines on every aspect of life. Techno-society "has one primary ethic: it works to destroy, eliminate and subdue the natural world and replace it with artificial conceits and managed monocultures." ~ Nikiforuk

31. Nikiforuk, Andrew. "Jacques Ellul: A Prophet for Our Tech-Saturated Times." *The Tyee*, 12 Oct. 2018. https://thetyee.ca/Analysis/2018/10/12/Jacques-Ellul-Prophet/

32. Urban Scout. *Rewild or Die: Revolution and Renaissance at the End of Civilization*, Urban Scout LLC, 2016.

Book description: Rewild or Die is a collection of essays written by Urban Scout exploring the philosophy of the emerging rewilding renaissance, in which civilized humans are thought to be "domesticated" through thousands of years of sedentary, agrarian life. This way of life is believed to be the root of all environmental destruction and social injustice. Rewilding is the process of un-doing this domestication, and restoring healthy, biologically diverse communities. Using thoughtful, humorously cynical and at times angry prose, Urban Scout explores how the ideology of civilization clashes with the wild and wild peoples, and how thinking, feeling and most importantly living wild is the only way to reach true sustainability.

33. Montana, Ria. "Untamed Unmasking of Permaculture: Debunk of Tao Orion's 'Beyond the War on Invasives.'" *Vegan Primitivist*, 8 June 2019, https://veganprimitivist.wordpress.com/2019/06/01/untamed-unmasking-of-permaculture/.

34. Montana, Ria. "Death of Hope." *Vegan Primitivist*, 25 Dec. 2019. https://veganprimitivist.wordpress.com/2019/12/25/death-of-hope/

35. Wolff, Robert. *Original Wisdom: Stories of an Ancient Way of Knowing.* Inner Traditions, 2001, pp. 156-7.

Book description: • Explores the lifestyle of indigenous peoples of the world who exist in complete harmony with the natural world and with each other. • Reveals a model of a society built on trust, patience, and joy rather than anxiety, hurry, and acquisition. • Shows how we can reconnect with the ancient intuitive awareness of the world's original people.

Deep in the mountainous jungle of Malaysia the aboriginal Sng'oi exist on the edge of extinction, though their way of living may ultimately be the kind of existence that will allow us all to survive. The Sng'oi--pre-industrial, pre-agricultural, semi-nomadic--live without cars or cell phones, without clocks or schedules in a lush green place where worry and hurry, competition and suspicion are not known. Yet these indigenous people--as do many other aboriginal groups--possess an acute and uncanny sense of the energies, emotions, and intentions of their place and the living beings who populate it, and trustingly follow this intuition, using it to make decisions about their actions each day.

Psychologist Robert Wolff lived with the Sng'oi, learned their language, shared their food, slept in their huts, and came to love and admire these people who respect silence, trust time to reveal and heal, and live entirely in the present with a sense of joy. Even more, he came to recognize the depth of our alienation from these basic qualities of life. Much more than a document of a disappearing people, Original Wisdom: Stories of an Ancient Way of Knowing holds a mirror to our own existence, allowing us to see how far we have wandered from the ways of the intuitive and trusting Sng'oi, and challenges us, in our fragmented world, to rediscover this humanity within ourselves.

36. Coetzee, 2003, p. 95.

37. Suzman, 2019, p. 167.

38. Ibid, p. 168.

39. Ibid, p. 164.

40. Ibid, p. 163.

41. Young, Jon, and Anna Breytenbac. "Tracking and Animal Communication: Jon Young and Anna Breytenbach." *YouTube,* https://www.youtube.com/watch?v=f-t5SaH8g3o.

Tracking and Animal Communication: Jon Young and Anna Breytenbach Professional animal communicator Anna Breytenback and master tracker Jon Young explore animal tracking in relationship to inter-species communication, nature connectedness and awareness.

Anna - "Animal tracking is the oldest form of interspecies communication. Connecting with an animal's footprint puts us in touch with the animal's body and mind... By just opening my awareness and softening my body and my mind, I started having intuitive experiences"

Jon – "You just stare into the footprint in a diffused kind of relaxed way, and in a certain sense begin talking. Something starts to come, and then out of the track comes a picture. And you mind is filled with a very clear image you couldn't have generated yourself. There's so much information in that one-billionth of a second. Even in the look of the face of the animal looking back at you…Sometimes it's a line of light appears on the landscape and I start following it, and then it disappears. It shows up long enough for me to know it's time to move. And then I start moving, and at that point the rest takes care of itself. My body wants to go that way, it wouldn't go any other way. And then I discover there's that fresh track, and I recognize that individual track, it's the same individual. When you have that moment of reconnecting with the animal physically at the end of that trail, there's a moment of grace." The line is connected to the spirit of the animal.

It is important to note that Jon Young has been taught to track for the purpose of hunting, and he feels it necessary to 'give thanks' in the mystical manner of rationalizing.

https://www.youtube.com/watch?v=f-t5SaH8g3o

42. Suzman, 2019, p. 169.

43. Ibid, p. 172.

44. Ibid, p. 171.

45. Ibid, p. 174.

46. Ibid, p. 173.

47. Ibid, p. 168.

48. Ibid, p. 164.

49. Ibid, p. 173.

50. Ibid, p. 174.

51. Ibid, p. 165.

52. Ibid, p. 166.

53. Tokarczuk, 2019, p. 10.

54. Montana, Rio. "My Wild Community." *Vegan Primitivist*, 14 Jan. 2020, https://veganprimitivist.wordpress.com/2020/01/14/my-wild-community

Fed up with civ, desperate to be without domesticates, I've taken to night walking. Each night of distinct tone, mostly nuanced differences, sometime stark like just now. A rare Salish lowland snow left a 1 inch white blanket, just icy enough to hold tracks precisely. I've never been much interested in tracks, as humans with broken compassion track to slay. But these tracks tell stories of new friends I've been seeing.

What first drew my attention is the young male coyote new to the neighborhood, just at my starting point. Not him, but his recent presence in paw prints. I checked to be certain – more oval than dog, small claw prints on two middle toes, yep coyote. I followed along where he'd done his rounds checking for food, just as I do rounds getting to know him and them. Turning up the snowy hill. First barely noticeable track on the falling snow had been a thin-tired bicyclist, slow & right down the middle of the hill, rear tire & front as one. From then, it had been a long while before the wild night community emerged.

Five-fingered raccoon had been meandering, also looking for food. A size 10 shoed homeless man, probably keeping warm by walking, set the coon slowly off his path into a drain ditch. Did he see raccoon as raccoon saw him? No pause or break in his steps. I see I was too late for the eastern rabbit that often hops up the hill beside me, leaving me wondering her intentions. Definitely not squirrel, as she stopped too frequently looking around, and the telltale sign – larger back feet outside & forward but staggering front feet behind (versus squirrels' symmetrical front feet). Did she instead walk along this size 6 woman, who walked from a house to another house? Uphill further, the size 10 man had stumbled almost falling, sped up & slippery stepped to the sidewalk. I didn't sense any fear in the man's track as he fell. He seemed to take it in stride moments before meeting raccoon.

At mid-hill plateau, a scurry that ended with coyote trotting off with a struggling possum in his mouth, a swipe of his tale on the ground didn't faze coyote's steady gate. I struggle to shift from deducing or imagining to intuiting possum and coyote's emotions, but can't. Will my new friends notice me noticing them in my tracks? Entering my home, my wildness melts like snow that holds wild stories, for a while.

55. Suzman, 2019, p. 168.

56. Tokarczuk, 2019, p. 56.

57. Good, Kenneth, and David Chanoff. *Into the Heart: One Man's Pursuit of Love and Knowledge among the Yanomama.* Touchstone, 1991, pp. 54-5.

  Book description: This is an absorbing, thrilling account of an anthropologist's foray into the heart of the Amazon, where for 12 years he lived among the Yanomama, learned their language, fell in love with one of their women, then found himself in a harrowing life-and-death struggle to keep from losing her.

58. Masson, J. Moussaieff, and Susan McCarthy. *When Elephants Weep: The Emotional Lives of Animals.* Dell Publishing, 1995, p. 145.

  Book description: From dancing squirrels to bashful gorillas to spiteful killer whales, Masson and coauthor Susan McCarthy bring forth fascinating anecdotes and illuminating insights that offer powerful proof of the existence of animal emotion. Chapters on love, joy, anger, fear, shame, compassion, and loneliness are framed by a provocative re-evaluation of how we treat animals, from hunting and eating them to scientific experimentation. Forming a complete and compelling picture of the inner lives of animals, When Elephants Weep assures that we will never look at animals in the same way again.

59. Ibid.

60. "The Life of Birds." *BBC Four,* BBC, https://www.bbc.co.uk/programmes/b007qn69.

61. Dietrich, William. *The Final Forest: the Battle for the Last Great Trees of the Pacific Northwest.* Penguin Books, 1993, p. 226.

  A telling of the human side of the struggle that looms as the fate of forests is determined.

62. Wilson, Peter J. *The Domestication of the Human Species.* Yale University Press, 1991, pp. 2-3.

  Book description: Peter J. Wilson takes domestication as the starting point for his continued inquiry into human evolution. Wilson argues that settling down into a built environment was the most radical and far-reaching innovation in human development and that it had a crucial effect on human psychology and social relations. The insights of this book point the way toward amendments to social theories that will challenge the professional reader and at the same time offer to the general reader an enriched understanding of human behavior and human history.

63. Collard and Contrucci, 1989, p. 53.

64. Eisler, Riane. *The Chalice and the Blade.* Thorsons, 1998, p. 170.

Book description: The Chalice and the Blade tells a new story of our cultural origins. It shows that warfare and the war of the sexes are neither divinely nor biologically ordained. It provides verification that a better future is possible— and is in fact firmly rooted in the haunting dramas of what happened in our past.

65. Ibid, p. 171

66. Defleur, Alban R., and Emmanuel Desclaux. "Impact of the Last Interglacial Climate Change on Ecosystems and Neanderthals Behavior at Baume Moula-Guercy, Ardèche, France." *Journal of Archaeological Science*, vol. 104, 2019, pp. 114–124, doi:10.1016/j.jas.2019.01.002.

Abstract: Earth's climate experienced a major warming during the last interglacial period.... The rapid climate change altered ecosystems causing a geographical redistribution of flora and fauna. Due to the scarcity of archaeological sites representing this period, the effect of these events on the behavior of Neanderthal hunter-gatherers in Western Europe has been poorly understood. New evidence from a well preserved archaeological layer (XV) at Baume (cave) Moula-Guercy in Southeastern France, attributed to the optimum Eemian Interglacial, unparalleled on the European continent, allows us to consider the challenges Neanderthals faced as these new ecosystems and ecological communities formed. We argue that, on the European continent, the human population collapsed, maintaining itself only in a few regions. We further suggest that these environmental upheavals, including depletion of prey biomass at the beginning of the Upper Pleistocene, contributed to the rise of cannibalistic behavior in Neanderthals, as exhibited among remains found at the Baume Moula-Guercy.

67. Farnish, Keith. *Underminers: a Guide to Subverting the Machine.* New Society Publishers, 2013, p. 21.

Book description: A user's guide for dismantling modern civilization.

68. Dietrich, 1993, p. 63.

69. Flower Bomb. "No Hope, No Future: Let the Adventures Begin!" The Anarchist Library, 2019. https://theanarchistlibrary.org/library/Flower-bomb-no-hope-no-future-let-the-adventures-begin

70. Young, Peter. *Liberate: Stories and Lessons on Animal Liberation Above the Law.* Warcry Communications, 2019, p. 355.

END QUOTES

1. Tallamy, Douglas W. *Bringing Nature Home.* Timber Press, 2016, p. 287.

Entomologist Douglas Tallamy presents hands on ways humans can assist wildlife recovery by returning indigenous biodiverse habitat, rewilding the land where you live. While it almost goes without saying, he lays out the case to rewild based on today's degraded in nature, and gives interesting lessons on the interdependence of plants, insects and other animals that evolved together, how humans need insects in our world for life to continue and how insect numbers are encouraged by diversity of indigenous plants specific to each area. It has taken thousands of years of evolution for communities of life to co-adapt. Many native insects do not eat nonnative plants, impacting the food chain at large. 'Gardens' can function as habitat for animals in desperate need. This is a guidebook for every gardener to reconnect with nature in a giving, beneficial way, to sense the urgency of Earth's declining conditions and help recover wildlife.

2. Shepard, 1997, p. 11.

3. Schlesier, 2013, pp. 10-11.

4. Hogan, 2011.

5. Luke, Brian. 1995, pp. 312–313, doi.org/10.1215/9780822381952-013.

6. Kheel, Marti. "Interview with Prominent US Writer Dr. Marti Kheel." *YouTube*, 2 May 2010. https://www.youtube.com/watch?v=DWghIE9a4TY

BIBLIOGRAPHY

Abbey, Edward. Desert Solitaire. University of Arizona Press, 2010.

Abbey, Edward. The Monkey Wrench Gang. Olive Editions, 2014.

AbdelRahim, Layla. Wild Children-Domesticated Dreams: Civilization and the Birth of Education. Fernwood Publishing, 2013. http://layla.miltsov.org/

Abete, Itziar, et al. "Association between Total, Processed, Red and White Meat Consumption and All-Cause, CVD and IHD Mortality: a Meta-Analysis of Cohort Studies." British Journal of Nutrition, vol. 112, no. 5, 2014, pp. 762–775, doi:10.1017/s000711451400124x.

Adams, Carol J. The Pornagrphy of Meat. Bloomsbury Academic; Little Simon Ed. Edition, 2004.

Adorno, Theodor W. "Culture Industry Reconsidered." New German Critique, no. 6, 1975, doi:10.2307/487650.

Adorno, Theodor. "Wozu noch Philosophie? [Why still philosophy?]," 1963, Critical Models, 1998.

Adovasio, J. M. The Invisible Sex: Uncovering the True Roles of Women in Prehistory. Routledge, 2017.

Agarwal, C. V., and Julie K. Wesp. Exploring Sex and Gender in Bioarchaeology. University of New Mexico Press, 2017.

Alvarez, Natasha. Liminal: a Novella. Black and Green Press, 2014.

Anderson, Kat. Tending the Wild: Native American Knowledge and the Management of California's Natural Resources. University of California Press, 2013.

Ardren, Traci. Ancient Maya Women. AltaMira Press, 2002.

Ardrey, Robert, and Berdine Ardrey. African Genesis: a Personal Investigation into the Animal Origins and Nature of Man. Story Design Limited, 2014.

Atjecoutay, Kerry Redwood. https://kredatjecoutay.wordpress.com/2017/04/04/kerry-m-redwood-atjecoutay/

Aubert, Maxime, et al. "Earliest Hunting Scene in Prehistoric Art." Nature, Dec 2019, doi.org/10.1038/s41586-0198-1806-y.

B., M. "Returning to Reality: A Response to Paul Shepard's 'The Vegetarians', by Michael B." Vegan Primitivist, 25 Aug. 2019. https://veganprimitivist.wordpress.com/2019/08/25/returning-to-reality-a-response-to-paul-shepards-the-vegetarians-by-michael-b/

Baba Yaga. "From Identity to Individualist: A Nihilist's Personal History in Leftism." The Anarchist Library, 2019. https://theanarchistlibrary.org/library/baba-yaba-from-identity-to-individualist-a-nihilist-s-personal-history-in-leftism?fbclid=IwAR20NtFWSxGca3ijDHAeWIMPwANiiecx80ysdBMHRKQ8IQFraVBRB48nFYU

Babbitt, Natalie. Tuck Everlasting. Square Fish, 2018.

Baker, Nick. Rewild: The Art of Returning to Nature. White Lion Pub, 2020.

Bar-On, Yinon M., et al. "The Biomass Distribution on Earth." Proceedings of the National Academy of Sciences, vol. 115, no. 25, 2018, pp. 6506–6511, doi:10.1073/pnas.1711842115.

Barnes, Simon. Rewild Yourself: Making Nature More Visible in Our Lives. Pegasus Books, 2019.

Barras, Colin. "Ancient Leftovers Show the Real Paleo Diet Was a Veggie Feast." New Scientist, 5 Dec. 2016. https://www.newscientist.com/article/2115127-ancient-leftovers-show-the-real-paleo-diet-was-a-veggie-feast/

Beauchesne, Patrick. Children and Childhood in Bioarchaeology: Bioarchaeological Interpretations of the Human Past: Local, Regional, and Global Perspectives. University Press of Florida.

Bekoff, Marc, and Jessica Pierce. The Animals Agenda: Freedom, Compassion, and Coexistence in the Human Age. Beacon Press, 2018.

Benítez-López, Ana, et al. "Intact but Empty Forests? Patterns of Hunting-Induced Mammal Defaunation in the Tropics." PLOS Biology, vol. 17, no. 5, 2019, doi:10.1371/journal.pbio.3000247.

Benzie, Iris, et al. "Effects of a Long-Term Vegetarian Diet on Biomarkers of Antioxidant Status and Cardiovascular Disease Risk." Nutrition, vol. 20, no. 10, 2004, pp. 863–866, doi:10.1016/j.nut.2004.06.006.

Berndt, Catherine H., "Interpretations and "Facts" in Aboriginal Australia" Woman the Gatherer, edited by Frances Dahlberg, Yale University, 1981.

Bernstein, Adam M., et al. "Major Dietary Protein Sources and Risk of Coronary Heart Disease in Women." Circulation, vol. 122, no. 9, 2010, pp. 876–883, doi:10.1161/circulationaha.109.915165.

Bickle, Penny, and Linda Fibiger. "Ageing, Childhood and Social Identity in the Early Neolithic of Central Europe." European Journal of Archaeology, vol. 17, no. 2, 2014, pp. 208–228, doi:10.1179/1461957114y.0000000052.

Bradley, Joan. Bringing Back the Bush: the Bradley Method of Bush Regeneration. New Holland, 2002.

Braudy, Leo. From Chivalry to Terrorism: War and the Changing Nature of Masculinity. Vintage Books, 2005.

Breytenbach, Anna. Tracking and Animal Communication: with Jon Young. https://www.youtube.com/watch?v=f-t5SaH8g3o

Briggs, Helen. "Human Impact on Nature 'Dates Back Millions of Years'." BBC News, BBC, 20 Jan. 2020. www.bbc.com/news/science-environment-51068816?fbclid=IwAR0CNooBYC-NWM-Jv0tdhW9Tm3LixsqqvqkpAOBOWdiTpZa4nEPtQDxanhE

Bruhns, Karen Olsen, and Karen E. Stothert. Women in Ancient America. Univ. of Oklahoma Press, 2014.

Budin, Stephanie Lynn, and Jennifer M. Webb. Gender Archaeology. American Schools of Oriental Research, 2016.

Butler, Octavia E. Dawn. Aspect, 1989.

Callenbach, Ernest. Ecotopia: a Novel about Ecology, People and Politics in 1999. Pluto Press, 1978.

Cameron, Anne. Daughters of Copper Woman. Press Gang Publishers, 1981.

Carlson, Kristen, and Leland Bement. "Organization of Bison Hunting at the Pleistocene/Holocene Transition on the Plains of North America." Quaternary International, vol. 297, 2013, pp. 93–99, doi:10.1016/j.quaint.2012.12.026.

Cartmill, Matt. A View to a Death in the Morning: Hunting and Nature through History. Harvard University Press, 1996.

Claassen, Cheryl, and Rosemary A. Joyce. Women in Prehistory: North America and Mesoamerica. University of Pennsylvania Press, 1997.

Chagnon, Napoleon A. Noble Savages: My Life among Two Dangerous Tribes - the Yanomamö and the Anthropologists. Simon & Schuster, 2014.

Clifton, Merritt, et al. "Killing the Female: The Psychology of the Hunt." Animals 24-7, 2 Jan. 2019. https://www.animals24-7.org/2018/12/29/killing-the-female-the-psychology-of-the-hunt/

Coetzee, J. M. Elizabeth Costello. Brombergs, 2003.

Collard Andrée, and Joyce Contrucci. Rape of the Wild: Mans Violence against Animals and the Earth. Indiana University Press, 1989.

Corby, Rachel. ReWild Yourself: Becoming Nature. Amanita Forrest Press, 2015.

Costello, Emily, editor. "Before You Vote, Read Mary Webb's 1917 Novel on the Barbarism of Fox Hunting." The Conversation, 7 June 2017. https://theconversation.com/before-you-vote-read-mary-webbs-1917-novel-on-the-barbarism-of-fox-hunting-78620

Craighead George, Jean. Julie of the Wolves. HarperCollins Publishers, 1972.

Daly, Martin and Margo Wilson, "Evolutionary Psychology of Male Violence." Male Violence, edited by John Archer, Routledge, 1994.

Damro, Kenneth. A Northwoodsman's Guide to Everyday Compassion. Wingspan Press, 2006.

Darimont, Chris T., et al. "The Unique Ecology of Human Predators." Science, vol. 349, no. 6250, 21 Aug. 2015, pp. 858–860, doi:10.1126/science.aac4249.

Darwin, Charles. The Origin of Species by Means of Natural Selection: or the Preservation of Favoured Races in the Struggle for Life ; The Descent of Man and Selection in Relation to Sex, Modern Library, 1872.

de Waal, Frans. The Bonobo and the Atheist. W.W. Norton & Company, 2014.

Defleur, Alban R., and Emmanuel Desclaux. "Impact of the Last Interglacial Climate Change on Ecosystems and Neanderthals Behavior at Baume Moula-Guercy, Ardèche, France." Journal of Archaeological Science, vol. 104, 2019, pp. 114–124, doi:10.1016/j.jas.2019.01.002.

Dennis, Stephen G. Homo Dominus: a Theory of Human Evolution. IUniverse, 2009.

Derricourt, Robin M. Unearthing Childhood: Young Lives in Prehistory. Manchester University Press, 2018.

Deur, Douglas Pacific Northwest Foraging: 120 Wild and Flavorful Edibles from Alaska Blueberries to Wild Hazelnuts. Timber Press, 2014.

Dietrich, William. The Final Forest: the Battle for the Last Great Trees of the Pacific Northwest. Penguin Books.

Doe, Jane. Anarchist Farm. III Pub., 1996.

Dunayer, Joan, "Sexist Words, Speciesist Roots." Animals & Women: Feminist Theoretical Explorations, edited by Carol J. Adams and Josephine Donovan, Duke University Press, 1995. https://nomorelockeddoors.files.wordpress.com/2013/12/sexist-words-speciesist-roots.pdf

"Earliest Roasted Root Vegetables Found in 170,000-Year-Old Cave Dirt." New Scientist, 2 Jan 2020. https://www.newscientist.com/article/2228880-earliest-roasted-root-vegetables-found-in-170000-year-old-cave-dirt/#ixzz69z24y5FA

Ehrenberg, Margaret R. Women in Prehistory. University of Oklahoma Press, 2005.

Ehrenreich, Barbara. Blood Rites: Origins and History of the Passions of War. Grand Central Publishing, 2020.

Eisler, Riane. The Chalice and the Blade. Thorsons, 1998.

Ellul, Jacques. The Technological Society. Vintage Books, 1967.

Emily Victoria. Vegan News. https://vegannewsnow.com

Farnish, Keith. Times up!: An Uncivilized Solution to a Global Crisis. Green Books Ltd., 2009.

Farnish, Keith. Underminers: A Guide to Subverting the Machine. New Society Publishers, 2013.

Faurby, Søren, et al. "Brain Expansion in Early Hominins Predicts Carnivore Extinctions in East Africa." Ecology Letters, 2020, doi:10.1111/ele.13451.

Foster, Judy, and Marlene Derlet. Invisible Women of Prehistory: Three Million Years of Peace, Six Thousand Years of War. Spinifex Press, 2013.

Fisher, Linda. "On the 'Right to Hunt' by a Native American Vegan." Scavenger. www.thescavenger.net/social-justice-sp-24912/animals/768-on-the-right-to-hunt-by-a-native-american-vegan.html

Flower Bomb. "No Hope, No Future: Let the Adventures Begin!" The Anarchist Library, 2019. https://theanarchistlibrary.org/library/Flower-bomb-no-hope-no-future-let-the-adventures-begin

Flower Bomb. "Vegan Means Attack: Fomenting A Wildfire Against Speciesism and Moral Anthropocentrism" The Anarchist Library, 2019. https://theanarchistlibrary.org/library/Flower-bomb-vegan-means-attack

Flower Bomb. "What Savages We Must Be: Vegans Without Morality." The Anarchist Library, 2019. https://theanarchistlibrary.org/library/Flower-bomb-what-savages-we-must-be-vegans-without-morality

Foreman, Dave, and Bill Haywood. Ecodefense: a Field Guide to Monkeywrenching. Abbzug Press, 2002.

Foreman, Dave. Confessions of an Eco-Warrior. Crown, 1993.

Foreman, Dave. Rewilding North America A Vision For Conservation In The 21St Century. Island Press, 2013.

Gaard, Greta. "Ecofeminism and Native American Cultures: Pushing the Limits of Cultural Imperialism?" Ecofeminism: Woman, Animals, Nature, Temple University Press, 1993, pp. 295–314.

Gasset José Ortega y. Meditations on Hunting. Wilderness Adventures Press, 2007.

Gero, Joan M., and Margaret W. Conkey, Engendering Archaeology: Women and Prehistory. Blackwell, 2002.

Gilmore, David D. Manhood in the Making: Cultural Concepts of Masculinity. Yale University Press, 1991.

Good, Kenneth, and David Chanoff. Into the Heart: One Man's Pursuit of Love and Knowledge among the Yanomama. Touchstone, 1991.

Gooley, Tristan. The Lost Art of Reading Natures Signs: Use Outdoor Clues to Find Your Way, Predict the Weather, Locate Water, Track Animals--and Other Forgotten Skills. The Experiment, 2015.

Gould, Stephen Jay. "On Replacing the Idea of Progress with an Operational Notion of Directionality." Evolutionary Progress, University of Chicago Press, 1988.

Hager, Lori. "Sex and Gender in Paleoanthropology." Women in Human Evolution, Routledge, 1997.

Hall, Lee. On Their Own Terms: Animal Liberation for the 21st Century. 2016.

Hance, Jeremy. "How Laos Lost Its Tigers." Mongabay Environmental News, 7 Nov. 2019. https://news.mongabay.com/2019/10/how-laos-lost-its-tigers/?fbclid=IwAR3IBGtv91-h03jrOgPu4EcdvT8nzN8ehi7JWkXUiawFtVoj94ueWH43N5g

Hardy, Karen, et al. "The Importance of Dietary Carbohydrate in Human Evolution." The Quarterly Review of Biology, vol. 90, no. 3, 2015, pp. 251–268, doi:10.1086/682587.

Harlan, Will. Untamed: the Wildest Woman in America and the Fight for Cumberland Island. Grove, 2015.

Harper, Breeze. "The Absence of Meat in Oankali Dietary Philosophy: An Eco-Feminist-Vegan Analysis of Octavia Butler's Dawn" The Black Imagination: Science Fiction, Futurism and the Speculative, Peter Lang, 2011.

Hart, Donna, and Robert W. Sussman. Man the Hunted: Primates, Predators, and Human Evolution. Westview Press, 2005.

Hegland, Jean. Into the Forest. Cornerstone Digital, 2016.

Heller, Chaia. "For the Love of Nature: Ecology and the Cult of the Romantic." Ecofeminism: Women, Animals, Nature. Temple University Press, 1993, pp. 219–242.

Henry, Amanda G., et. al. "The Diet of Australopithecus Sediba." Nature: International Journal of Science, vol. 487, 2 June 2012, pp. 90–93, doi: 10.1038/nature11185.

Hervey, Annette, et al. "Studies on Euglena and Vitamin B 12." Bulletin of the Torrey Botanical Club, vol. 77, no. 6, 1950, p. 423, doi:10.2307/2482180.

Hite, Shere. The Hite Report on the Family: Growing up under Patriarchy. Grove Press, 1994.

Hogan, Linda. "Our Animal Selves." Transcend Media Service, 21 Mar. 2011.
https://www.transcend.org/tms/2011/03/our-animal-selves/

Hockett, Bryan. "The Consequences of Middle Paleolithic Diets on Pregnant Neanderthal Women." Quaternary International, vol. 264, 2012, pp. 78–82, doi:10.1016/j.quaint.2011.07.002.

Honan, Kim, et al. "'Screaming Animals in Pain': Beekeepers Traumatised as They Check on Hives after Fires." ABC News, 20 Nov. 2019.
https://www.abc.net.au/news/2019-11-20/beekeepers-traumatised-by-screaming-animals-after-bushfires/11721756?pfmredir=sm&fbclid=IwAR1OO0VoOYBClu L2OkdAqD7_XHH3jo3TBYLVfeRfO_dxgnkXYsWY4zKHBvo

Hultman, Martin, and Pulé Paul M. Ecological Masculinities: Theoretical Foundations and Practical Guidance. Routledge, 2018.

Humboldt, Alexander von. Personal Narrative of a Journey to the Equinoctial Regions of the New Continent during the years 1799–1804. Translated by Jason Wilson, Penguin, 2006.

Huxley, Aldous. Ape and Essence. Heron Books, 1968.

Huxley, Aldous. Island. Heron Books, 1962.

IUCN Red List. "Unsustainable Fishing and Hunting for Bushmeat Driving Iconic Species to Extinction – IUCN Red List." IUCN Red List, 18 July 2019.
https://www.iucn.org/news/species/201907/unsustainable-fishing-and-hunting-bushmeat-driving-iconic-species-extinction-iucn-red-list

James, Tania. The Tusk That Did the Damage. Vintage Books, 2016.

Jamieson, Dale, "Animal Liberation Is an Environmental Ethic." Reflecting On Nature: Readings In Environmental Ethics and Philosophy, Edited by Lori Gruen, Dale Jamieson and Christopher Schlottmann, Oxford University Press, 2013.

Jensen, Derrick, "'If We Wish to Stop the Atrocities, We Need Merely to Step Away from the Isolation. There Is a Whole World Waiting for Us, Ready to Welcome Us Home."
https://www.derrickjensen.org/endgame/too-much-to-lose/

Jones, Pattrice. Aftershock: Confronting Trauma in a Violent World: a Guide for Activists and Their Allies. Lantern Books, 2007.

Joyce, Rosemary A. Ancient Bodies, Ancient Lives: Sex, Gender, and Archaeology. Thames & Hudson, 2009.

Kaczynski, Ted. "Ship of Fools." Crime Scene, 1999.
http://www.sacredfools.org/crimescene/casefiles/s2/shipoffoolsstory.htm.

Kelemen, L. E. "Associations of Dietary Protein with Disease and Mortality in a Prospective Study of Postmenopausal Women." American Journal of Epidemiology, vol. 161, no. 3, Jan. 2005, pp. 239–249, doi:10.1093/aje/kwi038.

Kheel, Marti. "Interview with Prominent US Writer Dr. Marti Kheel." YouTube, 2 May 2010, https://www.youtube.com/watch?v=DWghIE9a4TY

Kheel, Marti, et al. "License to Kill: An Ecofeminist Critique of Hunters' Discourse." Animals & Women: Feminist Theoretical Explorations, Duke University Press, 1995.

Kheel, Marti. Nature Ethics: an Ecofeminist Perspective. Rowman & Littlefield, 2008.

Kim, Hyunju, et al. "Plant-Based Diets Are Associated With a Lower Risk of Incident Cardiovascular Disease, Cardiovascular Disease Mortality, and All-Cause Mortality in a General Population of Middle-Aged Adults." Journal of the American Heart Association, vol. 8, no. 16, 2019, doi:10.1161/jaha.119.012865.

Kimmerer, Robin Wall. Braiding Sweetgrass: Indigenous Wisdom, Scientific Knowledge and the Teachings of Plants. Milkweed Editions, 2015.

Kover, T.R. "Of Killer Apes and Tender Carnivores." Studies in Religion/Sciences Religieuses, vol. 46, no. 4, 2017, pp. 536–567, doi:10.1177/0008429817735302.

Kropotkin, Petr. "Mutual Aid as a Factor in Evolution", 1902 in The Cry for Justice: An Anthology of the Literature of Social Protest, Upton Sinclair, The John C. Winston Co, 1915.

Lawrence, Andrew D., et al. "Construction of Fluorescent Analogs to Follow the Uptake and Distribution of Cobalamin (Vitamin B12) in Bacteria, Worms, and Plants." Cell Chemical Biology, vol. 25, no. 8, 2018, doi:10.1016/j.chembiol.2018.04.012.

Laws, Rita. "Choctaw Nation – a (Mainly) Vegetarian Tribe." The Lotus Post, 13 Jan. 2019.

https://www.thelotuspost.com/choctaw-nation-a-mainly-vegetarian-tribe/

Lerner, Gerda. The Creation of Patriarchy. Oxford University Press, 1986. https://radicalfeministbookclub.files.wordpress.com/2018/03/women-and-history_-v-1-gerda-lerner-the-creation-of-patriarchy-oxford-university-press-1987.pdf

Lewis, Jerome. "Ekila: Blood, Bodies, and Egalitarian Societies." Journal of the Royal Anthropological Institute, vol. 14, no. 2, 2008, pp. 297–315, doi:10.1111/j.1467-9655.2008.00502.x.

Lewis, Mary. Paleopathology of Children: Identification of Pathological Conditions in the Human Skeletal Remains of Non-Adults. Elsevier, Academic Press, 2018.

Liedloff, Jean. The Continuum Concept. Penguin, 2009.

"The Life of Birds." BBC Four, BBC. https://www.bbc.co.uk/programmes/b007qn69.

Livingstone, David. Missionary Travels and Researches in South Africa. National Trust for Scotland, 2013.

Livingston, John A. Rogue Primate: An Exploration of Human Domestication. Roberts Rinehart Publishers, 1994.

Luke, Brian. Brutal: Manhood and the Exploitation of Animals. University of Illinois Press, 2007.

Luke, Brian. "Taming Ourselves or Going Feral?: Toward a Nonpatriarchal Metaethic of Animal Liberation." Animals & Women: Feminist Theoretical Explorations, Duke University Press, 1995.

Luke, Brian. "Violent Love: Hunting, Heterosexuality, and the Erotics of Men's Predation." Feminist Studies, vol. 24, no. 3, 1998, doi:10.2307/3178583.

http://www.brown.uk.com/brownlibrary/luke.pdf

Macho, Gabriele A. "Baboon Feeding Ecology Informs the Dietary Niche of Paranthropus Boisei." PLoS ONE, vol. 9, no. 1, Aug. 2014, doi:10.1371/journal.pone.0084942.

Mandeville, Bernard. The Carnivorous Custom and Human Vanity: The Fable of the Bees; or, Private Vices, Publick Benefits, vol. 1, Oxford, 1705.
http://www.animal-rights-library.com/texts-c/mandeville01.htm

Marlowe, Frank W. The Hadza: Hunter-Gatherers of Tanzania. University of California Press, 2010.

Mason, Jim. An Unnatural Order: Why We Are Destroying the Planet and Each Other, The Continuum Publishing Company, 1998.

Mason, Sarah L. R., et al. "Preliminary Investigation of the Plant Macro-Remains from Dolní Věstonice II, and Its Implications for the Role of Plant Foods in Palaeolithic and Mesolithic Europe." Antiquity, vol. 68, no. 258, 1994, pp. 48–57, doi:10.1017/s0003598x00046184.

Masson, J. Moussaieff, and Susan McCarthy. When Elephants Weep: The Emotional Lives of Animals. Dell Publishing, 1995.

MacCaughey, Martha. The Caveman Mystique: Pop-Darwinism and the Debates over Sex, Violence, and Science. Routledge, 2008.

McKibbin, Phillip. "But What about Boil up? How Māori Are Embracing Veganism." The Spinoff, 16 Nov. 2018.
https://thespinoff.co.nz/atea/16-11-2018/but-what-about-boil-up-how-maori-are-embracing-veganism/

Medrano, Finisia. Growing Up in Occupied America. Lulu, 2013.
Melamed, Yoel, et al. "The Plant Component of an Acheulian Diet at Gesher Benot YaʻAqov, Israel." Proceedings of the National

Academy of Sciences, vol. 113, no. 51, May 2016, pp. 14674–14679, doi:10.1073/pnas.1607872113.

Merchant, Carolyn. The Death of Nature: Women, Ecology and the Scientific Revolution. HarperSan Francisco, 1980.

Merwe, Marcel Van der. Rewilding the Lost Wilderness: Green Heritage of the Forgotten Cape. Marcel Van Der Merwe II, 2017.

Messenger, Stephen. "Entire Village in India Relocates so Nature Can Move In." TreeHugger, 11 Oct. 2018.
https://www.treehugger.com/natural-sciences/entire-village-india-moves-out-so-nature-can-move.html

Mic the Vegan. "It's Official, There's a Plant Source of B12" YouTube, 27 Dec. 2019.
https://www.youtube.com/watch?v=QHvRArWglRY

Miles, Fayth L, et al. "Plasma, Urine, and Adipose Tissue Biomarkers of Dietary Intake Differ Between Vegetarian and Non-Vegetarian Diet Groups in the Adventist Health Study-2." The Journal of Nutrition, vol. 149, no. 4, 2019, pp. 667–675, doi:10.1093/jn/nxy292.

Milton, Katharine. "Diet and Primate Evolution." Scientific American: Becoming Human, Evolution and the Rise of Intelligence, 19 Sept. 2006.
file:///C:/Users/Robert/AppData/Local/Microsoft/Windows/INetCache/IE/FPGRDKVO/becoming_human from Scientific American.pdf

Milton, Katharine. "Hunter-Gatherer Diets—a Different Perspective." The American Journal of Clinical Nutrition, vol. 71, no. 3, 2000, pp. 665–667, doi:10.1093/ajcn/71.3.665.
https://academic.oup.com/ajcn/article/71/3/665/4729104

Miralles, Aurélien, et al. "Empathy and Compassion toward Other Species Decrease with Evolutionary Divergence Time." Scientific Reports, vol. 9, no. 1, 2019, doi:10.1038/s41598-019-56006-9.

Montana, Ria. "Anarcho-Primachismo: Primitivism Or Patriarchy?" Vegan Primitivist, 19 June 2019. veganprimitivist.wordpress.com/2019/06/01/anarcho-primachismo-primitivism-or-patriarchy/

Montana, Ria. "Death of Hope." Vegan Primitivist, 25 Dec. 2019. https://veganprimitivist.wordpress.com/2019/12/25/death-of-hope

Montana, Ria. "Dog Versus Wildlife." Vegan Primitivist, 2 Dec. 2017. https://veganprimitivist.wordpress.com/2017/12/02/dog-versus-wildlife

Montana, Rio. "My Wild Community." Vegan Primitivist, 14 Jan. 2020. https://veganprimitivist.wordpress.com/2020/01/14/my-wild-community

Montana, Ria. "Untamed Unmasking of Permaculture: Debunk of Tao Orion's 'Beyond the War on Invasives.'" Vegan Primitivist, 8 June 2019. https://veganprimitivist.wordpress.com/2019/06/01/untamed-unmasking-of-permaculture

Montana, Ria. "Us Before Cave Art." Vegan Primitivist, 16 Sept. 2017. https://veganprimitivist.wordpress.com/2017/09/16/us-before-cave-art

Moore, John. Anarchy & Ecstasy: Visions of Halcyon Days. Aporia Press, 1989.

Morris, Desmond. The Naked Ape: A Zoologists Study of the Human. McGraw-Hill Book Co., 1967.

Mowat, Farley. Never Cry Wolf. Langara College, 2019.

Nakos, M., et al. "Isolation and Analysis of Vitamin B12 from Plant Samples." Food Chemistry, vol. 216, 2017, pp. 301–308, doi:10.1016/j.foodchem.2016.08.037.

Native America Calling. "Monday, July 16, 2018 – Plant-Based Natives; What It Takes to Go Vegan » Native America Calling." 18 July 2018. https://www.nativeamericacalling.com/monday-july-16-2018-plant-based-natives/

Nelson, Sarah M. Gender in Archaeology: Analyzing Power and Prestige. AltaMira Press, 2004.

Nelson, Sarah M., and Myriam Rosen-Ayalon. In Pursuit of Gender: Worldwide Archaeological Approaches. AltaMira Press, 2002.

Nibert, David A. Animal Oppression & Human Violence: Domesecration, Capitalism, and Global Conflict. Columbia University Press, 2013.

Nikiforuk, Andrew. "Jacques Ellul: A Prophet for Our Tech-Saturated Times." The Tyee, 12 Oct. 2018. https://thetyee.ca/Analysis/2018/10/12/Jacques-Ellul-Prophet/

O'Dea, Kerin, et. al. "Traditional Diet and Food Preferences of Australian Aboriginal Hunter-Gatherers." Philosophical Transactions of the Royal Society of London. Series B: Biological Sciences, vol. 334, no. 1270, 1991, pp. 233–241, doi:10.1098/rstb.1991.0112.

Olsen, Jack. Slaughter the Animals, Poison the Earth. Manor Books, 1971.

Oppenlander, Richard A. Comfortably Unaware: Global Depletion and Food Responsibility... What You Choose to Eat Is Killing Our Planet. Langdon Street Press, 2011.

Paula, Rodrigo Martini. "Rethinking Human and Nonhuman Animal Relations in J.M. Coetzees Elizabeth Costello"

Perkins Gilman, Charlotte. Herland, The Forerunner, 1911.

Perlman, Fredy. Against His-Story, Against Leviathan! Active Distribution, 2016.

Pettorelli, Nathalie, et al. Rewilding. Cambridge University Press, 2019.

Plumwood, Val. Environmental Culture: the Ecological Crisis of Reason. Routledge, 2007.

Pointing, Charlotte. "Texas Hunter-Turned-Vegan Is Now Protecting 900 Acres for Wildlife." Live Kindly, 10 Apr. 2019. https://www.livekindly.com/former-hunter-vegan-activist/?fbclid=IwAR3RuUrNWDAM1h678X_ZIzD32SjvCVJEH Bc8f4quvDIbief93vXncotBRTU

Potts, Malcolm, and Martha Campbell. "The Origins and Future of Patriarchy: the Biological Background of Gender Politics." Journal of Family Planning and Reproductive Health Care, vol. 34, no. 3, 2008, p 171, doi:10.1783/147118908784734792. https://pdfs.semanticscholar.org/448b/3258e7b95b633d9f8b2ad4a4 4aa6c6fdf288.pdf

Power, Camilla. "Gender Egalitarianism vs Patriarchy Theory." Freedom News, 28 Jan. 2019. https://freedomnews.org.uk/gender-egalitarianism-vs-patriarchy-theory/

Powers, Richard. The Overstory: a Novel. W.W. Norton & Company, 2019.

Psihoyos, Louie, director. The Game Changers. 2018. https://gamechangersmovie.com/the-film/

Randall, Don. "The Community of Sentient Beings: J. M. Coetzees Ecology in Disgrace and Elizabeth Costello." ESC: English Studies in Canada, vol. 33, no. 1-2, 2008, pp. 209–225, doi:10.1353/esc.0.0054.

Rich, Adrienne, "Compulsory Heterosexuality and Lesbian Existence." Powers of Desire: The Politics of Sexuality, edited by Martha E.Thompson, Monthly Review Press, 1983. http://www.posgrado.unam.mx/musica/lecturas/Maus/viernes/Adri enneRichCompulsoryHeterosexuality.pdf

Robertson, Jim. Exposing the Big Game: Living Targets of a Dying Sport. Earth Books, 2012.

Robinson, Joshua R., et al. "Late Pliocene Environmental Change during the Transition from Australopithecus to Homo." Nature Ecology & Evolution, vol. 1, no. 6, 2017, doi:10.1038/s41559-017-0159.

Robinson, Kirk. "A Philosophical Critique of the North American Model of Wildlife Conservation." Rewilding, 26 Jan. 2020. rewilding.org/a-philosophical-critique-of-the-north-american-model-of-wildlife-conservation/?fbclid=IwAR1YgKlqGNU3JZjXN-fwW8MoXK4qL3zUC87nFFRvJbLxiI1xxqjn7U1Zsos

Robinson, Margaret. ELK, Earthling Liberation Kollective -. "Margaret Robinson - Indigenous Veganism: Feminist Natives Eat Tofu – Human Rights Are Animal Rights." YouTube, 10 June 2014, ww.youtube.com/watch?v=ahD6uz1mYJA

Robinson, Margaret and Michael Sizer. "Dr. Margaret Robinson at the AR Academy." YouTube, 22 Feb. 2014. www.youtube.com/watch?v=8t2mK92H63E

Rozema, Patricia, director. Into the Forest. Elevation Pictures, 2016.

Ryan, Christopher. Civilized to Death: The Price of Progress. Avid Reader Press, 2019.

Savoy, Ty. "Halifax Native Vegan Scholar Margaret Robinson on Cross Country Checkup 2019-01-28." YouTube, 28 Jan. 2019. https://www.youtube.com/watch?v=YESJ6daVg7U

Schipani, Sam. "13 Unlucky Animals That Are Killed for Fun." Sierra Club, 16 July 2018. www.sierraclub.org/sierra/thirteen-unlucky-animals-wildlife-killing-contests?fbclid=IwAR1Zcx7OMoVV6EREsABkHoc5jUeG2Vyyp IUwa35Xzgrfxe9aOFhQypwhMDA

Schlesier, Karl H. The Wolves of Heaven: Cheyenne Shamanism, Ceremonies, and Prehistoric Origins. University of Oklahoma Press, 2013.

Schmookler, Andrew Bard. The Parable of the Tribes. University of California Press, 1984.

Schreve, Danielle, et al. "Shoot First, Ask Questions Later: Interpretative Narratives of Neanderthal Hunting." Quaternary Science Reviews, vol. 140, 2016, pp. 1–20, doi:10.1016/j.quascirev.2016.03.004.

Scott, James C. Against the Grain: A Deep History of the Earliest States. Yale University Press, 2018.

Scott, James C. The Art of Not Being Governed: an Anarchist History of Upland Southeast Asia. Yale University Press, 2011.

Scott, James C. Two Cheers for Anarchism Six Easy Pieces on Autonomy, Dignity, and Meaningful Work and Play. Princeton University Press, 2014.

Seely, Mark. Anarchist by Design: Technology and Human Nature. OldDog Books, 2013.

Seely, Mark. Born Expecting the Pleistocene: Psychology and the Problem of Civilization. OldDog Books, 2012.

Seely, Mark. Civilization Heresies. Big Table Publishing Company, 2019.

Shai, Iris, et al. "Protein Bioavailability of Wolffia Globosa Duckweed, a Novel Aquatic Plant, a Randomized Controlled Trial." Clinical Nutrition, vol. 38, no. 5, 2019, p. 2464, doi:10.1016/j.clnu.2019.08.007.

Shelley, Percy Bysshe. "A Vindication of Natural Diet." Animal Rights Library, 1813.
http://www.animal-rights-library.com/texts-c/shelley01.htm

Shepard, Paul. Nature and Madness. Alfred A. Knopf., 1967.

Shepard, Paul. The Others: How Animals Made Us Human. Island Press, 1997.

Shepard, Paul. "A Post-Historic Primitivism." The Wilderness Condition: Essays on Environment and Civilization, edited by Max Oelschlaeger, Sierra Club Books, 1992.

Shepard, Paul. "Searching Out Kindred Spirits." Parabola, The Magazine of Myth and Religion, 1991.

Shepard, Paul. The Tender Carnivore and the Sacred Game. Scribners, 1973.

Spector, Janet. What This Awl Means: Feminist Archaeology at a Wahpeton Dakota Village. Minnesota Historical Society Press, 1993.

Shostak, Marjorie. Nisa: the Life and Words of a !Kung Woman. Routledge, 2015.

Smith, Felisa A., et al. "The Accelerating Influence of Humans on Mammalian Macroecological Patterns over the Late Quaternary." Quaternary Science Reviews, vol. 211, 2019, pp. 1–16, doi:10.1016/j.quascirev.2019.02.031.

Smuts, Barbara. "The Evolutionary Origins of Patriarchy." Human Nature, vol. 6, no. 1, 1995, pp. 1–32, doi:10.1007/bf02734133.

Solazzo, Caroline, et al. "Proteomics and Coast Salish Blankets: a Tale of Shaggy Dogs?" Antiquity, vol. 85, no. 330, 2011, pp. 1418–1432, doi:10.1017/s0003598x00062141.

Song, Mingyang, et al. "Association of Animal and Plant Protein Intake With All-Cause and Cause-Specific Mortality." JAMA Internal Medicine, vol. 176, no. 10, Jan. 2016, p. 1453, doi:10.1001/jamainternmed.2016.4182.

Sonnenblume, Kollibri terre. The Failures of Farming and the Necessity of Wildtending: a Collection of Essays by Kollibri terre Sonnenblume. Macska Moksha Press, 2018.

Spielvogel, Jackson J. Western Civilization to 1500. Wadsworth, 2014.

Spikins, Penny. "Goodwill Hunting? Debates over the 'Meaning' of Lower Palaeolithic Handaxe Form Revisited." World Archaeology, vol. 44, no. 3, 2012, pp. 378–392, doi:10.1080/00438243.2012.725889.

Spikins, Penny. How Compassion Made Us Human: the Evolutionary Origins of Tenderness, Trust and Morality. Pen & Sword Archaeology, 2015.

Spikins, Penny, et al. "From Homininity to Humanity: Compassion from the Earliest Archaics to Modern Humans." Time and Mind, vol. 3, no. 3, 2010, pp. 303–325, doi:10.2752/175169610x12754030955977.

Stabile, Carol A. Feminism and the Technological Fix. Manchester University Press, 1994.

Stark, Philip B., et al. "Open-Source Food: Nutrition, Toxicology, and Availability of Wild Edible Greens in the East Bay." Plos One, vol. 14, no. 1, 2019, doi:10.1371/journal.pone.0202450.

Stowe, Harriet Beecher. Uncle Toms Cabin. Wordsworth Classics, 2002.

Sturtevant, William C. Handbook of the North American Indians. Smithsonian Institution, 1978.

Sussman, Robert. "The Myth of Man the Hunter/Man the Killer and the Evolution of Human Morality." The Evolution of Human Behavior: Primate Models, State Univ of New York Press, 1985, pp. 121–129.
https://www.unl.edu/rhames/courses/current/readings/sussman.pdf

Suzman, James. Affluence without Abundance: What We Can Learn from the World's Most Successful Civilisation. Bloomsbury, 2019.

Tallamy, Douglas W. Bringing Nature Home. Timber Press, 2016.

Taylor, Timothy. The Artificial Ape: How Technology Changed the Course of Human Evolution. Palgrave Macmillan, 2010.

Tharrey, Marion, et al. "Patterns of Plant and Animal Protein Intake Are Strongly Associated with Cardiovascular Mortality: the Adventist Health Study-2 Cohort." International Journal of Epidemiology, vol. 47, no. 5, Feb. 2018, pp. 1603–1612, doi:10.1093/ije/dyy030.

Thomas, Elizabeth Marshall. The Harmless People. Vintage Books, 1989.

Thompson, Jessica C., et al. "Origins of the Human Predatory Pattern: The Transition to Large-Animal Exploitation by Early Hominins." Current Anthropology, vol. 60, no. 1, Feb. 2019, pp. 1–23, doi:10.1086/701477.

Thompson, Randall C., et al. "Atherosclerosis Across 4000 Years of Human History: The Horus Study of Four Ancient Populations." Journal of Vascular Surgery, vol. 58, no. 2, 2013, p. 549, doi:10.1016/j.jvs.2013.06.006.

Tokarczuk, Olga, translated by Antonia Lloyd-Jones. Drive Your Plow over the Bones of the Dead. Fitzcarraldo Editions, 2019.

Torres, Bob. Making a Killing: the Political Economy of Animal Rights. AK Press, 2007.

Toynbee, Arnold Joseph. Mankind and Mother Earth. A Narrative History of the World. Oxford University Press, Incorporated, 1984.

Turnbull, Colin M., "Mbuti Womanhood." Woman the Gatherer, edited by Frances Dahlberg, Yale University, 1981.

Turnbull, Colin M. The Mountain People. Simon & Schuster, 2007.

Urban Scout. Rewild or Die: Revolution and Renaissance at the End of Civilization. Urban Scout LLC, 2016.

Van Arsdale, Adam. Introduction to Human Evolution, Wellesley College, EdX.

Vierich, Helga. "Addendum to Gardening in Eden." Anthroecologycom, 1 Dec. 2019. https://anthroecologycom.wordpress.com/2019/12/01/addendum-to-gardening-in-eden/

Vogt, Benjamin. A New Garden Ethic: Cultivating Defiant Compassion for an Uncertain Future. New Society Publishers, 2017.

Wadley, Lyn, et al. "Cooked Starchy Rhizomes in Africa 170 Thousand Years Ago." Science, vol. 367, no. 6473, Feb. 2020, pp. 87–91, doi:10.1126/science.aaz5926.

Walia, Arjun. "Anthropologists & Scientists Explain How Ancient Humans Were Predominantly Vegan" Collective Evolution, 1 Nov. 2019. https://www.collective-evolution.com/2019/11/01/anthropologists-scientists-explain-how-ancient-humans-were-predominately-vegan/

Washburn, Sherwood, "The Evolution of Hunting." Man the Hunter, edited by Richard Lee and Irven DeVore , Aldine, 1968.

Weaner, Larry, and Thomas Christopher. Garden Revolution: How Our Landscapes Can Be a Source of Environmental Change. Timber Press, 2016.

Webb, Mary. Gone to Earth. 2020. Originally published in 1917.

Weyrich, Laura S., et al. "Neanderthal Behaviour, Diet, and Disease Inferred from Ancient DNA in Dental Calculus." Nature, International Journal of Science, vol. 544, 2017, pp. 357–361. https://www.nature.com/articles/nature21674

White, E. B. Charlotte's Web. Harper & Brothers, 1952.

Whiten, Andrew, and David Erdal. "The Human Socio-Cognitive Niche and Its Evolutionary Origins." Philosophical Transactions of the Royal Society B: Biological Sciences, vol. 367, no. 1599, May 2012, pp. 2119–2129., doi:10.1098/rstb.2012.0114. https://royalsocietypublishing.org/doi/full/10.1098/rstb.2012.0114

Wiber, Melanie. Erect Men/ Undulating Women: the Visual Imagery of Gender, Race and Progress in Reconstructive Illustrations of Human Evolution. W. Laurier U.P., Canada, 1999.

Wilder, Laura Ingalls, and Renee Graef. Deer in the Wood: My First Little House Books. Harper Collins, 1995.

Wilkinson, Todd. "A Death Of Ethics: Is Hunting Destroying Itself? From Killing Baboon Families to Staging Predator-Killing Contests, Hunters Stand Accused of Violating the North American Model of Wildlife Conservation. Now They're Being Called out by Their Own." Mountain Journal, 12 Dec. 2018. https://mountainjournal.org/hunting-in-america-faces-an-ethical-reckoning?fbclid=IwAR2AxsoWzhRvEhkveJTw_RN6ReGzPYsE Y62aruGxZQbC5rwd8Drr6wQ3d-w.

Williams, Cara. "Ecofeminism in the Speculative Fiction of Ursula K. Le Guin, Octavia Butler, and Margaret Atwood", 2018.

Williams, Joy. "The Killing Game: Why the American Hunter Is Bloodthirsty, Piggish, and Grossly Incompetent." Esquire, 1 Oct. 1990. https://classic.esquire.com/article/1990/10/1/the-killing-game

Wilson, Peter J. The Domestication of the Human Species. Yale University Press, 1991.

Wolff, Robert. Original Wisdom: Stories of an Ancient Way of Knowing. Inner Traditions, 2001.

Woodburn, James, and Richard B. Lee "An Introduction to Hazda Ecology," Man the Hunter. Routledge, 2017.

Wrenn, Corey. "Human Supremacy, Post-Speciesist Ideology, and the Case for Anti-Colonialist Veganism." Animals in Human Society, University Press of America/Hamilton Books, 2015.

Wright, Laura. "A Feminist-Vegetarian Defense of Elizabeth Costello: A Rant from an Ethical Academic on J.M. Coetzee's The Lives of Animals" J. M. Coetzee and the Idea of the Public Intellectual, Ohio Univ. Press, 2008.

Wright, Ronald. A Short History of Progress. House of Anansi Press, 2019.

Young, Peter. Liberate: Stories and Lessons on Animal Liberation above the Law. Warcry Communications, 2019.

Young, Jon. Tracking and Animal Communication: with Anna Breytenbach. https://www.youtube.com/watch?v=f-t5SaH8g3o

Young, Jon, and Dan Gardoqui. What the Robin Knows: How Birds Reveal the Secrets of the Natural World. Mariner Books, 2013.

Zakin, Susan. Coyotes and Town Dogs: Earth First! and the Environmental Movement. Markham Books, 2018.

Zerzan, John. "Patriarchy, Civilization, and the Origins of Gender" 2008. http://theanarchistlibrary.org/library/john-zerzan-patriarchy-civilization-and-the-origins-of-gender.html

Zerzen, John. Running on Emptiness: The Pathology of Civilization. Feral House, 2002.

Zerzan, John. Why Hope? The Stand Against Civilization. Feral House, 2015.

Zihlman, Adrienne, "The Paleolithic Glass Ceiling: Women in Human Evolution." Women in Human Evolution, edited by Lori D. Hager, Routledge, 1997.

Zihlman, Adrienne, and Nancy Tanner. "Gathering and the Hominid." Female Hierarchies, Lionel Tiger, 2017.163–188, doi:10.4324/9780203792018-7.

Anti-Hunting Books

Classical
"Gone to the Earth" by Mary Webb
"The World is a Mighty Slaughterhouse" by William A. Alcott

Contemporary
"The American Hunting Myth" by Ron Baker
"Children's Literature, Domestication, and Social Foundation: Narratives of Civilization and Wilderness" by Layla AbdelRahim
"Drive Your Plow over the Bones of the Dead" by Olga Tokarczuk, translated by Antonia Lloyd-Jones
"Exposing the Big Game: Living Targets of a Dying Sport" by Jim Robertson
"Man Kind?" by Cleveland Amory
"A Northwoodsman's Guide to Everyday Compassion" by Kenneth Damro
"Slaughter the Animals Poison the Earth" by Jack Olsen
"Wild Children — Domesticated Dreams: Civilization and the Birth of Education" by Layla AbdelRahim

Children's
"Bambi" by Felix Salten
"Bear Hunt" by Anthony Browne
"Bless the Beasts and Children" by Glendon Swarthout
"Carly's Buck" by C. S. Adler
"Curse of the Squirrel" by Laurence Yep
"Danny, the Champion of the World" by Roald Dahl
"Dr Doolittle's Circus" by Hugh Lofting
"A Fabulous Creature" by Zilpha Keatley Snyder
"The Fox and the Hound"by Daniel P. Mannix
"The Gnats of Knotty Pine" by Bill Peet
"Harald and the Great Stag" by Donald Carrick
"The Henry Williamson Animal Saga: Tarka The Otter, Salar The Salmon, The "Epic Of Brock, The Badger, Chakchek, The Peregrine" by Henry Williamson
"The Hunter" by Paul Geraghty

"The Hunter and the Animals: A Wordless Picture Book" by Tomie De Paola

"Hunter and His Dog" by Brian Wildsmith

"The Hunter I Might Have Been" by George Mendoza

"The Hunting Trip" by Robert Burch

"Jenny's Corner" by Frederic Bell

"The Magic Finger" by Roald Dahl

"Rascal" by Sterling North

"Sandy and the Rock Star" by Walt Morey

"Saving Lilly" by Peg Kehret

"Sniper" by Theodore Taylor

"Song of the Golden Hare" by Jackie Morris

"The White Seal" by Rudyard Kipling

"Wringer" by Jerry Spinelli

ABOUT THE AUTHOR

Ria is a folio-frugivore, anarcho-primitivist
tending Salish lowland forests and wetlands
for wild life.

Some indigenous wild discoveries while wild tending:

Banana Slug

Northwestern Salamander

Stumbled on these babes when clearing introduced invasive bramble.
Wild discoveries still inspire compassion and blissful awe,
but now that I understand what's at stake,
there's a motivation with a purpose.

Before-After midslope wetland 2014 – 2017.

Rewilding forests and wetlands rewilds my entire being.
To facilitate shifting from humans' domesticated agriculture to
wild foraging, I foray into prospects of returning wild abundance,
for wilding humans and other animals.

Prior to contact,
Wapato grew abundantly... managed in carefully tended family garden patches
and gathered throughout the fall and winter as a staple root vegetable.
Stó:lō elder Ralph George told me he remembers raking away the detritus from
sloughs near Chilliwack BC so the Wapato would grow better, and Melissa
Darby writes of family owned patches being carefully cleared of large woody
debris by the Chinook near Sauvie Island (formerly known as Wapato Island) on
the Lower Columbia. During the winter of 1805-1806, Lewis and Clark noted
that Wapato was the "principal article of trade" along the Columbia. In 2007
archaeologists from Simon Fraser University excavated a 3000 year old Wapato
garden along the shores of the Fraser River. They discovered a conspicuous
rock layer at the bottom of the Wapato bed that likely limited the depth that the
tubers could burrow, making them easier to harvest during the cold winter
months. Unfortunately habitat loss due to the construction of dams and dikes as
well as predation from introduced carp has severely restricted the abundance of
Wapato throughout much of its former Northwest range. Native American use of
Wapato for food has suffered a similar fate due to loss of access to the tubers
and the hyper-availability of introduced foods.
http://arcadianabe.blogspot.com/2012/10/wapato-cultivating-native-tubers.html

A wild growing lush patch of Wapato, *Sagitaria latifolia,*
in a cutoff oxbow,
home to a river otter.

To minimize disturbance, first I try gathering seed clusters to cast into similar habitats. If they don't grow, then I'll pull up tubers to transplant, taking few, leaving most.

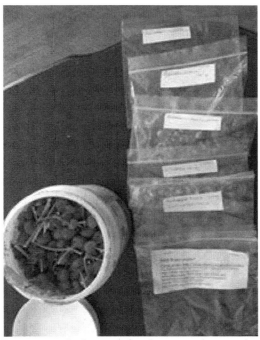

Wapato seed clusters in the round container.

Propagating by seed.

Water Pepper, *Persicaria hydropiperoides*
blended with Wapato up shore on which salamanders lay eggs.
I gather seeds to spread into other similar conditions with nearby
struggling salamanders to invite their expansion.

Planting toxin filtering species at low tide in a Duwamish estuary.
The health indicator goal here is return of herring.
An osprey nests nearby.

Planting natives along the forest edge of what was once prairie.
Golden Paintbrush, *Castilleja levisecta*, now endangered, once
flourished here. When domesticated humans stop using this space
to run domesticated dogs, prairie can be recovered to replace lawn.

Pulling back introduced invasive Morning Glory,
liberating an indigenous Douglas Fir sapling struggling beneath,
tagging the young conifer to monitor its health and growing space.

My wild tending tool kit.

Recently fallen dead tree covered in lichen.
When trees fall we do inexpert tree autopsies on possible causes.

Logs are so vital, we liberate them from invasive bramble.
Down woody debris is vital to wildlife habitats and soils.

Log covered in several species of mushrooms.
Decomposition cycle is full of stages of life-converting dynamics.

Organizing habitat restoration work parties.

Perhaps the most satisfying is wild tending with children.
This boy started coming when he was four. He's now eight.
He observes and loves all animals, mentoring me in insects.

Cooking in La Gran Sabana while visiting with Pemón people *(Domingo, Tamara, Margarite, Antonio, Blanca, Wili, Rosi & Enya Manila and their village)* in southeast Venezuela. Alongside their indigenous foodways, they practice slash & burn jungle gardening, with the main staple being cassava tubers (*Manihot esculenta*). They report no introduced invasive species, but their vast land is beginning to be encroached and degraded for diamond and gold mining.

Drinking fresh glacier melt. I often wonder why humans seem ok with other animals drinking water we deem unfit for us.

This essay, a blending of ideas of many caring humans,

is a living document of inspiration,

an ever emerging story

inciting feral future.

Nuts Jōmon gathered and stored in the fall 14,500 years ago:
chestnuts (*Castanea crenata*)
buckeyes (*Aesculus turbinata*)
walnuts (*Juglans sieboldiana*)
deciduous acorns (*Quercus*)
evergreen acorns (*Cyclobalanopsis and Castanopsis*)

Tokyo Maibun Archaeological Center

VeganPrimitivist.wordpress.com
Feel free to give input for an update of this essay.

From hominin to *Homo sapiens*, the story of the human ape's relationship with other species and Earth has been more tragic than not. From human origins, ever emerging brutal lifeways turned humans' predators into prey, paving a blood path of conquest over the planet.

As the growing human brain honed inventiveness of the hunt, it too cultivated an intensified compassion. This palpable incongruence sparked a mind adaptation utilizing language to rationalize killing. Rationalizing through mythologies and rituals served as an evolutionary strategy to overcome anxiety in slaying other animals. 'Man the Hunter' entwined humans with other animals onto an apocalypse-bound course.

This thesis picks up from the 1990's debate between Feminists for Animal Rights (FAR) and Deep Ecology. Through the lens of resistance anthropology observing wildness, the 'Man the Hunter' narrative is reinterpreted as eco-patriarchy, a trap set in the roots of the origins of early humans' adaptation into hunting.

"Ria Montana takes us closer to truths about human nature. She sees that hunting (and later domestication) stifled human empathy for and kinship with our animal cousins and contributed to false ideas of male supremacy and female inferiority. Her stuff is vital now in this era of re-defining gender and discarding the lies and myths of patriarchal culture."
~Jim Mason, author of
"An Unnatural Order: Why We Are Destroying the Planet and Each Other"

"If there is a meaning to humanity and our being here, our journey here, this is it, without a doubt."
~Kenneth Damro hunter turned vegan and author of
"A Northwoodsman's Guide to Everyday Compassion"

"This intense essay hits hard, tearing apart years old analysis of hunter-gatherer absurdity."
~Flower Bomb, creator of *Warzone Distro*
and co-organizer of *Green Scare Anarchist Bookfair*

"Let animals be our teachers… a radical change that Ria is promoting, for which many thanks."
~Yi-Fu Tuan, author of *"Dominance & Affection: The Making of Pets"*

"… informative, original, and we'll researched. If you are interested in the feminist and ecological implications of hunting give this a read!"
~Joshua Harper, National organizer & spokesperson, SHAC USA; former crew member, Sea Shepherd Conservation Soc.; producer, Breaking Free animal rights videos

Made in the USA
San Bernardino, CA
24 June 2020